CAROLINE GNAGY

TEXAS JAILHOUSE MUSIC

A PRISON BAND HISTORY

THE History PRESS

Published by The History Press
Charleston, SC
www.historypress.net

Front cover: The Goree All-Girl String Band, circa 1942. *Texas Prison Museum.*
Back cover, top: Members of an African American musical group from Goree strike poses in their full western dress. *Texas Department of Criminal Justice.*
Back cover, bottom: The Wynne Unit Band in the early 1960s. *Texas State Library and Archives Commission.*

First published 2016

Manufactured in the United States

ISBN 978.1.62619.867.8

Library of Congress Control Number: 2015960004

This book is dedicated to all the men and women who have served time in the prisons of our nation. So many of their forgotten voices, talents and stories will never be adequately conveyed to the world. And to my late father, Allan Stephen Gnagy, who in my girlhood drove for hundreds of miles, several times a week, to teach hundreds of prisoners the value of self-expression.

CONTENTS

ACKNOWLEDGEMENTS

Words cannot adequately express the depth of gratitude I have for the many individuals and institutions that have contributed to the writing of this book. Without any of you, this book simply would not be. First of all, I'd like to thank my loving fiancé, Kevin Fontenot. Historian, teacher and friend, you have listened to me yammer on and on about this project since we first met. Without you, I wouldn't have been able to accomplish nearly so much or have as much fun doing it.

I thank the staffs of the Texas Prison Museum, the Texas State Library and Archives Commission, the Texas Department of Criminal Justice and the Dolph Briscoe Center of American History at the University of Texas for allowing me access to an enormous wealth of information. Your archives form the backbone of this work—and the work of many others—so thank you for taking such good care of these important historical documents.

I've presented portions of this research at various academic conferences, and I thank the International Country Music Conference (ICMC), the East Texas Historical Association (ETHA), the Texas State Historical Association (TSHA) and others for the opportunity to speak; I appreciate all the comments, encouragement and contributions. The University of Texas, Sam Houston State University, Lamar University, Victoria College, Texas State University at San Marcos and other educational institutions have also been of great assistance at various times.

Thanks to my very patient editor at The History Press, Christen Thompson—you are a gem! Jim Willett and Sandy Rogers of the Texas

Prison Museum in Huntsville have gone above and beyond with their generous assistance, for which I'm very grateful. I'd also like to thank Kirby Pringle for introducing me to the presence of these unique musical acts and Skip Hollandsworth, whose May 2003 *Texas Monthly* article about the Goree All-Girl String Band served as the best possible jumpstart I could have wished for.

I know that I've neglected to mention some of you by name, but please know I am no less grateful, only temporarily forgetful. Thank you to the following individuals (and their families) for giving me all manner of support over the years—professional, academic and personal: Ethan Blue; Robert Perkinson; James Akenson; Kris McCusker; Diane Pecknold; Travis Stimeling; Penny Clark; Mitchell Roth; Gayle and Bill Royer; Becky Tucker; Elizabeth Cook; Tom Cook; Steve Dean; Deidre Lannon; Norma and Neil Lewi; Joe and Sue Fontenot; Monica Keller; Rachel Wilson; Barb Clifford; Rachel Decker; Laurie Gallardo; Joey Armon; Dave Anderson; Mike Buck; Ted and Linda Branson; my singularly inspirational brother, Mathew Gnagy; and all the rest of my family and friends.

Introduction

THE MYTH AND THE MUSIC

Texas brings together vital threads of the American fabric. Its hardscrabble folk and wide-open spaces symbolize individual liberty. Yet this freedom has always traveled with a wrathful twin.[1]
—*Robert Perkinson,* Texas Tough

For over 150 years, the very phrase "Texas state prison" has elicited a shake of the head and a whistle of acknowledgment that Texas wields a crushing hand when it comes to justice. In a nation widely known for its tough approach to law enforcement, the state of Texas reigns supreme as both a poster child and cautionary tale of justice with its long prison sentences, high percentage of executions and "we ain't gonna put up with it" attitude toward crime.

However, for a time, the Texas prison system represented hope, serving as a symbol of physical and/or personal freedom—through a weekly half-hour radio show of music and entertainment. Nationwide and beyond, people tuned in to clear-channel station WBAP Fort Worth to listen to the sweet sounds of the men and women who earnestly performed the popular music they loved: songs of patriotism, sentimentality and home sweet home.

Soon after the first episode aired in March 1938, *Thirty Minutes Behind the Walls* received thousands of fan letters each week, all addressed to the Huntsville unit of the Texas state prison. The radio show became an unprecedented hit, and for a decade, it served as a public relations tool for state officials. In addition to the music, *Thirty Minutes* also conducted interviews with state and prison officials. From the print shop manager to various governors of Texas, the show operated as a platform for political rhetoric. Through the show, officials communicated their political and social attitudes to hundreds of thousands of Americans as they worked to climb out of hardship wrought during the Great Depression. Not just a political platform for the elite, the most intriguing aspect of *Thirty Minutes* was surely the musical performers: all were inmates of the Texas state penitentiary; men and women who were serving years-long sentences for various crimes.

Public demand to see these acts in person intensified as the performers' popularity grew. Before long, these inmate performers took the songs they played on the radio and in the rodeo arena to state fairs, fiddle contests, homecoming celebrations and more. Music spread happiness and good cheer; it did not incite fear. It garnered curiosity from a public who began to see the prisoners as not so different as themselves and, for some, to care for some of the inmates as if they were their own kin.

The stars of *Thirty Minutes* were convicted cattle thieves, drug addicts, bootleggers, car thieves, forgers, robbers, murderers and more. Some were also jazz stars, bona fide rock stars, notorious exotic dancers and champion fiddlers whose stories will be recounted in this book. Most importantly, however, all of these inmates were fathers, mothers, daughters, sons, husbands and wives of real people. All fervently hoped that one more song on a guitar, one more yodel or one more interview about their lives would get them ever closer to freedom and back into the arms of those they loved.

As a musician and writer who studies early forms of twentieth-century roots music, I couldn't help but be entranced by the images of these young women in stylish cowgirl outfits with perfect curls and dimpled smiles. I was drawn to the respectable-looking young men in dapper suits who posed stiffly with their instruments. My imagination went wild as I looked upon their forgotten faces, and I heard their songs in my mind. I wondered where one dark-haired girl was born and what that tall, good-looking young man did to land himself in the brutal Texas prison. I marveled about all they were up against in one of America's toughest prison systems. I wondered if any of their children ever knew about this part of their lives.

When I delved more deeply into the research, I discovered that every inmate in those photographs has a story worth telling. All of these men and women—or at least, *almost* all—were imprisoned for crimes they committed many decades ago. Some of these criminal acts were borne out of impoverished desperation and some out of love for the wrong person. Many crimes represented foolish or accidental acts committed in a haze of drugs, alcohol or even plain old hunger. And yes, one or two were committed in cold blood.

The stories of these men and women are utterly fascinating, and collectively, they represent myriad mad, bad decisions resulting in a nightmarish, oppressed existence behind prison bars. For some of the inmates, joining a prison band was the start of a long, slow climb toward reclaiming some forgotten part of themselves.

The music itself, however, wasn't often the primary goal. Instead, the music acted as a conduit through which positive feelings could grow. On a tangible level, the music gave these young people a chance—even if temporarily—to be admired or to eat better food or see the great Texas sky, unfettered by steel bars. Many of the inmates felt not only the rhythm of the songs but also a sense of accomplishment, of belonging to a group and—strongest of all—a fervent hope for release. How rich and little-known a history it is!

Texas Jailhouse Music will focus on this historically important era within the Texas prison system and take a brief look into later decades and the eventual decline of its rehabilitative music programs. At the heart of this book, however, are the stories of its inmates: the music they made, the music's impact on their lives and the lives they touched. Sometimes shocking, often entertaining, these narratives provoke intense compassion, insight and inspiration as we explore why and how such frequently ostracized, marginalized men and women managed to provide such widely lauded creative expression in such literally confining circumstances.

Music in the Texas Prisons

Early Years

One might question how such an inspired period of creative expression could have even come about, given what is generally known of the Texas prison system. The mythology surrounding Texas has always reveled in the icons of its maverick lawmen, if not its outlaws. Doled generously from those maverick lawmen, an iron-heavy hand of justice has seemingly been called for in order to crush the maverick outlaws. This pervasive attitude toward crime and punishment evidenced itself before Texas's development of its justice system and even before its establishment as a state. Though legislation for a statewide penal system passed shortly after Texas was admitted to the Union in 1846, it was not implemented immediately due to the Mexican War. Revised legislation passed in March 1848, and the legislature determined Huntsville as a base for the new prison. Construction on the prison began in the fall of that same year.

In these earliest years, it appears that the Texas prison management disallowed musical expression under any circumstances, since the prisoners were managed under the Auburn system. One of the most frequently adopted penal methodologies, the Auburn system originated in the early 1820s in Cayuga County, New York, at the Auburn Prison. It proscribed that the prisoners worked in groups by day and retired to individual cells by night. The primary tactic of the Auburn system was to prevent the prisoners from interacting with one another, whether verbally or non-verbally. Communication between inmates was completely prohibited, even as they worked together.[2]

The objective of the Auburn system was to remove a sense of self or individuality from every prisoner, so that no one prisoner could "corrupt" another. This was only achieved by strict maintenance of the silence, violation of which was punishable by whip. Personal expression (creative or otherwise), relationships and, essentially, the prisoners' humanity were removed from the picture altogether. Therefore, no music would have been officially sanctioned when the Texas prison system first began.

The Auburn system remained in place through the Civil War, even as the Texas prison was the only one in the eleven Confederate states to remain standing. Following the war's chaos, the Auburn system began to dismantle, due in large part to the efforts of Thomas Jewett Goree, who was appointed first to the prison board in 1874 and then superintendent of the Huntsville prison in 1877. Goree, a former Confederate captain, ushered in an era of punitive practices that resulted in Texas's first prison classification system and explored some rehabilitative aspects, such as better education and religious study for the prisoners.[3]

Whether music played a formal role in Goree's rehabilitative efforts is unclear at this time. However, with the restrictions of silence lifted, prisoners were able to express themselves creatively—even if this only meant singing old "slave songs" and hymns while they worked the fields of the prison farms. Field labor songs such as these endured for centuries on the farms and plantations of the South and carried on as the inmates continued what was essentially slave work, laboring in the fields and on other convict labor projects. Coincident with the abandonment of the Auburn system (and thus, the resumption of the field song) was the rise of the convict lease system in Texas, which lasted until 1912.

INTRODUCTION

The practice of singing while working the prison farm fields is a post–Civil War parallel continuation of the southern slave tradition, one that persisted well into the twentieth century. Beginning with folklorist John Avery Lomax's exploration of early twentieth-century African American musical traditions, southern prison work songs are well documented by historians and ethnomusicologists. They remain one of the most fascinating and unique forms of music to come out of United States prison history.

Aside from the field songs collected later, evidence of sanctioned, organized musical acts by prisoners between the Civil War and the early twentieth century is rare in the United States, even more so in the rural and less "cultured" setting of Texas. However, by World War I, many prisons throughout the country used music as a diversion for the prisoners, even if rehabilitation was not the primary objective. Coast to coast, military-style marching bands and classical orchestras blossomed in prisons of the early years of the twentieth century.

Often documented in old postcards and other souvenir-style ephemera, early prison bands were a curiosity to the general public. In the latter half of the nineteenth century, the respectability of Sousa-style military marches and classical music made these early prison bands popular within their communities. With support from prison officials and the public, these early bands often performed for the surrounding communities and, thereby, created a precedent for prison bands of other soon-to-be-popular genres to develop, aided immensely by the advent and increasing accessibility of radio.

By 1938, when *Thirty Minutes Behind the Walls* took to the airwaves, prison reform in Texas was well underway. A public beset by hardships for years became enamored with the fairly inexpensive radio. It not only delivered the news but also allowed people to discover far-off places both known and unknown. It enabled the president to have intimate "fireside chats" and offered aural glimpses into worlds they could not fully access through letters and newspapers. What *was* it like in a state prison? One inmate, a soft-spoken, elegant-sounding young woman named Reable Childs, answered to her own experience in an on-air 1940 interview on *Thirty Minutes*. She said:

> *When I first knew I had to come, I was filled with dread. I had never been in trouble before in my life, and, like others whose knowledge of the penitentiary is based on magazine articles and the movies, I looked forward to a living death. I pictured cold, lonely cells, calloused companions, a tight-lipped matron without feeling.*[4]

When the announcer asked her if her fears were confirmed when she entered the penitentiary, Reable replied, "No, sir…Those fears were foolish. I found, instead, a small group of girls who were bravely striving to climb back up the ladder. It's harder for a girl to make up for her mistakes than it is for a man to live down his past…but these girls are all trying."[5]

1
PITCHFORKS AND BASEBALL BATS

On the whole, the inmates of the penitentiary are happier and in better spirits than ever before, especially in view of the fine modern hospital facilities now available. Texas still has its prison problems however. Out here perhaps 150 or 200 feet, five men are in the solitary waiting for their call to go to the little green chamber. All around us here are thousands of these young men, to see them here, most of them you could not tell but what they were just out of college. It is a problem which society has to deal with and it is up to us to make the best of it.[6]
—Thirty Minutes Behind the Walls

Rehabilitation Efforts of the Texas Prison System

Though many have tried to generate a positive spin on the Texas prison system over the years, the reality of life within its walls, especially of decades long past, is beyond the imagination of most people. In Texas, the first prison units were formed under a plantation design, and the inmate work performed to keep them functioning was literally backbreaking. Male inmates of all races (and some of the African American female inmates) toiled in the plantations and gardens of the Texas prison units—Sugarland, Darrington, Wynne, Blue Ridge, Harlem, Ramsey and Eastham to name a few—for ten hours a day or more. Guards carried guns and sat atop their horses, eagle-eyed as they watched the inmates, all too ready to strike the butt of their gun against a "lazy" or "insolent" head that dared lift up to take a moment of rest during that time. The Texas prisons were hot, brutal and antiquated even after numerous reforms occurred earlier in the twentieth century, particularly for the men.

Since the convict lease era ended in 1912, Texas government officials faced issues with management of the prison system from the top managers of the prison board down to the inmate "building tenders." The Progressive era and the issues faced by the country after the 1929 stock market crash ushered in renewed, more substantial efforts to improve the system in the 1920s and 1930s. The goal was to improve the Texas prison system's brutal public image, one rife with reports of both systematic and arbitrary acts of torture on both male and female inmates perpetrated by prison guards, including beatings, whippings and even rape. One of the major moves made during this time occurred when the previous board of prison commissioners was retooled in 1926 and expanded to become the nine-member Texas Prison Board. W.H. Mead was appointed as the prison system's first general manager. In 1927, newly elected Texas governor Dan Moody proposed an extensive reform project within the prison system,

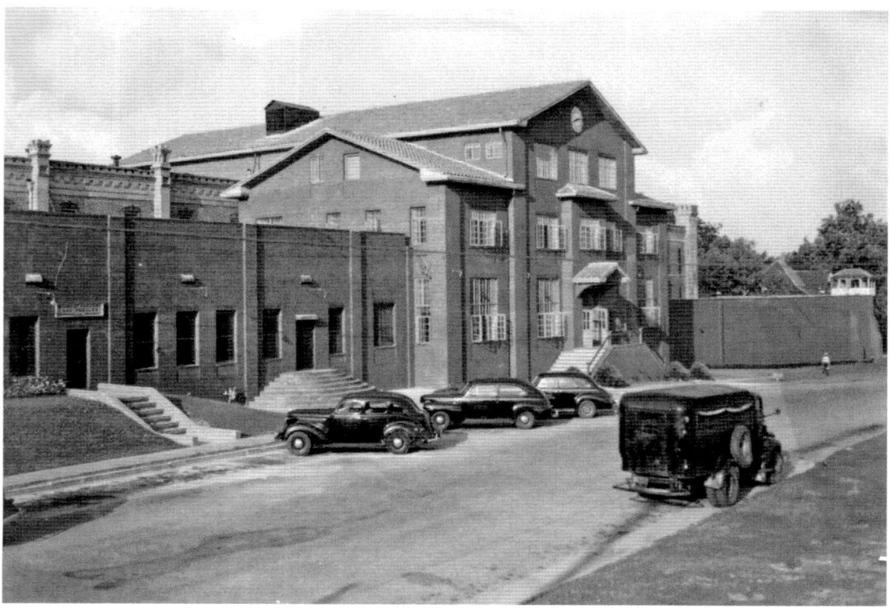

The main unit of the Texas state prison at Huntsville (also called "the Walls") in 1943. Note Bud Russell's famed "One-Way Wagon" (also called the "Black Betty," "Black Annie" or the more standard "Black Maria") parked in front of the unit. *Texas Department of Criminal Justice.*

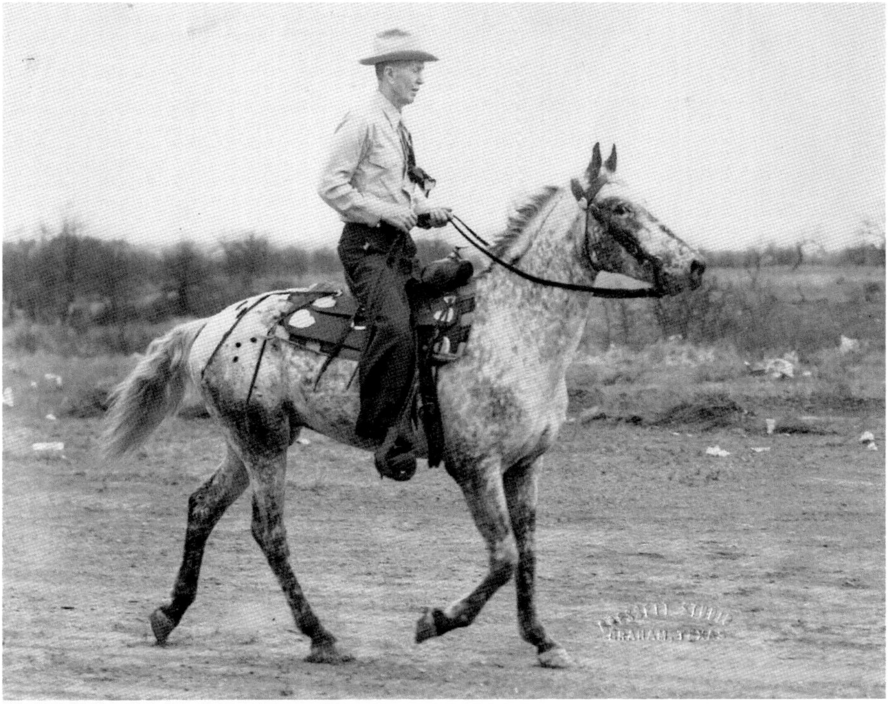

Prison manager Lee Simmons atop his horse Dan. *Texas Department of Criminal Justice.*

guided in part by the national Committee on Prisons and Prison Labor (CPPL) and supplemented by shocking findings within the *Texas Prison Survey*, released in the mid-1920s.[7]

In 1930, former sheriff Marshall "Lee" Simmons was appointed by the Texas Prison Board to become the next general manager of the prison system. He had been involved with the prison system for some time, first serving on a committee, at the invitation of Governor Pat Neff, to inspect the prison system, look into the welfare of the inmates and offer suggestions for improvement. In his autobiography, Simmons said one of the reasons he was initially hesitant to join this committee was because "there was a woman on it. But when I met Mrs. [W.C.] Martin, I found that she was a well-to-do landowner and business woman of good sense and experience."[8] Statements such as this were typical of Simmons, described by Robert Perkinson as a proponent of "manly planter justice."[9]

Following that committee's inspection of the prisons and documentation, Simmons presented its report to the Joint Penitentiary Committee of the

Senate and House of Representatives. This report put him on the radar of the government officials and the prison board. The board made him a consultant and, in March 1930, general manager of the system.

During his administration, Simmons adopted a strict authoritarian approach to prison management, eschewing what he felt were unrealistic propositions for reform. As he saw it, his responsibility was to help whip the antiquated prison system into shape. This primarily involved transformation of the seventy-three thousand acres of farmland on multiple plantation-style prison units into viable, self-sustaining profit for the entire prison system.[10]

Simmons did not shrink from much. "Whipping" the system into shape also included the idea of using violence as a punitive tool, with Simmons maintaining that the bat was still occasionally a viable form of punishment for deserving inmates. Beset by a number of mutinies before and during his appointment, Simmons brooked zero tolerance or sympathy for such goings-on, even quoted by Parkinson as saying that he would use "pitchforks and baseball bats" to tamp down the uprisings, even if the inmates were "carried out feet first."[11]

His tyrannical tactics drew strong criticism during his administration, but some improvements occurred after his appointment to general manager, and after so many years of ineffectual management due to various circumstances, Lee Simmons later received praise from the prison board for the majority of his efforts. Charismatic and authoritative, Simmons masterfully employed public relations, embarking on an all-out campaign to tout the state's rehabilitation efforts during the first few years of his administration. Earlier efforts toward prisoner rehabilitation programs were maintained and expanded on, including sports; music programs; the recently implemented prison newspaper, the *Texas Prison Echo*; and holiday celebrations—all shrewdly acknowledged with publicity photos and disseminated to the local media.

The Texas Prison Rodeo

Most significantly, in 1931, Simmons rolled out one of the most enduring and successful endeavors in the Texas prison system history: the Texas Prison Rodeo. Appealing to the masses through "blood sport, with the prison setting intensifying the element of lurid fascination,"[12] the rodeo made its rip-roaring debut in 1931 and soon became a major regional tourist

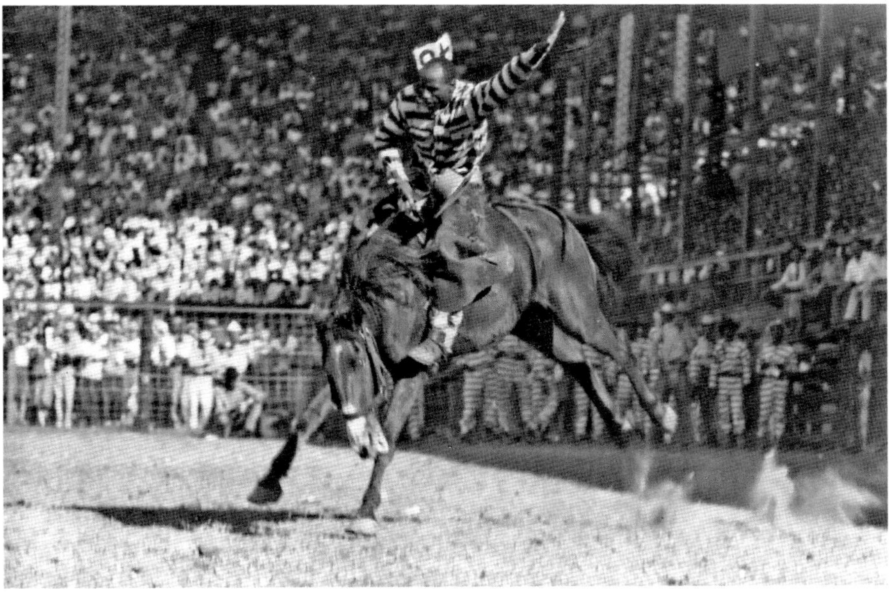

An inmate rodeo contestant rides for glory in the bareback competition. *Texas Department of Criminal Justice.*

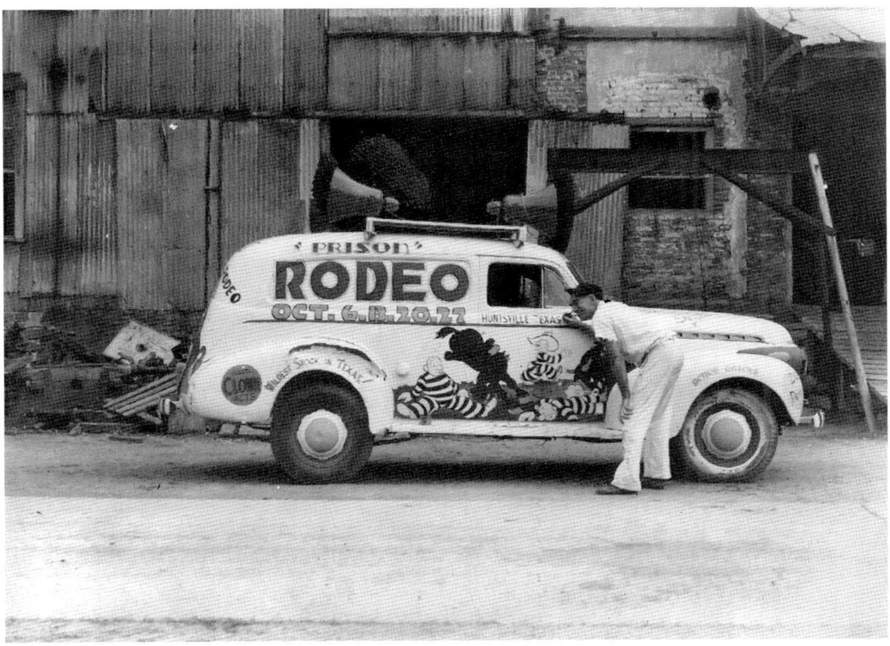

A wagon is prepped for a Texas Prison Rodeo parade. *Texas Department of Criminal Justice.*

attraction, aided by extensive, provocative media coverage. The rodeo was a dangerous, exciting opportunity for (untrained) inmates of all races to "reform" themselves via daring stunts such as the "Mad Scramble," "Wild Mare Milking" and "Convict Poker" (played in the middle of the ring with a bull loosed and out for blood). Even African American female convicts participated, however degraded and vaguely sexualized, in the mud-heavy "Greased Pig Sacking Contest." Perkinson notes that, in terms of popular entertainment, the rodeo portrayed "nostalgia for not just the frontier, but the Old South. It brought the minstrel show to the cattle drive."[13]

Using themes of minstrelsy, the Wild West and bloodthirsty ancient Rome, the rodeo's publicity materials did not want for sensationalism either, and the attendance grew exponentially each year. By 1933, around fifteen thousand free-world spectators walked through the prison gates; by 1935, it was twenty-five thousand. By the time *Thirty Minutes Behind the Walls* began in 1938, the Texas Prison Rodeo was a firmly established event and a monstrously effective jumping-off point for the prison's musical groups to display their talents to thousands of people.

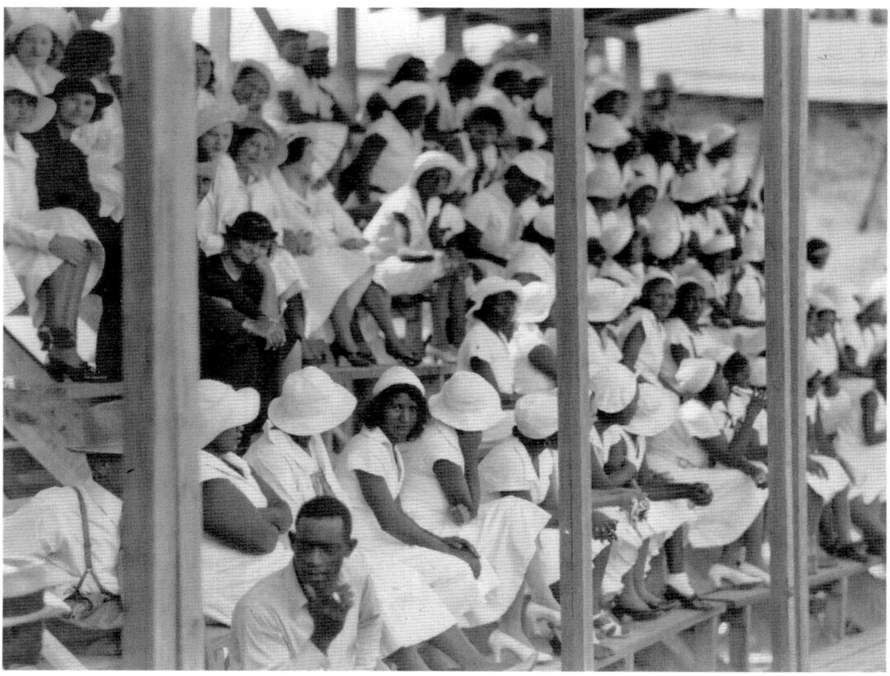

Spectators from the Goree State Farm for Women attend the rodeo as Mrs. Heath (in the dark suit, middle left) looks on. *Texas Department of Criminal Justice.*

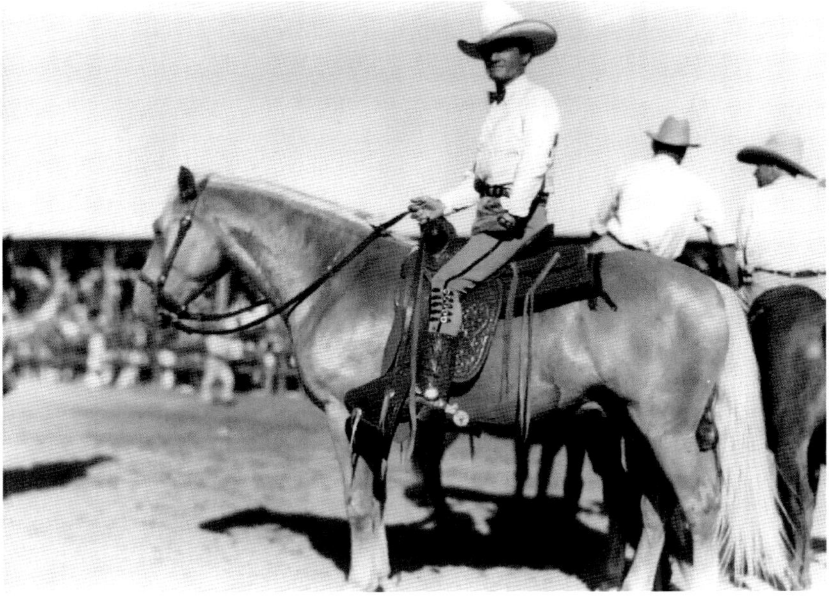

Tom Mix poses at the Texas Prison Rodeo. *Texas Department of Criminal Justice.*

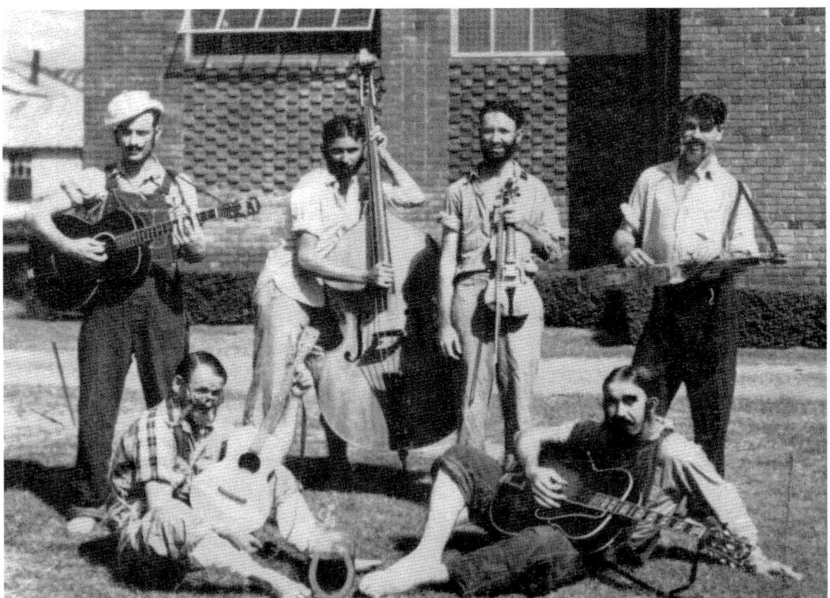

One prison band, the Hillbillies, performed at the 1944 prison rodeo. *Texas Prison Museum.*

Music at the rodeo first began with performances by the already-established prison orchestra, which—along with Sousa-style marching bands—were common recreational pastimes in most U.S. prisons by the 1930s. The Texas prison's orchestra was composed of white male inmates. Also present at the earliest rodeos was the "Cotton-Pickers' Glee Club," an obvious reference to the race of the inmates who sang their own traditional songs of labor, love and praise of the Lord. Simmons, ever the master of equal-opportunity exploitation, took credit for assembling this group of African American male inmates and for presenting them to the public with great fanfare. Women began to join the rodeo's musical ranks a few years later, singing popular western songs and hymns. By 1939, even African American female inmates became star attractions on the rodeo's musical bill. Also featured every year were big-name cowboy and hillbilly stars from the outside world, such as Ernest Tubb, Tom Mix, Eddy Arnold, Curly Fox and Texas Ruby. Even the governor himself, Wilbert Lee "Pappy" O'Daniel, performed with his band. Later decades brought country stars like Ray Price, Dolly Parton and Johnny Cash.

While Simmons's savvy use of public relations drew widespread acclaim from government officials and made it appear that the rehabilitative efforts were paying off, all was not what it seemed. Reports of brutality to inmates remained rampant, with Simmons feeding the fire with statements like "Bring 'em more axes, boys!" in response to questions on the self-mutilations occurring at various units. Simmons resigned as general manager in November 1935, succeeded by Texas Prison Board member Dave Nelson. Nelson passed away two weeks after his appointment, however, and thus, Simmons was truly succeeded by O.J.S. Ellingson. Ellingson continued in much the same vein regarding inmate management. Simmons soon moved on to become clerk of the United States Court for the Eastern District of Texas. However, Ellingson also continued the public relations work and image improvement that Simmons began, including an increased focus on the prison music programs. It was under O.J.S. Ellingson's term as the prison's general manager that *Thirty Minutes Behind the Walls* first aired.

Prisoner Classification in Texas Prisons

One other interesting development that came out of the Texas prison system's rehabilitation efforts occurred beginning in 1936, when prison official Carl Basland conducted a survey of (mostly white male) inmates. Based on his findings, he implemented a revamped inmate classification system that designated each inmate to a subsection—using race, age and rehabilitative potential—within a few major classifications: "Physically Defective," "Insane," "Feeble Minded," "Drug Addicts" or "Homosexuals."[14]

Basland's rationale for the new classification system was scientific in nature, noting that, prior to a true scientific psychological study, there was a "failure to recognize that the offenders are products of situations and not persons possessed by the devil, filled with the evil spirit, or born criminals."[15]

With this, he determined that classification, segregation and a true psychological study of each inmate's case would help correct this archaic misinterpretation. Subsequently, he set about modernizing the existing system, utilizing progressive psychological philosophies. In Basland's words, for the prison system, it was separation time. He said:

> *That prisons have been popularly referred to as "schools of crime" is not hard to understand when the vicious, the habitual offenders, the drug addicts, the sex perverts and the youthful first offenders have been given a like custodial and a like general treatment and have been housed together.*[16]

The classification system was published in 1938, with classes divided into the following:

Classification	Description
Classification 1A	First offenders under age twenty-six with indication of good rehabilitative prospects and no evidence of "undesirable" traits.
Classification 1B	First offenders over age twenty-six with indication of good rehabilitative prospects and no evidence of "undesirable" traits.
Classification 2A	Repeat offenders under age twenty-six with little indication of good rehabilitative prospects or first-time offenders with one of the "undesirable" traits.
Classification 2B	Repeat offenders over age twenty-six with little indication of good rehabilitative prospects or first-time offenders with one of the "undesirable" traits.
Classification 3	"Lifers" or death row inmates with no foreseen prospects for rehabilitation.

On one of the earliest episodes of *Thirty Minutes Behind the Walls*, Basland declared to the public that careful mental and physical examinations were conducted on each inmate "so that special problem cases, such as the insane and the feeble-minded may be treated according to their problems."[17] Within each of these classifications, however, existed a rather broad interpretation of what was permissible treatment for an inmate based on the results of such examinations.

On one hand, these classifications represented a desire on the prison administrators' part to create a more growth-oriented, humane environment for the inmates. Unfortunately, classification under these parameters, while positive in intent, ended up being rather vague and subjective, essentially creating a loophole that enabled those with sufficient power to wield it in any way they chose. In the end, if an inmate was classified incorrectly or perhaps not classified at all—for instance, an African American or female inmate—the well-intentioned Basland classification system had the potential to foster the exact opposite of a humane, growth-oriented environment.

Although discussed in the 1938 classification report as inclusive within the prison system's full inmate population, prison population in the 1930s numbered around 6,500 total inmates, with the female inmate population around only 150. Although not explained explicitly within the report, there were likely several reasons that female inmates were not given the above-noted alphanumeric classifications. First, since they were housed in the single Goree unit, full segregation was not logistically possible. Secondly, violence on the part of the female inmates occurred less frequently, although, of course, inmates occasionally proved the exception.

Basland's classification impacted the makeup of the Texas prison bands because the male inmates were not allowed to participate in the prison bands or appear on *Thirty Minutes* unless they were in one of the superior classifications. Inmates who fell within the lower echelon of Basland's classification system were also frequently relegated to prison farms and units other than Huntsville. As such, they were unable to participate regularly in the largely Huntsville-based broadcasts of *Thirty Minutes*—regardless of their talent. Only when the WBAP—and, later, KPRC—broadcasts occasionally aired from one of the other units were the lower classifications allowed to showcase their talent on the radio; but even then, they had to be in good standing within the system.

Texas Prison Echo

Throughout all the changes occurring in the Texas prison system from the late 1920s on, the prison newspaper, the *Texas Prison Echo*, captured it all. Thanks in part to the on-site print shop at the Huntsville unit, each month, the *Echo* provided information and commentary from prison officials and inmates in the form of editorials, unit-specific regular columns, humor and features on popular culture such as radio shows, movies and, later, television.

Furthermore, this prison-run newspaper has endured in some form to almost the present day, which means it was the longest-lasting rehabilitative program developed within the Texas prison system. The *Echo* provides firsthand commentary from the inmates themselves, in the form of editorials and columns, and adds unique personal insight and sentiment into the goings-on of the prison bands.

Print shop manager S.E. Barnett oversaw the publication of the *Texas Prison Echo* and participated in running *Thirty Minutes* when the radio show first began. Not surprisingly, quite a lot of newspaper coverage of *Thirty Minutes*, from its development on to its great fanfare later, is found in the prison newspaper—live shows, sports recaps, reprints from other newspapers, text and photographic documentation of the fan response, public opinion and notations of radio industry sociopolitical critical acclaim are all documented heavily.

As *Thirty Minutes* episodes progressed through the years, the *Echo* turned toward supporting the war effort, fostering a patriotic spirit in its readers and continuing to document the radio show. Later, as other vocational, addiction-focused and faith-based programs developed at the prison in the 1950s and 1960s, the newspaper faithfully documented the changes and continued featuring the music, entertainment and sports programs within the changing prison system.

Although the inmates of the Texas state penitentiary did exist within a harsh, brutal environment, there was improvement of the quality of life for most of the white male inmates. Basland's classifications, however faulty, improved conditions for the higher-ranked male inmates at the various units—even as lower-ranked, African American and Hispanic inmates continued to suffer.

Similarly, the physical conditions improved for female inmates when construction on a new main building at the Goree State Farm for Women was completed in 1937, replacing the barracks-style prison farm in which the women had previously been housed. Dormitory-style living was the new plan for the women of the Goree Farm, with "vocational space" built in via a new garment factory and beauty shop classroom. Slowly, very slowly, the agonies of reform were stabilizing to some degree. Similarly, the national consciousness grew more compassionate in the face of hard times. Compassion was the fashion with the public—but in Texas, it was lost on the majority of law enforcement officials like the Texas Rangers, sheriffs, lawyers and judges.

2
THE WIDOW AND THE REPORTER

The prison commission stepped far ahead of other states when it inaugurated the calory [sic] *system of feeding prisoners. It has done a fine job in backing the building of a new $40,000 prison structure, with its shining locks, new bars and stronger cells, in which to hold the state's female prisoners. But until it gives them a matron, trained in penal and social welfare work, to whom women prisoners can take their fears of the future, their problems of the present, their utmost thoughts of rebellion without fear of immediate punishment without a fair hearing, the state will have done nothing to make them better than when they became its charges.*[18]

—*Melba Newton George,* Houston Post

Convict #83327

On the night of April 23, 1936, in the small town of Center, Texas, near the Louisiana border, thirty-five-year-old Marlie Childs died from a gunshot wound to the back of his head. Sitting in the living room, Marlie's wife, Reable Childs, jumped up upon hearing the gunshot and rushed toward its source to find the still figure of her murdered husband on the kitchen floor. She ran to a neighbor's house screaming for help. There, the sobbing young wife and her supportive neighbors made a report to the police department. Across a field from the scene, an idling car roared to life and drove off down an obscure little lane shortly after the shot sounded.

At the scene, Shelby County sheriff J.B. Samples and Deputy Officer Grover Poplin found former Shelby County treasurer Marlie James Childs lying on the kitchen floor of his home. They found a toothbrush and tooth powder on the floor near his body; he had been preparing to brush his teeth at the kitchen sink when he was shot once through the head with what was later determined to be a .22-caliber rifle. Finding the bullet holes in his head but no weapon at the scene, the police called for their bloodhounds and embarked on a search for the perpetrator. The hounds took off but lost the trail on the small, dark lane across the field from the Childses' home. Meanwhile, other law enforcement officials found a man's footprints on the ground outside the kitchen window. They concluded that the killer shot Childs through the window and escaped across the field to the waiting car. They combed the area while an inconsolable Reable wept in a neighbor's arms.[19]

During the next few days, community members came forth to assist with the disquieting new case. A high schooler named Tom McElroy reported that he saw the car parked in the lane for some time that evening and then gave the officers their first real lead: not only did he see the car that night, but he actually recognized it as one he'd seen several times before at a Civilian Conservation Corps (CCC) camp not far from the town. The next day, they tracked it to a home fifty miles away in Jefferson, Texas, where a twenty-one-year-old man named Terence Bramlett lived with his sister and her family. Bramlett didn't appear alarmed at the police questioning and voluntarily agreed to go to the station for a more detailed interrogation.[20]

Questioning of the suspected car's driver commenced after a night in jail. They first discovered that the car belonged to Bramlett's brother-in-law and that he often borrowed it in order to get to his job at the camp infirmary. They were further encouraged when the young man described his knowledge of the family stricken by the week's horrific events. Yes, he knew the Childs couple; he'd met the wife two years ago at the CCC camp. As the interrogation intensified, Bramlett buckled under the pressure and unleashed a torrent of statements that led the police to believe unequivocally that they had their man. He spoke of a two-year affair that he and Reable Childs maintained, of Reable's distress at the state of her marriage, of her desire to be free of her husband and of their combined efforts to plot her escape. In the end, he was quite matter-of-fact as he described how he had borrowed his brother's shotgun and car, drove to Center and shot Marlie Childs from outside the kitchen window just a few days earlier. According to one account of the questioning, "The youth signed the statement just before daybreak and then Mrs. Childs, who had not known of his arrest, was brought to the sheriff's office."[21]

During this time, officials pieced together a timeline of events for the deepening investigation that brought the actions of the lugubrious young widow, Reable Childs, into sharper focus. The coroner's report made the alleged timeline of events impossible. According to the report, the order of events as Reable told it left a gap of at least thirty minutes from the time of the gunshots to the time the police call was placed. A November 1936 article in the *Salt Lake City Tribune* stated, "Common sense told the sheriff that the reason why she delayed reporting the death would bear investigating." With the damning confession of the now unraveling Bramlett, twenty-three-year-old Reable soon became another target of the investigation. Both were arrested and held for the murder of Marlie Childs. As they got wind of the increasingly scandalous criminal case, the media went wild.

Over the next few months, newspaper reports on the investigation exploded not only throughout Texas but also the nation. The reporters were clearly fascinated with the seeming black widow duplicity of the "auburn-haired, comely young widow"[22] Reable Childs and her fiendish young lover. Did she lure Terence Bramlett into pulling the trigger? Had she dreamt of poisoning Marlie herself or otherwise causing his death? Did she only marry him for his money, or did she kill him to try to get it? After all, Marlie Childs was an upstanding citizen. He was a former treasurer of Shelby County, where they lived. He was older than Reable by twelve years, and a childhood bout of "infantile paralysis," better known as polio, left him impaired through adulthood, forcing him to walk with the assistance of a cane. How could this lovely young woman have done such an abominable thing to her caring, unsuspecting invalid husband? In retrospect, all may not have been what it seemed.

Reable Sapp was born in rural Shelby County on May 1, 1912, one of six girls and one boy born to Ulvia and Annie Sapp. The close-knit farm family worked hard to provide for one another as well as they could, but even so, the children grew up with only one pair of shoes each per year. Once they wore out, the Sapp children simply went without. However, Reable's impoverished life did not affect how others perceived her, and by the time she was a teenager, her intelligence, poise, kindness and good looks caused her to be well liked by everyone she came in contact with. At sixteen, she caught the eye of Marlie Childs, a wealthy local man. Before long, he proposed to her. Given her circumstances, Reable likely considered the prospect of marriage to Marlie a very attractive one. In addition to advancing her own social and financial status, their marriage would allow her to raise her children with opportunity and comfort and contribute to her family's care.[23]

Marlie James Childs and Reable Sapp wed not long after her seventeenth birthday on June 30, 1929. They settled in Marlie's hometown of Center, Texas. Marlie's well-to-do family vehemently disapproved of the match, and his mother in particular set about making his young wife miserable. Reable attested during the murder trial that their marriage was unhappy from the outset. Later in life, she explained to her daughter that even though they lived in a beautiful home with an opulent yard (complete with a koi pond), Marlie turned out to be a cold, domineering and mean-spirited man. For example, early in the marriage, Reable asked her wealthy husband for money to pay for a vital medical surgery needed for Reable's younger sister. Her request was denied: "I didn't take in all your family to raise," Marlie told her. Her dreams of helping her family through the marriage were dashed, but nonetheless, Reable quietly cobbled together what money she could out of the household funds and gave it to her sister, saving her life.[24]

Further bringing a stark reality to her youthful dreams of marriage, Marlie unyieldingly refused to have any children; Reable cited this as one of the reasons for her unhappy marriage in news reports and trial testimony. Privately, Reable told her daughter later in life that she actually did become pregnant twice during her marriage to Marlie. Both times this occurred, Marlie's mother came over and "made her some tea." Each time, Reable trustingly drank down the kind of tea that causes a woman to miscarry. When the second miscarriage occurred after drinking Marlie's mother's tea, Reable finally comprehended that even in marriage, she was essentially alone and without recourse. Her desire to have a close-knit family of her own, like the one she'd grown up in, would never happen. No children would ever be born if she and Marlie remained married.[25]

Perhaps not surprisingly, these early seeds of dissent bloomed into an unfortunate alliance a few years into the marriage. When her cousin Ellis was hospitalized at the CCC camp infirmary, Reable Childs met the strapping young Terence Bramlett. Almost three years her junior but a good-looking, earnest-appearing young man, Bramlett worked at the infirmary as a medical assistant. He was immediately taken with the brown-eyed beauty and begged Reable's cousin to tell him all about her. Even though he received the unfortunate news that Reable was married, he pumped Ellis for more information. Before long, he borrowed his brother's car to drive to Center, where he waited at the local drugstore, sure he would run into Reable. His persistence paid off as he reintroduced himself to Reable and

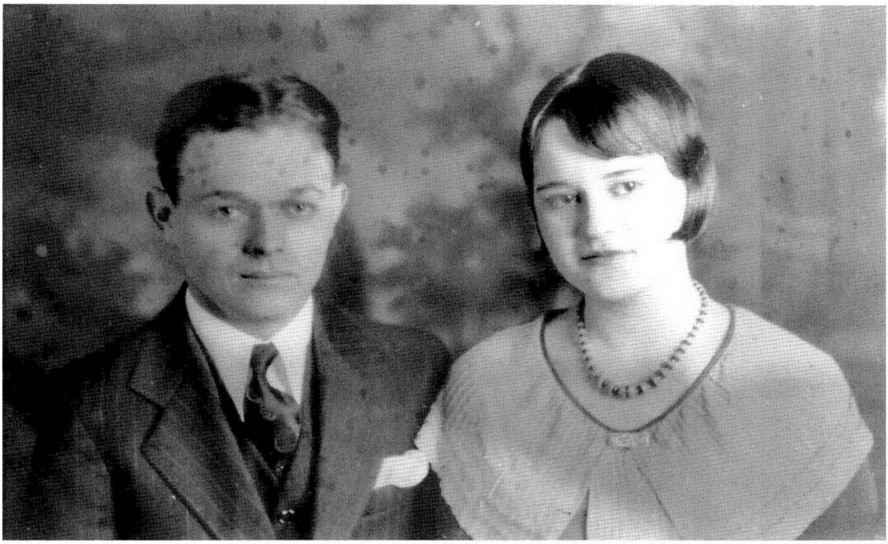

Above: Marlie James Childs and Reable (Sapp) Childs's wedding portrait, circa 1929. *Gayle Royer.*

Right: Terence Bramlett with a puppy, circa 1935. *Gayle Royer.*

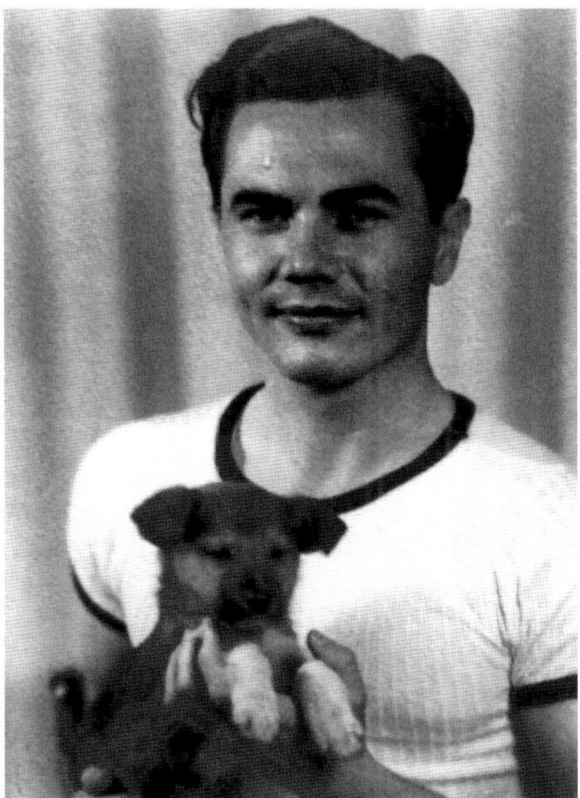

befriended her. The young, unhappily married woman eventually warmed to Terence Bramlett, and in time, the friendship turned romantic. They began a love affair that lasted for around two years, up until the night Marlie Childs was killed.[26]

The few available photographs of Childs from the media coverage show a well-heeled, ladylike and attractive young woman dressed in a prim, embellished black hat and a fur collar. With all the media frenzy, her glamorous appearance in the newspapers didn't benefit her many claims of innocence and, in fact, cemented her public image as a conspiratorial black widow. With Reable's story trailing on the heels of Texas's notorious criminal duo Bonnie and Clyde, a number of newspapers relayed with salacious detail the story of their affair, even behind bars.

When Reable's twenty-fourth birthday rolled around on May 1, 1936—one week after Marlie was found dead on the kitchen floor—the *Port Arthur News* front page blazed: "It's Her Birthday! Confessed Slayer Buys Present." The article detailed, "The boy's cell is one tier above that of the woman for whose love he killed." It went on to say he'd given two dollars to a "negro trusty" to go purchase Reable candy and "some attractive lingerie" for her birthday. Their romance was portrayed in a sexualized manner, as a lust—or, at the very least, a blind love—stronger than what held them apart. Neither steel bars nor even certain guilt could stand in their way.[27]

A newly minted legend for helping rid East Texas of some major criminal activity, Texas Ranger Dan Hines was assigned to the Childs case and opined to the *Port Arthur News* reporter, "They still love one another and always will." Rather than garnering sympathy, this statement probably cemented Reable Childs and Terence Bramlett—referred to in one article as the "young widow and her tree army lover"—as both callous and foolhardy in the public mind, but their daring to love each other so much after having killed in cold blood was not without its own romantically ironic undertones.[28]

The truth is, Reable Childs and Terence Bramlett once found themselves deeply in love and wanted a future together. Keepsakes—photos, jewelry and love notes that are still in the possession of Reable's children—show the devotion she and Bramlett felt at one time, despite her marriage. Reable testified repeatedly that she tried to leave Marlie Childs on multiple occasions, but he would not grant her a divorce. This statement is supported by her family's reports of Marlie's coldness to them and to her and his attempts to isolate Reable from others. With no money of her own and the times being what they were, it appears Reable felt unwilling or unable to shake things up by leaving Marlie outright, regardless of his wishes.

Perhaps she and Bramlett talked wildly one night about all the ways she could be free of her marriage; maybe there would be an "accident" to remove the impediment to their love. Perhaps Reable tried to push Bramlett away so she could make a fresh start, either with her husband or alone, but there is no solid evidence to support either notion. What is certain is that whether or not Reable ever knew about Terence Bramlett's intent to kill Marlie, after his death and the subsequent trial, their romance died as well.

In the first days after his arrest, Terence Bramlett confessed to shooting Marlie Childs and provided great detail on how he performed the act. Reporters quoted Bramlett's initial testimony as such:

> *On the afternoon of April 23 I borrowed by* [sic] *brother-in-law's .22 rifle and his 1928 Chevrolet sedan and started toward Center. I did not drive into Center until night. I stayed on the highway between Teneha and Center before I drove directly to the home of Marlie Childs. When I reached his home I could not see a light in the back part of the house, but Mr. and Mrs. Childs were sitting in the front room of the house talking. I stood on the outside of the house in the yard, near the window just like I done many times before when I was there to see Mrs. Reable Childs. Marlie Childs got up and walked into the kitchen. I then went around to the back of the house and when Childs came in view under the light I shot him one time. I never shot but once and Childs dropped to the floor. I carried the gun back to Jefferson with me and arrived in Jefferson by eleven o'clock that night. When I reached Jefferson I stayed all night at the home of my sister there.*[29]

However, he soon recanted his confession, and by the time the *Port Arthur News* reported on the trial in September 1936, his story became thus:

> *He pictured Mrs. Childs as a pretty, pleasure-starved young wife of a wealthy, middle-aged cripple. She "pursued" him, he said, after their first meeting, and soon had him enmeshed in a love affair. The youth said he went to Chicago to study engineering, in an effort to avoid her advances, but she besieged him with love letters, begging him to return because she was "lonesome and blue."*[30]

This was only the beginning of Bramlett's recantations. Soon, his accounts began to fluctuate wildly, and not a little desperately, about the nature of their affair and the chain of events leading up to the shooting. In another article, he stated that Reable presented him with a gun to shoot Marlie Childs with and that he refused. Other news reports contain statements he made saying Reable fired the fatal shot while he stood next to her outside the window. One article even reported that a state witness, Bramlett's fellow CCC camp worker Dartis Wyndham, claimed Bramlett offered him $3,000 to kill Marlie Childs. Examination of multiple news reports on Bramlett's repudiation show a general shift of focus to Bramlett's lack of credibililty and frantic story-changing, implying a sort of cowardice—if not outright guilt—on his part. Conversely, news coverage of Reable's testimony began to lean toward sympathetic, even as she was sexualized and portrayed as a fallen—or at least misguided—young woman.

In the case's early days, Reable Childs claimed she had no knowledge of Terence's intent to kill her husband, although under oath she admitted to having a two-year affair with him. The news reports of Reable's initial statements show no apparent bias or questioning of her claims of innocence. A couple of weeks into the investigation, however, Reable also changed her story, stating that she and Bramlett conspired with each other to rid her of her husband, thus freeing them to be together. News articles reported varying discussions between her and Bramlett about how to carry out the murder of Marlie Childs. Headlines blazed with phrases such as "Love Murder"; the articles focused on their love triangle, primarily depicting Bramlett as the leader and Reable as the misguided co-conspirator.

At the same time, other articles reported about Reable's own recantations of previous testimony in which she stated that all her admissions of involvement were coerced after being denied food, water, sleep and other basic physical rights by her interrogators. The police were questioned about it and, not surprisingly, denied such a thing occurred. Still, the existence of a number of reports like this show more sympathy for Reable; and with no further comments on the police's denial of ill treatment, this could further be interpreted as the reporters' potential mistrust of police and a growing support for Reable's innocence.

The trial itself was a madhouse. Due to the extensive news coverage, authorities determined that a fair trial in Shelby County would be impossible and moved it about thirty miles from Center to Carthage, Texas, in Panola County. In a 2003 *Texas Monthly* article, author Skip Hollandsworth found reports of seats in the courtroom being sold to reporters for as much as five dollars (just over eighty dollars by today's standards). By this judgment, perhaps even Panola County was not able to offer a fair trial.[31]

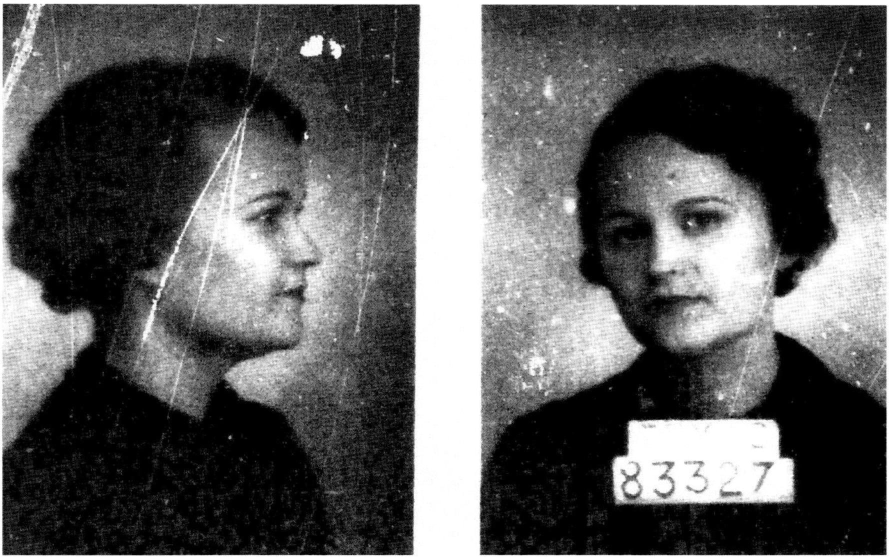

Mug shot of Reable Childs. *Texas Department of Criminal Justice.*

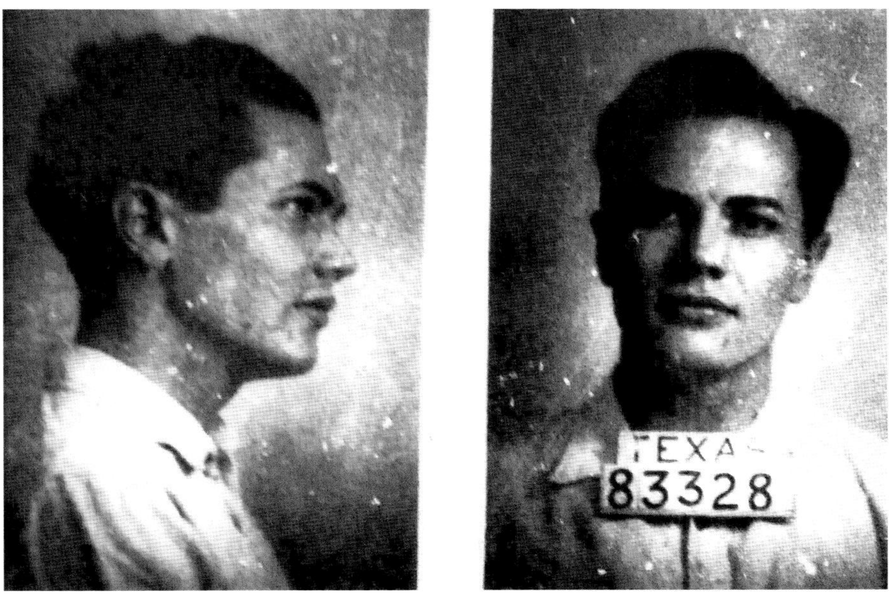

Mug shot of Terence Bramlett. *Texas Department of Criminal Justice.*

Nonetheless, Reable's trial began in mid-September 1936, with Bramlett's taking place just a few days afterward. At Reable's trial, forensic evidence was admitted and subsequently accepted that showed that Reable herself could not have been the shooter that night. The debate about her level of participation in Marlie Childs's murder, however, raged on as the jury tried to decide just how much, if anything, Reable knew beforehand. Bramlett's trial was no less dramatic, as he continued to assert that, due to his unswerving love for Reable, he was essentially a slave to her whims and desires, including participation in the heartless dispatch of her husband.

After hearing all sides, the juries seemed to decide that Bramlett held infinitely more sway than he claimed, and also that Reable knew plenty about the murder beforehand. Both were found guilty of "murder with malice aforethought" and given appropriately harsh sentences. As the shooter, Bramlett received a sentence of up to fifty years in prison at the main Huntsville unit of the Texas state penitentiary. Reable was given a twenty-five-year sentence, to be served at the Goree State Farm for Women. She walked through the prison gates on October 2, 1936, and registered as convict #83327, sentenced to a life on the Goree Farm until September 29, 1961—unless somehow, some way, she was freed before that time.

Convict #86388

On October 6, 1937, one year and four days after Reable Childs entered the Goree State Farm for Women, a young woman identified as convict #86388 was entered into the prison system. Her name was Dorothy Thompson, and she was twenty-nine years old; five feet, six inches tall; had dark blue eyes and auburn hair; and was serving a two-year sentence for a forgery conviction. As a woman being entered into the Texas prison system in the 1930s, her experience was typical. She was brought to the Huntsville unit and fingerprinted by "Ace High," a tall, handsome male convict. Her mug shot was taken and entered in the prison ledgers before she was loaded into the front seat of a prison van with a guard behind her and brought to Goree Farm.[32]

After Thompson arrived at Goree, she was given a medical examination, vaccinated and tested for syphilis. Only after receipt of a negative result would she be allowed to bunk with the general population. Women with venereal diseases were confined to a single dormitory. Mrs. Heath, wife of the prison manager and also the Goree prison matron, confiscated her few allowed belongings and ordered for a delousing for the new convict through a harsh application of coal oil, during which the new inmate complained bitterly about the treatment.[33]

Her dissent during the delousing process led to retaliation from the prison manager, Captain Heath. That evening, Heath called for the new prisoner and told her that he heard she was "being a bully" and that bullies were not tolerated in his prison; how dare she have spoken to Mrs. Heath in such a manner! At his behest, Thompson's long hair was cut off against her will, and Captain Heath even threatened to shave her hair entirely off. He asked Mrs. Heath if she preferred he do so, and she stated that an apology would be sufficient. Thompson apologized and attempted to shake hands on the matter but was told, "We don't shake hands with prisoners…you ain't nobody to us now."[34]

Understandably, those who oversaw the Goree unit of the Texas state prison felt they needed to enforce their authority to any inmates they felt did not understand acceptable behavior. But Dorothy Thompson, aka convict #86388, was not simply any inmate. She was Melba Newton George, a reporter with the *Houston Post*, who had received prior approval from the Texas Prison Board and the prison system's general manager to enter the prison on an undercover assignment. She arranged her illusory incarceration with the prison system's general manager, O.J.S. Ellingson, and provided conviction papers, signed by a judge, to the prison admission team so that she could be booked in true undercover status—and just then, she was taking notes. "You better not get smart again or I'll spank your —," the Captain told her, unknowingly. "Say—you're so big and strong I think I'll put you out with the niggers digging ditches."[35]

The threats from Captain Heath and the treatment resultant of her "sassing Mrs. Heath" led the reporter to decide to leave much sooner than her original plan, which was to stay at Goree for two weeks in order to get her story about prison life and those of some of the women incarcerated there. That first night as she lay with the others in the "syphilitic" dormitory—she had not yet received the results of her own test—Melba wrote a letter to O.J.S. Ellingson letting him know of her experiences so far and, as was allowed per the rules posted on the wall for the inmates to see, sealed it shut before sending. The other inmates watched and whispered among themselves of the trouble she was going to get herself into. Confident that her letter would arrive unhindered, she went throughout the morning as scheduled, noting that a "[*Houston*] *Chronicle* correspondent visited our sewing shop and I secretly enjoyed the thoughts of how I was scooping him."[36]

After the inmates were given their lunch, she was called into the office, where she hoped Ellingson would be waiting with the other prison officials, but it was only Captain Heath and his wife. They'd seen she sent a sealed letter to Ellingson, and they didn't like it one bit. "What'd you want to write to the General Manager for? You must have a complaint of some kind." Melba, not yet ready to blow her cover, was vague about her reasons for writing. They responded, "Dorothy, you're so smart I think I'm gonna put you in solitary confinement."[37]

Now she was ready to blow her cover. She explained to Captain and Mrs. Heath who she was, what she was doing there and how she had arranged it with the prison system and Ellingson. Unfortunately, Melba's disguise was too thorough, and Captain Heath did not believe her.

Having been thoroughly briefed by the other inmates on the horrors of solitary confinement and knowing she'd told them her story plainly, Melba refused to go to "sol," as it was referred to at the time. The conflict ended with "six Negro inmates" dragging Melba off to the solitary confinement cell block, where she stayed for several days on the floor with a thin blanket, being fed stale water and one slice of bread per day, bread that Reable Childs later described as being "alive with maggots" for the entire time she was at Goree.[38]

Several days into her "sol" stint, a visiting doctor believed what Melba imploringly told him and looked into it for her. After her story checked out with Ellingson and discovering that the name "Dorothy Thompson" (her undercover alias) only belatedly ever reached Ellingson, Melba was finally brought out of confinement, but not before a disbelieving Captain Heath telephoned and verified everything with the judge whose name appeared on the false conviction papers. One can only imagine what must have been going through the minds of Captain and Mrs. Heath as they proceeded to return Melba's belongings to her and give her a tour of the prison, this time as a reporter.

Melba Newton George's two-part exposé made the front page of the *Houston Post* on October 11, 1937, five days after she entered the prison. While she did write extensively about the prison surroundings and the impressions made by the inmates and her stories (including a glowing description of Reable Childs), she also recounted in lurid, humiliating detail the bullying tactics she experienced at the hands of Captain Heath. After all, they thought she was just another inmate, and her experience was of no account to them.

The Texas media took notice. In a reprint by the *Brownsville Herald* on October 21, 1937, the *Austin American* summarized the serious implications for the prison system:

> *What her study revealed, and wherein it should be of public value, is that the former dog sergeant who manages the farm, and his staff, know and do utterly nothing toward the salvage of those capable of staying above the level of the inmates, and nothing in the world toward making those who come out any better than those who come in.*[39]

Conditions at Goree State Farm for Women

Melba Newton George's frightening undercover operation made newspaper headlines, bringing to light yet another account of inmates in the Texas prisons systematically receiving impassive, harsh treatment at the hands of

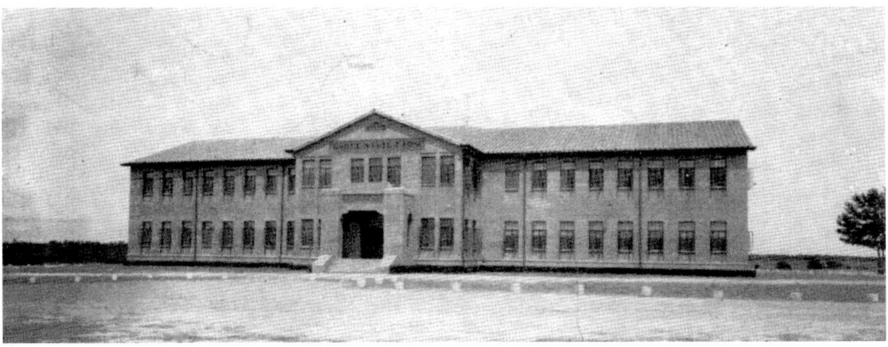

Above: Goree State Farm for Women, circa 1937. *Texas Department of Criminal Justice.*

Right: A portrait of prison official Captain Marcus Heath from a 1944 Texas Prison Rodeo souvenir program. *Texas Prison Museum.*

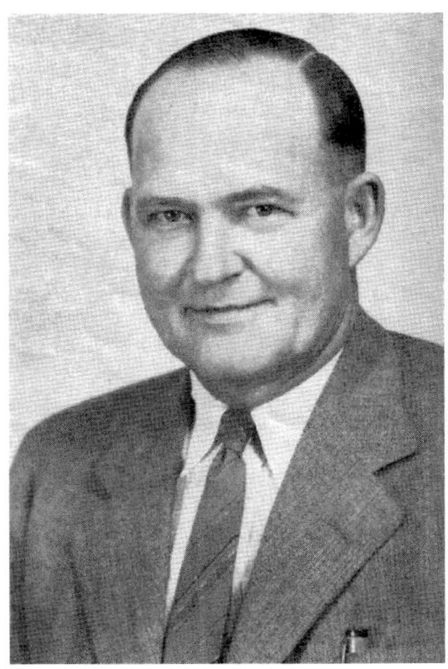

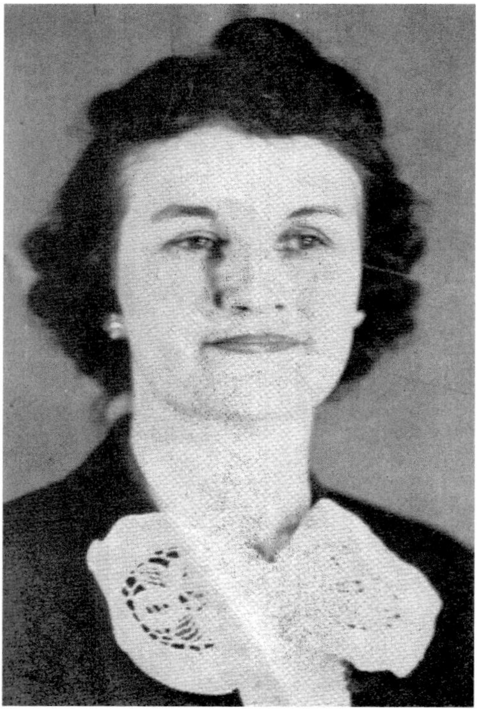

Left: A portrait of Mrs. Clyde Oree Heath from a 1944 Texas Prison Rodeo souvenir program. *Texas Prison Museum.*

Below: A personalized dormitory at the Goree State Farm for Women, circa 1940. *Texas Prison Museum.*

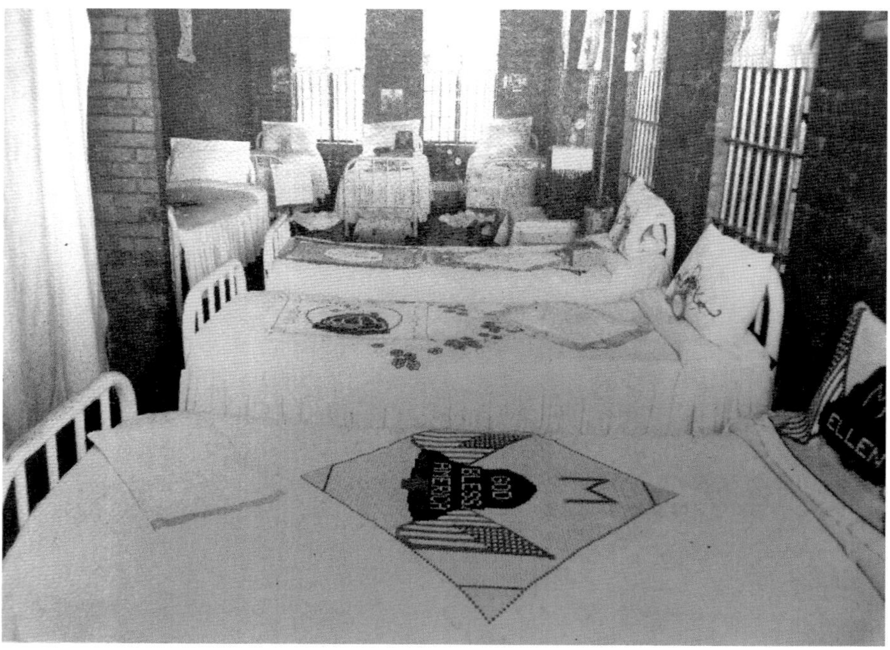

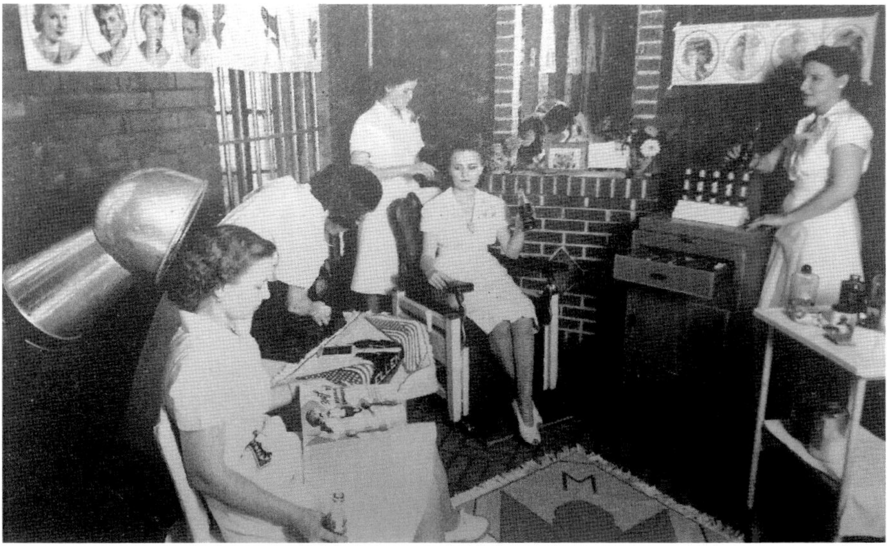

Goree inmates relax at the beauty shop classroom, where they learned vocational skills for after their release. *Texas Prison Museum.*

the guards and officials. Until her article, however, what may have been shoved under the carpet was that this was not just the case for male inmates. Female inmates suffered as well, and Melba Newton George's personal experience was a window into the issues commonly encountered by female inmates at the Goree unit.

Curiously, a detailed study of the Goree unit resides within a 1932 Texas A&M student master's thesis, a copy of which is housed at Huntsville's Texas Prison Museum. The graduate student, Kelly E. McAdams, met at length with prison officials, conducted interviews with them and toured the grounds of the unit, much like what occurred—albeit more sheepishly—with *Houston Post* reporter Melba Newton George. This thesis, while in no way an official document, provides a glimpse into not only the Texas prison system but also rural sociology studies of the Great Depression and New Deal era. Along with this glimpse come voices that are sharp with the pervading attitude of the time: sweeping statements of benevolent, compassionate prisoner management that completely contradict the undercover reporter's story just a few years later. Here is an excerpt from McAdams's thesis that summarizes the prison officials' way of thinking:

> *The treatment which the convicts receive is the vest* [sic] *that can be given to a person who is in the penitentiary. The manager and guards are not overbearing. The inmates get food that is far above what the average farmer gets in this section of Texas. Medical treatment is given to every convict, free of charge. All dental work is also given free. Punishment is given, only as a last resort. The treatment is not such that will cause the inmates to rebell* [sic]. *They merely submit and go ahead to their work. The work that the inmates are required to do is not strenuous, but is mostly of the domestic nature such as sewing, cooking, milking, caring for chickens, working in the cardens* [sic] *and canning.*
>
> *The managers of the various units of the prison system who the writer has talked with say the most important thing in dealing with convicts is discipline. The women in the Texas prison are handled with an iron hand. If a woman disobeys the rules and regulations of the prison she either gets thirty-six hours in "solitary" on bread and water, or "The Red Heifer" (a term that means the leather strap). This is employed only as a last resort and is not administered except in small amounts.*[40]

Obviously, all McAdams could do in the case of his thesis was repeat what he was told by the prison management. Concealment of the real conditions of the prison through generalized, euphemistic terms was a common practice for prison officials skilled in public relations, such as Lee Simmons and, later, O.J.S. Ellingson. However, in 1937, George was relegated to solitary confinement for a minor infraction, one that clearly did not represent a "last resort." George adhered to the rules and regulations of the prison and was punished for it. One can conclude that, in fact, such punishments were commonplace and overutilized in order to keep the inmates submissive enough for the officials' satisfaction.

Medical care and other concerns, such as inmate pregnancies, homosexuality and sexual abuse, were also addressed in detail. The thesis stated that, concerning medical care, preference was given to the white female convicts, who were allowed to convalesce in a dorm next to the hospital after any procedures; African American inmates were removed to their own beds in the cell-block dormitories. Homosexuality within the women's unit was treated as if it were a thing of the past through McAdams's proclamation that "sodism [*sic*], homo-sexuality and self-abuse were practiced to a great extent among the inmates up until recent years. However, from all investigations it has found to be not so prevalent as formerly."[41] McAdams does not expound on what investigations drew him to this dubious conclusion.

In his book *Doing Time in the Depression: Everyday Life in Texas and California Prisons*, scholar Ethan Blue discusses at length the power struggles within the relationships of inmates, guards and "building tenders" (inmate trusties). Both McAdams's thesis and Blue's texts note that expressions of dominance were mostly achieved through sexual means, including rape and other forms of sexually charged "ownership" between inmates, both male and female. Blue's book includes a deeper exploration of gender and race negotiations, illustrated by several graphic inmate accounts. McAdams, however, examines the sexual dominance aspect of prison life in the form of a salacious cautionary tale of the worst kind of inmate: the violent female recidivist. This takes the form of near legend in an inmate called "Cocaine Nora."

Convict #41391

Nora Harris, alias "Cocaine Nora" was one of the worse cases which has ever been on the Goree Farm. She was a dope fiend and unless she was under the influence of dope she was a regular demon. She was fifty years of age and serving her third term in prison; having been recaptured on other charges and returned, after each release.

Being a member of one of the worst gang of thieves in San Antonio, she was a dope peddler, a prostitute, receiver of stolen goods, one of the most nimble thieves in the gang, and a professional "bull-daggerer."[42]

Since she enjoyed this sort of copulation between another and herself to such an extent, the other women in the barracks were never safe against her persecutions. Because of this, the prison officials built a cell where she was forced to sleep each night and was looked in by a guard before retiring. She was one of the most unruly women who has ever been there, and and led the other women in all sorts of escapades. She was put in "solitary" a number of times for disobeying the prison rules, leading other women in disobeying, and for trying to escape.[43]

Prison records of "one of the most unruly women who has ever been there" show that the inmate was a short, slight African American woman. Her real name is difficult to ascertain, since she served her terms under three different names: Effie Johnson, Nora Johnson and the infamous Nora Harris. Harris served three terms between 1900 and 1920, with the first two for theft of varying levels of offense. Her second offense, in 1906, made local newspapers when she was charged with theft for "fleecing a white man out of $75 in money."[44] For the third offense, in 1917, Effie Johnson was sentenced to serve ten years for assault with intent to murder and was released on April 18, 1925.

Nora Harris's conduct registers in the Texas prison system show numerous pages of infractions, for which she received multiple punishments of solitary confinement and lashes with the Red Heifer. No mentions of sexual improprieties exist in her conduct register, but these were not typically noted within the inmate conduct registers, so the extent or "professionalism" of her bull-daggering remains unverified. By the time the young graduate student Kelly McAdams arrived, Cocaine Nora was long gone, leaving behind a boogey man–style legend that was documented in enough detail to become historical record.

The thesis also documented discussions held about women and babies in the prison, instances of rape and so on. Apparently, this was still somewhat of a taboo topic when he attempted to learn more. Regarding pregnancies and male sexual abuse of female inmates, McAdams himself acknowledged that it was a difficult topic to discuss and implied that he knew he was not being told the whole story.

Involuntary Sterilization of Female Inmates

One question that has repeatedly arisen during historical research of the prison system is whether female inmates of the Texas prison system were subjected to involuntary sterilization during their incarceration. Rampant speculation has abounded through the years on whether the female inmates underwent this type of surgery during their incarcerations and how frequently this occurred. This speculation includes past and recent avowals from family members of the female inmates of the Texas prison bands and even one startling personal account from the notorious burlesque performer Candy Barr (imprisoned for several years on a marijuana-related conviction) of a hysterectomy given to her—without permission or consultation—as late as 1959.

The eugenics movement in the United States had lost steam by the late 1930s, and Texas never passed official legislation sanctioning the practice of compulsory sterilization on women (or men) in its own penal system. Theoretically, involuntary sterilization of inmates could not have occurred without legislation to justify it, but upon investigation of some claims, along with examination of what little documentation is available, quite a bit of evidence exists to support this theory. As discussed later with the stories of Candy Barr, members of the Goree All-Girl String Band and other female inmates of the Texas prison system, evidence exists that suggests not only did involuntary sterilization occur, but it was commonplace for female inmates to be given hysterectomies against their will.

Even recently, how prisoners are treated in regard to reproductive rights is a hot topic. In 2013, news reports abounded with the explosive, divisive discovery that medical staff in California prisons had been performing sterilization procedures on hundreds, even thousands of female inmate patients that very year, with either coerced consent or no consent at all. When examined contextually today, a time when prisoners remain one of the most marginalized populations in the United States, the theory that most female inmates underwent involuntary sterilization as a normal part of their incarceration within a southern penitentiary in the 1930s has even more support.

The debate regarding involuntary sterilization in prisoners remains an important gender issue then, as well as today. Although involuntary sterilization of the female inmates is not directly related to music in the Texas prisons, it provides context and a scope for how tightly these inmates' lives were controlled. Incidentally, the sterilizations have had an indirect impact on the depth of research for this book. Historical research of the prison bands has been more difficult due to the absence of immediate relations in the form of children or grandchildren.

Research into the personal lives of both men and women, all inmates of the Texas prison system, can be a difficult topic to broach. Similarly, hard evidence regarding the extent of inmates' treatment—both medical and punitive—while in the care of the Texas prison system in the 1930s is challenging to unearth. Some documents have been lost, some destroyed and some never written down in the first place. However, right around this time, discoveries at the prison were made that brought prisoners' lives—and their experiences—to the attention of ethnomusicologists, scholars and archivists throughout the world. Through the music recorded by these ethnomusicologists and the films made and books written on these few musical inmates, the Texas prison system was, in turn, brought to the attention of a nation—this time, through its music.

3

YOU BE MY BIG BOSS, I'LL BE YOUR MAN

My son and I conceived the idea this summer that the best way to get real Negro singing and Negro idiom, and the music also in Negro idiom, was to find the Negro who had had the least contact with the whites... We had to record in most cases under very unfavorable conditions and our records are not at all perfect. But they did give us what we wanted: the tunes to the songs. And a fairly accurate representation of what the real Negro, in the South—removed from white influence—had given us in the way of folk songs.[45]
—*John A. Lomax*

Convict #42738

A single song, performed for Texas governor Pat Neff, decided the fate of penitentiary inmate Walter Boyd, convict #42738. "Walter Boyd" was an alias. The inmate's real name was Huddie Ledbetter, later known to the world by his Texas prison nickname, "Lead Belly."

In January 1924, Governor Neff toured the Texas prison camps with his wife and an entourage of other philanthropic women. As convict #42738, Lead Belly was already well known in the prison system as a talented musician and was summoned to perform for the governor and his guests.

Since his 1918 incarceration into the Central unit of the Texas prison system—also known as Sugarland—and despite his seven- to thirty-year conviction for the murder of one of his friends, Lead Belly enjoyed special

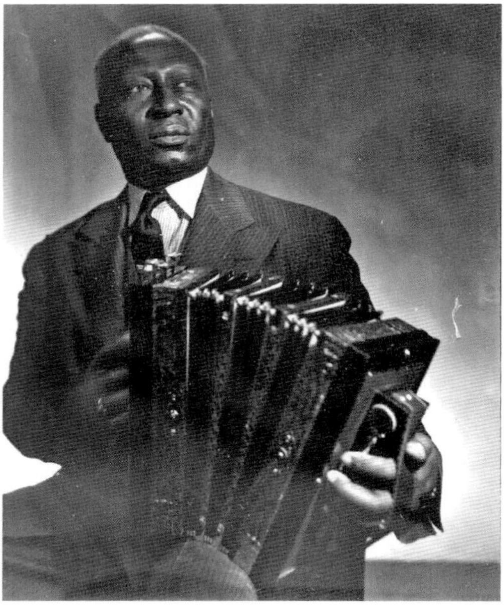

Lead Belly and his accordion. *Library of Congress, Prints & Photographs Division, Lomax Collection.*

privileges related to his talent. He had been playing guitar and singing as a professional musician since his early adolescence, and the music he played was well loved. On Sundays, the Sugarland manager, Captain Flannagan, allowed him to travel from unit to unit to tell stories and perform songs for the inmates and officials. Therefore, Lead Belly had plenty of time to build his craft, hone his already considerable entertainment skills and learn how to please the men who currently controlled his fate even better. No doubt using the presence of the women to further his cause, Lead Belly skillfully played on the sympathies for the governor and the assembled throng. He later described his calculated approach:

> *The way I made this song up* ["Governor Pat Neff"], *I lay down at night trying to get the right words, you know, kept a pencil and paper under my pillow. I'd be laying there, everybody'd be snoring and I'd doze off a little. I'd dream of a good word and I'd write it down a little... When we went up there that night, Governor Pat Neff and the women was sitting on the front porch. He was sitting with his legs crossed and his arms folded. He wore these tall collars and a bow tie, looked a little like a priest, you know. When I go in I wouldn't tell nobody what was on my mind. I put my guitar on my shoulder, had my twelve-string Stella... We sang "Midnight Special" and then the captain said, the Governor wants to hear a song. I sat down at a place where I could really see him. I was watching him, but I was watching the women, too. Before I start to sing that song, he talked to me. Then the women would ask me some questions...Finally I started my song. I put Mary in it, Jesus's mother, you know. I took a verse from the bible, around about the twenty-second chapter of Proverbs, around the fourteenth verse: if*

you forgive a man his trespasses, the heavenly father will also forgive your trespasses. But if you not forgive man of his trespasses, the heavenly father will still forgive you of your trespasses. Then I start singing.[46]

"Governor Pat Neff (Sweet Mary)," the song that Lead Belly had shrewdly honed in his cell by night and guilelessly performed for his entranced audience that January evening, goes like this:

Oh Mary, sweet Mary. Yes, Miss Mary, oh Mary

Nineteen hundred and twenty-three
When the judge took my liberty away from me
Nineteen hundred and twenty-three
When the judge took my liberty away from me
I left my wife wring her hands and cryin'
Sayin' Lord have mercy on that man of mine
I left my wife wring her hands and cryin'
Sayin' Lord have mercy on that man of mine

Told my wife before I left the land
If I never no more see her do the best she can
I told my wife before I left the land
If I never no more see her do the best she can
Goodbye Mary, sweet Mary. Oh Mary, ooo ooo ooo

I know my wife would jump and shout
When the train rolls up, I come a-stepping out
I know my wife would jump and shout
When the train rolls up, I come a-stepping out
Say what you gonna say?
Oh hello Mary, sweet Mary. Oh Mary, ooo ooo ooo

Had you Governor Neff like you got me
I'd a-wake up in the mornin', I'd set you free
If I had you Governor Neff like you got me
I'd wake up in the mornin', I would set you free
If I had you Governor Neff like you got me
I'd wake up in the mornin', I would set you free
Where you going?

I'm goin' back to Mary, ooo ooo ooo
Oh, Mary, ooo ooo ooo. Oh Mary, ooo ooo[47]

Lead Belly's forethought to his lyrics and performance paid off, and Governor Neff was well pleased. That very evening, Governor Neff vowed to give a pardon to Lead Belly, although he made it clear that he wouldn't do so right away. Instead, Lead Belly was to remain at the prison and serve his time but continue to perform for Neff whenever he visited until such time as the pardon was granted.

Governor Neff did not grant many pardons during his administration, so his willingness to pardon a convicted murderer is a testament, of sorts, to his belief that Lead Belly deserved a place in free society. But first, he wished to ensure that Lead Belly was willing to "play the game," remaining available and willing to provide music and entertainment on later penitentiary visits. Secondly, by waiting to give the pardon until his last few days in office, Neff avoided any major political controversy (historically a common practice for governors). By the time Neff stepped down in January 1925, Lead Belly was very close to completing seven years in the prison system, which was the minimum amount of his sentence.

At the Sugarland unit, Lead Belly kept out of trouble by working the fields and playing his music as directed (while no doubt wondering if the governor was going to keep his promise). Finally, true to his word from nearly a year before, Neff set Lead Belly free in one of his very last acts as governor of Texas. Convict #42738 was granted a full pardon by Governor Neff on January 16, 1925, having served six years, seven months and eight days of his sentence. Lead Belly left the prison with $115 (saved up from his performances) and made a beeline for Houston, staying there for a few months before heading back to his family and friends in Shreveport, Louisiana.

Lead Belly made a living in Shreveport for a few years working day jobs and performing around town. He took care of his mother and gained a new girlfriend named Era Washington. In 1927, Lead Belly also gained a new daughter named Jesse Mae, born to a woman who was not Era Washington. Life was hard, but Lead Belly did what he could with his music and work, carrying out a few bootlegging stints when things got really tough. The path Lead Belly took wasn't exactly straight and narrow, but it was respectable enough for the Great Depression, and he managed to keep a low profile until January 15, 1930.

That night, an altercation took place that, depending on the originating source, had different scenarios and in which Lead Belly had varying degrees of involvement. In the end, he was arrested for stabbing a white man named Dick Ellet; it was an "assault with intent to kill." A rushed trial was held, and five weeks later, the verdict was in: six to ten years for Huddie Ledbetter, to be served as convict LSP #19469 in the Louisiana State Penitentiary in Angola.

Life in Angola was three pits of hell below that of Sugarland. Relentless, backbreaking fieldwork had no limits as the inmates worked while chained together. The air was cloying and swampy, and there were no heating or air conditioning provisions in place. It was hellfire hot, sticky and damp in the summer and cold, damp and clammy in the winter. For the first several years of his sentence, the only respite Lead Belly enjoyed was one similar, albeit more informal, to the arrangement he'd had at Sugarland: he was allowed to play the guitar and sing during the inmates' relaxation time on Sundays. Word of mouth about his musical talent spread, eventually trickling up to the warden. And in 1933, when well-known folk song collector John A. Lomax and his son, Alan, drove up to the gates of Angola looking to record African American folk music untainted by what John Lomax called "white influence," Lead Belly was one of the warden's first recommendations for them to hear.

John Lomax was deeply impressed with Lead Belly's music and recorded him straightaway. The relationship deepened as Lomax returned to Angola on later trips to visit with Lead Belly and record more music. At one point, Lead Belly even wrote a song for Louisiana governor O.K. Allen. Clearly, he recalled the success he'd had with the Texas governor and hoped to receive some form of sentence commutation or clemency in Louisiana, as well. He entreated Lomax to record this song on one of his visits and send the recording to Baton Rouge, to which Lomax acquiesced. No evidence exists that the governor received that particular recording (even though the Lomaxes did deliver it), but nonetheless, Lomax believed in Lead Belly's talent immensely. In Lead Belly, Lomax saw the embodiment of living African American folk music.

The rest, as they say, is history. In 1934, Lead Belly finally obtained release from prison, due to accrual of enough "good time" to satisfy a specified number of hours toward his sentence. Lomax arranged for Lead Belly to accompany him to New York and other cities as a performer, as well as his traveling companion and chauffeur. Contrary to popular belief, Lomax did not arrange for Lead Belly's clemency in any way, and the song Lead Belly wrote for Governor Allen did not secure his release from prison.

Together, Lomax and Lead Belly traversed the well-appointed lofts and penthouses of the upper echelon. Almost all who heard him were transfixed by what they heard and embraced Lomax's "find," even if all did not approve of Lomax's treatment of Lead Belly (which was paternalistic at best and arguably reprehensible at worst).

Lomax's discovery of Lead Belly's music and its path to the Library of Congress can be found in a *March of Time* newsreel from 1935. Produced by *Time* magazine and video pioneer Fred Smith, these newsreels were semi-documentarian in nature, featuring news along with reenactments of the events they covered. In this video, African American convicts are huddled together in a dark, prison-like location noted simply as "Angola, LA." Lomax hilariously mimes recording Lead Belly singing "Goodnight, Irene" and then stands up and woodenly delivers his lines. Lead Belly responds enthusiastically in the exaggerated "yassuh, no suh" dialect that was de rigueur for 1930s film portrayals of African Americans.

> *LOMAX: That's fine, Lead Belly! You're a fine songster. I never heard so many good Negro songs.*
> *LEAD BELLY: Thank you, sir boss! I sure hope you send Governor O.K. Allen a record of that song I made up about him, 'cause I believe he'll turn me loose.*
> *LOMAX: Lead Belly, I don't know this governor. You might expect too much of me.*
> *LEAD BELLY: But Governor Pat Neff of Texas, he turned me loose when he heard this song that I made up about him.*
> *LOMAX: The Texas penitentiary too, Lead Belly?*
> *LEAD BELLY: Yes sir, it was thirty-five years for murder, but it wasn't my fault. A man was tryin' to cut my head off.*
> *LOMAX: Mighty bad, Lead Belly.*
> *LEAD BELLY: I believe Governor O.K. Allen, if you'll just send him a record of this song, I believe he'll turn me loose.*
> *LOMAX: Lead Belly, I'll try it.*
> *LEAD BELLY: Thank you, sir boss, thank you, sir, thank you!* [strikes chord on guitar for emphasis]

The newsreel then cuts to Lead Belly, guitar in hand, barging in on Lomax as he works at a desk in a respectable hotel. He shouts, "Yes sir, you be my big boss and I'll be your man!" Lead Belly's travels with Lomax are featured, as is a wedding to his "sweetheart, Martha Promise," and a final, glowing extolment on the significance of Lead Belly's contribution to the Library of Congress, where his music—"along with the original copy of the Declaration of Independence"—was committed to the archives of "this great, national institution."[48]

The newsreel wholeheartedly contributes to the mythology surrounding Lead Belly and Lomax's discovery of his music. It also convolutes the story of how he was freed from prison due to a song, implying that he was set free by the Louisiana governor, as had occurred in Texas in 1925. The pair's video reenactment is strikingly vaudevillian in tone between the paternalistic attitude of Lomax toward African Americans and Lead Belly's willingness to play the well-meaning, childlike role typically expected of the "good" African American, albeit imbued with a smattering of the trickster and a heavy dose of Lead Belly's natural talent and charm. Lead Belly played the game he needed to play to succeed and, thereby, played this role to perfection.

Through Lomax's recordings of him and the stardom that followed his prison release (which later cemented into legend), Lead Belly became an archetype of sorts for African American social elevation during the Jim Crow era and still maintained a "real deal" mystique. Long after his relationship with John Lomax came to a grindingly painful, lawsuit-laden end, Lead Belly's name is virtually synonymous with the definition of African American folk music, through the force of his personality and his musical contributions.

A distinct irony lies in Lead Belly's legendary status as an icon of American folk and blues music. He was pardoned for his crime by a powerful Texas governor, based on the strength of his music. However, had Lead Belly only played his music and cleaved to the straight and narrow path from the time of his 1925 pardon to the end of his life, today, most people would not know of him or of the songs he made famous—songs like "Midnight Special" or "Goodnight, Irene."

He probably would have remained in Texas or Louisiana, frequently performing live locally, just like he'd done before he landed in the Texas penitentiary. He would have made at least a few commercial recordings for "race music" labels, since public demand for blues music records had exploded during the early 1920s, while he was playing his own blues in the Texas penitentiary.

Today's collectors would discuss him, revere him, as an obscure yet titanic talent and vie fiercely for rare Lead Belly 78 rpm recordings. One could argue that had Lead Belly taken the high road, the lawful road, he might have remained a tremendously talented, yet obscure, regional bluesman, rather than the scion of American folk music that he came to be. Nonetheless, parlaying the power of his personality and his music into a governmental pardon by the governor of Texas not only affected his future and his fame but also foreshadowed events to come in the Texas prison system.

Convict #57469

Central State Farm, No 1.
Sugar Land, Texas
December, 24 1935.

Mr. John A. Lomax,
Austin, Texas,

I got your Xmas Card all O.K. Sure appreciate you thinking of me, I got it to [sic] *late to write you before Xmas. But will write you just the same and maybe you will think of me on New Years Day. Now if you will come around to see me in the near future, May be I can fix up a few songs for you I have a man working with me now he is very good. Try to come by some time and we will see what we can do for you. Wishing you and all the happiest Xmas you ever had. I have often wondered as I am a lone some Prisnor* [sic] *and glad to know that someone in Old Texas is taken me as thier* [sic] *old Friend yet. And I am forgotten as to know that you write me yet in all the Family my best wishes and regards & Merry Xmas a Happy New Year. Wishing you the best in health. In Life. I am,*

Yours very truly,
James Baker, Iron Head[49]

The above letter was written to John Lomax from another Texas penitentiary inmate: convict #57469, James "Iron Head" Baker. Lomax describes in detail his work with Iron Head in his 1946 book, *Adventures of a Ballad Hunter*. As was common in his writings, the details do not corroborate existing documentation. For example, Lomax begins by stating that Iron Head is "aged 63, convict #3610," both of which are inaccurate according to public and prison records.[50] Cross-examination of these records show that "Iron Head" was a prison nickname given to James Baker—which, in turn, was an alias for Tom Barkley—born to Tom and Ise Barkley on March 18, 1884, in Dallas, Texas. Thus, Iron Head was forty-nine years old when John Lomax and his son, Alan Lomax, came to the prison in 1933. The age of forty-nine also matches more closely the approximate age of the man in Lomax's own photographs from that trip, identified as "Iron Head" Baker.[51]

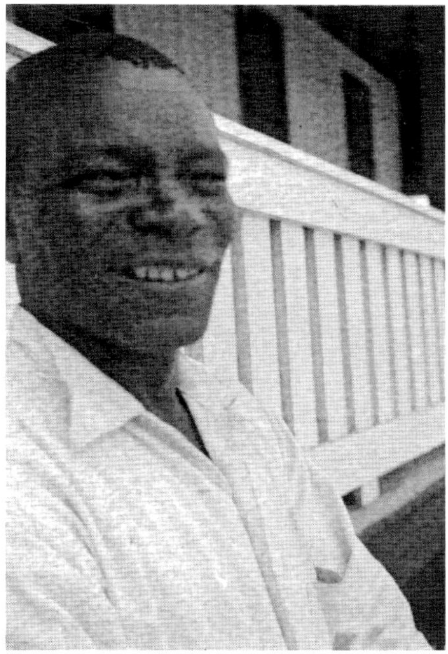

James "Iron Head" Baker poses for John Lomax. *Library of Congress, Prints & Photographs Division, Lomax Collection.*

Iron Head's prison records are extensive, and by the time the Lomaxes encountered him in 1933, he was serving his sixth term in the Texas prison system. First as convict #29046; then as #36275, #42161, #47166 and #53680; and, finally, as convict #57469. Iron Head personified (and self-identified as) an "H.B.C." (habitual criminal).[52] His sixth conviction of theft and burglary (mostly within the impoverished Dallas neighborhoods in which he lived) bestowed upon him a ninety-nine-year term, meant to unequivocally put him away once and for all.

A "lone some Prisnor," Iron Head was eager to perform his music for Lomax. "I know lots of jumped-up, sinful songs—more than any of these niggers," he bragged to Lomax through a window on Lomax's first foray behind penitentiary walls.[53] Lomax recorded Iron Head and Moses "Clear Rock" Platt on this trip. Fascinated by the mystique of it all, Alan Lomax described the experience in his book *Land Where the Blues Began*: "Despite our own pale faces, which must have seemed like masks of indifference to so many of them, the convicts filled our records with a thousand moving songs, an epic of hot sun and brutality and human courage, mounted upon sincere and profound melodies."[54]

One of the most moving epics of "hot sun and brutality" that the Lomaxes recorded by Iron Head was "Ol' Hannah" (referring to the sun). "Ol' Hannah" was not just sung in the Texas prisons but also in a number of other plantation-style prisons throughout the South. Iron Head sang while documenting the lyrics with his characteristic "eye dialect"—phonetic interpretation and spelling—for southern African American speech patterns.

Been a great long time since Hannah went down,
Oh Hanna[h], *go down;*
Been a great long time since Hannah went down,
Oh Hannah, go down!
She's gone behin' dem western hills, (etc.)

I wonder where is de Capt'in gone? (etc.)
He's gone to de house to ring de bell (etc.)

Bullies, did you hear what de Capt'in said? (etc.)
Bullies, if you work I'm goin' trust you well
An' if you don't, I'm goin' give you hell. (etc.)

You orta come on dis river in Nineteen-fo',
You'd find a dead nigger on ev'ry turnrow. (etc.)

You orta come on dis river in Nineteen-ten,
Dey was workin' de wommens like dey was workin' de men. (etc.)

Go down, Old Hannah, don't you rise no mo',
Oh, Hannh, go down;
If you rise any mo', bring Jedgement Day,
Oh, Hannah, go down![55]

Lomax took a liking to Iron Head and his songs, and they struck up a friendly acquaintance with Lomax visiting the prison while in the area and, later, sending one another cards and letters. In 1936, Lomax shrewdly proposed to the authorities to release Iron Head into his custody for a time, taking him along to be a "chauffeur and companion on a hunt for folk songs among the Southern penitentiaries and remote Negro communities. Iron Head's singing was to inspire other Negro songsters to strive to excel him." If he behaved appropriately on the trip, Lomax determined to ask the governor for an extension on the parole or possibly even a pardon. Soon enough, a four-month furlough for convict #57469 was granted on March 24, 1936, one week after Iron Head's fifty-second birthday. Lomax drove Iron Head to his home on 34th Street in Austin, Texas, before hitting the road with Alan.

Lomax's paternalistic—if not patronizing—desire to provide an opportunity for inmate exoneration and companionship for himself was a driving force in his later life. He had already made societal inroads with notorious bluesman and former convict Huddie "Lead Belly" Ledbetter. Even though Lomax's association with Lead Belly ended badly, he apparently hadn't had enough and sought to improve yet another convict's lot in life by taking him out on the road. This was a naïve, albeit well-intended approach, for on that trip, Lomax was presented with Iron Head's true nature. Much to Lomax's chagrin, Iron Head was nothing if not frank when divulging his criminal tendencies. He said:

> *I jes' took what I wanted. I never done no work. My grandma raised me. Ev'ry day she giv' me my dinner in a bucket an' sent me to school. I never got there. But mos'ly I stole from niggers. De law don't pay no 'tention when niggers lose their things. I'd watch a house till de womenfolks go away. Den I'd go in an' take what I wanted.*[56]

Lomax was also privy to what he perceived as Iron Head's singularly selective philosophies on life, including an admission not only that he had committed all crimes for which he was imprisoned but that he was also helpless to stop. According to Lomax, Iron Head essentially took what goodwill Lomax had to offer him without making any promises to stay above the law in the future. In retrospect, Lomax wrote of his disappointment at how Iron Head's story played out, not excluding his own responsibility in the matter:

> *When we finished our work among the Negroes where Iron Head's singing had been useful, I proposed to send him back to Austin where, according to promise* [to prison officials], *I was to set him up in the business of weaving rugs from corn shucks. He was bitterly resentful and hinted at reprisals on my family. Neither was he willing to find a job and work in Washington. So I bought a ticket, gave him money, and sent him back to Texas.*
>
> *He never showed up at my home in Austin. Another friend found work for him in the country. But he couldn't stay away from Austin honkytonks* [sic] *and low company. Finally, I learned, he had deserted his job on the farm and become a street-corner bum. Then quickly followed the "pen" for the seventh time—and life.*
>
> *Last time I saw him, it was a sad meeting and a sad separation. Ramsey Farm is the State's home for the long-termer and incorrigibles. I should have left him at Sugar Land to weave from corn shucks horse collars and rugs.*[57]

Lomax lamented the consequences of his decision to give Iron Head money and a modicum of trust that he would "do the right thing," but Iron Head was a man who never claimed to be above the law. Lomax himself had done what he perceived as "the wrong thing"—he had set Iron Head, an admitted repeat offender, free to commit more crimes and, thus, end up with an even bleaker future. Embarrassingly, everyone knew that Lomax's kind assistance had come to naught, evidenced by a 1937 Associated Press (AP) blurb that appeared in newspapers throughout the nation. It was quite a change from the accolades Lomax had received when he brought Lead Belly to national prominence just two years earlier. He wrote:

> *James "Iron Head" Baker, who sang his way out of the Texas penitentiary, is back inside its walls. Gove. James V. Allred, impressed with the negro's ability to sing folk songs, granted him a reprieve last year from a life sentence for habitual burglary so he could accompany John A. Lomax, curator of folk songs for the Library of Congress, on a tour. When the tour ended he worked several jobs, he says, but easier money beckoned. After Baker was charged with burglarizing several Austin residences, the governor revoked his furlough.*[58]

Even back in 1936, convict #57469, by all accounts, seems to have accepted that he'd never be able to beat the law and would forever be behind bars. James "Iron Head" Baker, born Tom Barkley, died of kidney cancer in the Texas prison system on February 23, 1944, several weeks before his sixtieth birthday. He is buried in the prison cemetery at Huntsville.

Convict #46474

"Gimme room, niggers, gimme room. Let me git at dat singing machine. I'se de out-singin'est nigger on dis here plantation. I's been in de pen forty-nine years off and on, an' I ought to know all de songs. Git out o' my way!"

I saved the microphone of the recording machine from being overturned by the big, eager, confident, self-important copper-colored man as he pushed through the throng of Negro convicts.

"Wait, Clear Rock," I said. "Later we will try you out."

"Ready right now," he insisted, and I hardly had time to start the machine before he plunged into a patting song, "Dat's All Right, Honey," where his big hands helped carry the song.

"Way up yonder, darlin', 'bove the sun, sugar,
Girls all call me honey, sugar plum, sho' nuff!
Got a horse, sugar; buggy, too, baby;
Horse's black, darlin'; buggy's blue, sho' nuff!
Dat's all right, honey, dat's all right, baby."

The crowd cheered, for the tune was catchy. Where he got the words and tune he did not know. I have not found the song elsewhere. Here was evidence that among Negro convicts, Alan and I were to find an easy source of folk songs, for Clear Rock was among the first group of Negro convicts in our search.[59]

Lomax's patronizing yet mesmerizing account of his initial encounter with convict #46474, Moses "Clear Rock" Platt, nonetheless extolled the ability of this "seventy-one year old water boy, a satisfied prisoner for life," to recall an unheard of number of folk songs. "He had a store in equal to continuous length to the *Iliad*," Lomax wrote years later in *Adventures of a Ballad Hunter*.[60]

Although the general implication in Lomax's account is that Clear Rock was in the prison continuously, for close to a full fifty years, Clear Rock was more accurate when he said he was in there "forty-nine years off and on." When Lomax first met Clear Rock on their first penitentiary recording trip in 1933, Clear Rock was serving the last of many terms in the Texas prison—a life sentence for assault and attempted rape—and he was sixty-six years old.

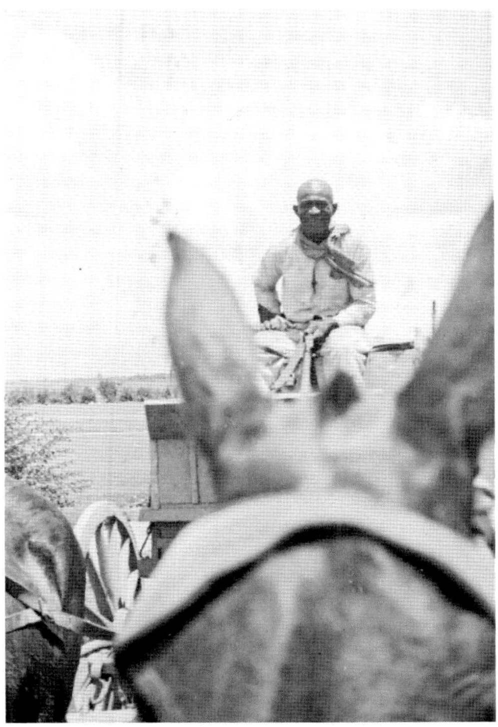

Moses "Clear Rock" Platt works the fields. *Library of Congress, Prints & Photographs Division, Lomax Collection.*

Prison records for Clear Rock abound, with stints from 1909 to 1910 and again from 1910 to 1919. Before 1900, his records appear to be under various names—"Jim Robinson" or "Moses Robinson"—and conduct registers from the prison system show that Clear Rock committed many infractions during his prison stints. For these transgressions, Clear Rock received numerous punishments, including the "pole," the "barrel," time in the hole (solitary) or in chains. The punishments ranged from twelve to forty-eight hours. And on October 25, 1912, Clear Rock even escaped the Ramsey state farm and managed to stay out of sight for over a year. He was recaptured on April 30, 1914, and his sentence extended thusly.

Unlike Lead Belly and Iron Head, Lomax showed no interest in removing Clear Rock from the penitentiary during his 1930s visits. Perhaps this was due to Clear Rock's criminal history, for which he was not likely to have been granted any furlough by the authorities.

Hoping to record some more of Clear Rock's impressive repertoire (this time with better equipment), Lomax wrote to the prison looking for Clear Rock while preparing for his 1939 Southern States Recording Trip. Much to his surprise, he was told that Clear Rock was long gone from behind bars. As it turned out, Clear Rock had never needed a furlough from Lomax, for he'd gone one better: he was granted a conditional pardon by Ma Ferguson on November 27, 1934.

Using his connections at the prison, Lomax learned that the illiterate Clear Rock was living in Taylor, Texas, working as a local preacher. Lomax seemed surprised but pleased that the illiterate convict had done so well for himself after he left prison. While Lomax and his wife, Ruby Terrill Lomax, toured the southern penitentiaries and small communities in the South on their 1939 recording trip, he made sure to stop in Taylor. With an indomitable faith in Clear Rock's ability to sniff out a good opportunity, Lomax was certain he could locate Clear Rock and get some of that immense folk music repertoire documented. He wrote:

> *Clear Rock on earlier recording trips had been one of the most fruitful sources of Negro stories and songs, especially work-songs and other secular songs. And so the search was on: on the promise of a dime a boy conducted us to Clear Rock's home, only to hear from neighors* [sic] *that Clear Rock and his wife had been seen going up the tracks towards town just ten minutes ago; twenty-five cents was to be the reward for bringing him to our hotel. No word had come by breakfast time, and so Mr. Lomax started out afoot in earch* [sic]. *When he returned to the hotel two hours later, there he found Clear Rock, sitting on the running board of the Lomax automobile; with him was his two-hundred-fifty pound wife, his "seventeen wife," as he told Mrs. Lomax later. They had been waiting at the car from six o'clock. The wife, looming too large for our small hotel room, was dismissed with*

> *breakfast money…Mr. Lomax wished to re-record some of the Negro's best songs with the improved machine. At first Clear Rock was slow at entering into the spirit of the old work-songs, "disremembering" the words of some of them, because perhaps of two circumstances: Clear Rock was now "The Reverend Mose Platt," devoted to hymns and spirituals, and what secular songs he indulged in were mostly modern jazz, sung for the entertainment of his white friends. But Mr. Lomax's cajoling words and a substantial contribution to the next Sabbath's collection helped Clear Rock to overcome his handicaps, and he was off. For four hours he told stories and sang and preached and prayed.*[61]

John Lomax

Method and Myth

Clear Rock never needed Lomax to negotiate for his own release, which must have been somewhat surprising to Lomax, given his antiquarian and inaccurate perception of African Americans as childlike and incapable of navigating complex social dynamics (even as he worked closely with them).

Lomax's intentions and methodology regarding the subjects and music he recorded is well documented by eminent scholars. One of these scholars, Jerrod Hirsch, noted that Lomax's "own accounts were repeated so often in so many different versions that they too can be treated as narratives, as the lore about John Lomax that he chose to offer the public."[62] Lomax essentially constructed a mythology for not only the music he recorded but also for himself.

After he achieved acclaim with his documentation of cowboy songs in the early 1900s, Lomax eagerly promoted the idea of collecting "folk songs of the Negro." His considerable efforts came with an oft-quoted qualifier that the folk songs he collected needed to be "the least contaminated by white influence or by modern Negro jazz." Despite the qualifier, Lomax's documentation of this music was vast and successful, and his work in the southern penitentiaries was unequivocally groundbreaking for the study of African American folklore.

Lomax sought out African American outlaws and laborers and recorded their music under very specific parameters, which generally excluded the Anglo culture. In the African American folk songs, freedom is an intangible

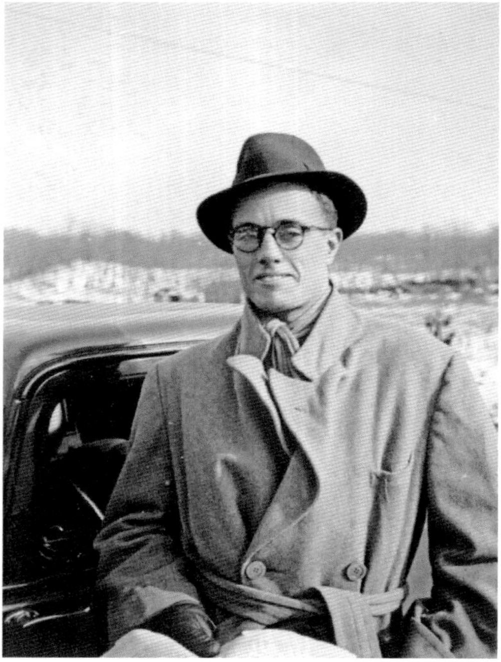

Folklorist John A. Lomax on the road. *Library of Congress, Prints & Photographs Division, Lomax Collection.*

desire of those dependent on others. In the prison system, freedom lies in the hand of the (mostly white) prison and government officials. However, the African Americans who were documented by Lomax—like Lead Belly, Iron Head and Clear Rock—also played a role in this mythology. Whether consciously or unconsciously, African Americans were discouraged from attaining such freedom themselves. With a painful yet intriguing polarity, they contributed to his developing mythology in that they were allowed to sing about the desire for their home as well as freedom and individuality, universally human traits that connected them with the Anglo culture and allowed some insight into their world, if from a safe distance.

On May 14, 1939, Lomax returned again to the Huntsville prison to record the music of African American inmates. He'd already found Clear Rock and gotten what he could from him on this trip—but when he got to the penitentiary, Lomax found that the music had shifted since he was last there.

Huntsville

1939 Southern States Recording Trip

"I Ain't Got Nobody"

Now I ain't got nobody
And there's nobody cares for me

'Cause I am sad and lonely
Won't somebody come on and take a chance with me?
I sing sweet songs all the time
Won't you come be a pal of mine
'Cause I ain't got nobody
And there's nobody cares for me

There's a saying going around this town
And I began to think it too
It's mighty hard to love someone and that someone don't love you
Once I had a loving man, the sweetest man in this town
But now he's gone and left me, he has thrown me down
Now I ain't got nobody, and there's nobody cares for me.

'Cause I am sad and lonely
Won't somebody come on and take a chance with me
I sing sweet songs all the time
Won't you come be a pal of mine
'Cause I ain't got nobody
And there's nobody cares for me.[63]

John Lomax cut the recording off after the song but caught a fast-talking, sweet-voiced woman with a high-pitched, infectious laugh before the sound cut out. Comparing field notes of the 1939 Southern States Recording Trip with his wife, Ruby Terrill Lomax, with that of other folk music he recorded, Lomax's impression of the inmate and her singing is clear: he doesn't find her musical contributions to be of much value. He wrote:

> *Hattie Ellis is a blues singer who is very popular on the radio program sent out from the Texas State Penitentoary* [sic]...*The Captain Heath told us that in one week Hattie received 3,000 "fan" letters. She is in for thirty years for killing a man. Another Dallas, Texas Negro girl who "come visitin' in Arkansas and got took up for somethin' I didn't do", told us that Hattie wouldn't have got such a long term if she hadn't sassed the judge when he brought her boot-legging activities into the murder case. Hattie's voice is fast becoming "throaty" as she strives to imitate the professional "blues" singers...both of these blues were accompanied by Jack Ramsey. Ramsey is a white convict within "The Walls."*[64]

Hattie Ellis, also known as convict #73126, was a huge star on the radio by the time the Lomaxes came back through the prison in 1939. Prison records show she was African American, born in 1912 and hearkened from Rockdale, Texas. By the early 1930s, she was in Dallas working in the bootlegging trade. A tricky line of work, bootlegging was lucrative enough, although dangerous—and, often, deadly. Hattie Ellis shot and killed Henrietta Murphy on February 8, 1932, and was sentenced to thirty years in prison. *Texas Monthly* writer Skip Hollandsworth unearthed a few details about the crime:

> *According to trial testimony, Henrietta and some other woman had come to Hattie's house, wanting to buy whiskey for a dollar from Hattie's boyfriend. Hattie didn't sell them any whiskey and she and Henrietta got into an argument. Henrietta, who was apparently drunk, urinated on Hattie's floor. Later, Hattie drove up to Henrietta's house in a little black roadster, talked to her for a few minutes while sitting in the car, then opened the front door, got out, grabbed Henrietta by the coat, drew a pistol, and shot her in the stomach and then in the back. There was a testimony that Henrietta had threatened Hattie during an earlier argument over a dollar. Hattie herself testified that she had not pulled out her pistol until Henrietta came after her with a razor. But a judge and jury were not convinced.*[65]

Hattie performed every week on the radio with *Thirty Minutes Behind the Walls* and sang every year at the radio show, as well as at fiddle contests and other engagements outside the prison walls, until her conditional pardon from Governor O'Daniel in 1940. In 1944, she was released from making parole reports. Her conduct register at the prison also states that this conditional parole was revoked in 1955 but does not give any reason and does not have another prisoner number assigned to her name. This generally indicates that she was not returned to the prison and assigned another inmate number, but the notes on her "good hours" accrued toward her term show a last date of March 22, 1956.

Who was Hattie Ellis? How did she come to sing as well as she did? Did she ever sing or record music after prison? She was certainly talented enough to have a considerable career in singing. Unfortunately, all public records aside from the prison registers are unclear. Hattie Ellis's scintillating voice—one that rivals the greats of the era—can be forever heard in the annals of the Library of Congress, but the woman behind that incredible voice remains a mystery.

As for the guitar player who accompanied Hattie Ellis on her Lomax recordings, "Cowboy" Jack Ramsey's presence is an anomaly since those two songs were very likely the only penitentiary recordings the Lomaxes made in which a white prisoner was treated as part of the African American folkloric story.

It's an unfortunate happenstance that throughout his life, John Lomax repeatedly—and quite thoroughly—chose not to forge the human connections further and challenge established definitions of "authentic" folk music. If he had chosen to expand this connection and include representatives of other races and ethnicities in more areas of his fieldwork, Lomax might have found some surprising connections. It can be safely assumed that for Hattie Ellis's recordings, Lomax would have preferred an African American convict as accompanist, rather than a white convict.

Deemphasizing the presence of white musicianship was a clearly stated intent of Lomax's and likely grew out of his desire to present his African American convict recordings as representative of an authentic musical tradition. Lomax's lofty proclamation of searching for African American music uncontaminated by "Negro jazz" is absolutely contradicted not only by Ramsey's presence on the 1939 Lomax recordings but also by the songs Hattie Ellis actually recorded for him. Hattie's version of "I Ain't Got Nobody"—a perfect example of "Negro jazz" if there ever was one—is truly unique because it is not authentic in the way that Lomax envisioned.

A popular song with many early renditions by stars such as Marion Harris, Bessie Smith, Louis Armstrong, the Mills Brothers and more, Hattie Ellis's version of "I Ain't Got Nobody" stands on its own among them as a perfect blend of black and white, of blues and jazz. Furthermore, lyrics and vocal style for Hattie Ellis's version of "I Ain't Got Nobody" indicate that she may have had other influences. Her vocal tone and vibrato are reminiscent of popular blues and jazz singers like Billie Holiday. But the rhythm of the song; the lyrics; the tempo; and, most importantly, her phrasing are most similar to western swing vocalist Tommy Duncan's style, as sung in the 1935 Bob Wills version of the song.

Far-fetched as it may be, Hattie might have been familiar with Bob Wills's version of the song. Another possibility is that she learned to sing the song from the white inmates who played on the radio show, who would have been familiar with Wills's version and perhaps played it themselves with a male vocalist. It's unfortunate that Lomax was so close-minded and so quick to denigrate Ellis as "striving to imitate the professional blues singers," because the voice on the recording is entirely professional in delivery. Furthermore, it is her own interpretation, colored by any variety of sources.

So why did Lomax choose to record Hattie Ellis? He may have acquiesced simply to comply with the prison officials' recommendations. A more optimistic theory is that he made an exception to their collecting philosophy because of Hattie Ellis's astonishing vocal talent.

Nonetheless, Lomax's decision to exclude white inmates from his prison field recordings created a pattern of omission unchallenged and perpetuated by folklorists who followed his lead. Lomax only recorded the music of non-white prisoners—as if the cowboy songs, Anglo ballads and sea shanties that he'd found extremely significant earlier in his career were of no merit if they were collected inside prison walls. Furthermore, later folklorists such as Bruce Jackson, Harry Oster and Alan Lomax evidently followed the precedence that John Lomax established regarding folk song collection in prisons. There is no doubt that these men all made monumental, valuable contributions to folklore studies and exceptional field recordings in the prisons. But in general, the recordings they made exclude white inmates from folk song collection within Texas penitentiaries.

4

THIRTY MINUTES BEHIND THE WALLS

Before the advent of radio, prisoners were exiled. Citizens outside paid little attention to them. But now you hear them talk; you hear them sing; you find out they are sons and daughters of good mothers. You find out that they made mistakes, thus proving that they are human; and thus recalling to our minds that He who gives us the radio, and everything else we have, is the same One who gave us the assurance and the hope of redeeming our souls after we had made even the greatest mistakes. And if the Great Benefactor…can forgive the most terrible sinner spiritually, isn't there some reason in believing that we as human beings should find some method of permitting men and women who make mistakes to redeem themselves and reestablish themselves among us[?][66]

—Governor Wilbert Lee "Pappy" O'Daniel, on Thirty Minutes Behind the Walls

Convict #86043

Mention Jack Purvis to any musician who came up playing hot music in those days [the 1930s]*, and the reaction was invariably the same: wonderful, sometimes brilliant. A madman, probably a con artist. But brother, could he ever play. He's part of the mythology, one of those figures around whom musicians' tall tales seem to cluster…Purvis near, Purvis far; Purvis fleeing the cops over*

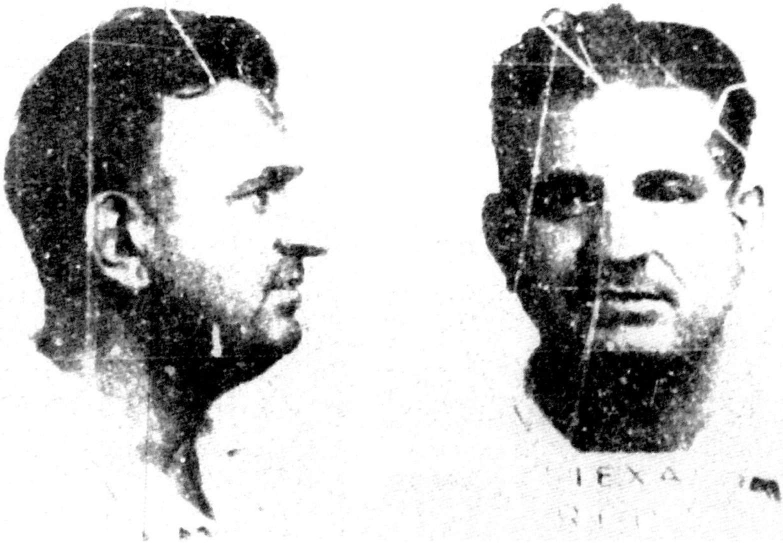

Mug shot of Jack Purvis during his second prison stint, in the mid-1940s. *Texas Department of Criminal Justice.*

rooftops in southern France; Purvis climbing the Alps barefoot, or running guns in Mexico; Purvis giving flying lessons in the South Pacific and "Greek dancing lessons" to scantily clad maidens in Miami.

But that at least partly obscures—or at least deflects attention from—the more important reality of his playing. Rhapsodic, almost operatic in its breadth of conception, Purvis's trumpet, at its best, captures a sense of drama…unconventional, against the grain, he danced to nobody's tune but his own.[67]

For convict #86043—a jazz trumpet legend—living high and laying low was his immediate nature. Jackson "Jack" Purvis was born in Kokomo, Indiana, on December 11, 1906, to Sanford B. Purvis and Waneta "Nettie" Purvis (née Jackson). According to the 1910 census, Sanford B. Purvis was a sales manager at Stove Works and, according to other sources, a prominent local real estate mogul. Sanford Purvis was thirty years older than his young wife, with one marriage and two grown children under his belt. The two married in 1904, less than a year after the death of Sanford's first wife, Mary. Although not wanting for money, Jack Purvis was not born into a happy environment. In 1910, Waneta attempted to divorce her husband on grounds that "he had abused her not less than 100 times in the last few years."[68] She was granted a temporary restraining order, but she was not granted a divorce, and a younger son, J. Richard Purvis, was born in 1911. In 1912, Waneta died, and Sanford was left with two young boys to raise. Some sources say that Sanford married again, but this information is unclear, although the 1920 census states that the family had a live-in housekeeper. As a teenager, Jack's escapades became legendary at the reformatory where he was dispatched in 1919 on the order of a local judge. A 1919 *Kokomo Tribune* article devoted entire page sections to his restless wiliness:

> *Little Jack Purvis has staged another stunt. As per usual, he has not only staged it but gotten away with it. He was caught, but is gone again. Jack Purvis, about three weeks ago, was sentenced by Judge Overton, sitting as a juvenile court to a term at the Indiana School for Boys at Plainfield, he having been convicted of repeated lapses into petty pilfering. He was taken to the institution by his father, S.B. Purvis, long a prominent figure in broker circles of Kokomo. When the father left him there, the lad promised him he would be dutiful and earn his release as soon as possible.*[69]

Three parts exasperation and one part grudging admiration, the article goes into an extended blow-by-blow account of Purvis's escape from the reformatory shortly after his incarceration there and the subsequent trials of his family and police as they searched for him. Even as a teen, Jack Purvis's cunning and audacity evidenced themselves. The article's description of his success in fooling a reformatory guard into thinking that he was not Jack Purvis but some other, "half-witted" charge is particularly telling, especially when his family came to identify him, and he actually attempted to fool them, too—this time unsuccessfully.

The Indiana School for Boys at Plainfield was a notorious reformatory with many deaths and startling accounts of brutality and abuse—one most notably laid forth by convicted murderer Charles Manson, who was sent there in the late 1940s; he escaped in 1951. Yet with all its notoriety, at the Indiana School for Boys, Jack Purvis managed to get his hands on some musical instruments. Through the brass of the trumpet and the trombone, he found his life's true calling—that is, if petty pilfering could be discounted. During his years at the reformatory, Jack Purvis planned and plotted, escaped the reformatory and was sent back. All the while, his talent on the trumpet and trombone developed. Soon, he was playing in local jazz bands. In 1923, the same year his father, Sanford B. Purvis, passed away from a stomach disorder, Jack took a job playing with regional jazz star Hal Denman and his Carolina Cotton Pickers. From there, he hit the road—running.

For the remainder of the 1920s, Jack Purvis played trumpet with various jazz stars of the era. In 1926, he landed in New England, playing with the Original Pennsylvania Serenaders, and by 1928, he was a cornet player on the cruise ship circuit. It was at this point that Jack went wild with invention of new identities and personae for himself, ingratiating himself with first-class passengers. Most often, he referred to himself as "Jacques" Purvis and assigned himself the pretentious-sounding "Fræmac" as a middle name, with the *a* and the *e* combined in a diphthong, like in the archaic spelling of "aeroplane." Fitting with his new name, Jack's escapades in Europe achieved legendary status in 1928 and 1929 while he performed with American jazz bands at various French resorts and consorted with the "local color." In *Lost Chords*, Sudhalter wrote of him:

> *Working…at the Hotel Negresco, on the seafront at Nice, Purvis fell in with some local Arab boys who sold everything from rugs to pornographic postcards, learned some Arabic from them, and wound up affecting Turkish garb on the stand complete to fez and turned-up slippers. Later, on the top floor of a cheap hotel in Montmartre, Purvis…vaulted the rail, and leaped to the roof of the neighboring Bal Tabarin, with all the gendarmes in hot pursuit.*[70]

These "gendarmes"—French police officers—chased Purvis because he had reportedly relieved an American tourist of his American Express travelers' checks, either by con or a good old-fashioned pickpocket job. This event foreshadowed events to come.

After a few months in Europe, Jack returned to the United States and accepted a job with jazz great Hal Kemp. Through his connections with Kemp, on December 17, 1929, Jack Purvis recorded for Okeh Records. Some of these recordings survived until the present day and can be heard on the Internet or on CD. Of these recordings, jazz scholar Richard Sudhalter pointed out that Jack Purvis imitated the African American trumpet players—most notably Louis Armstrong and Cladys "Jabbo" Smith—but also that Jack Purvis sounded "like no other white trumpet player of 1929."[71]

Despite his talent, a "too hot to handle" reputation—compounded by difficulties with getting work during the Great Depression—dried up the jazz gigs for Jack Purvis, and in the 1930s, he began to rely on his "disarming" brand of conning and pilfery on a full-time basis. While working as a hotel cook, but also presumably while working his gun running jobs in El Paso, in

June 1937, the charming smuggler made a grievous error when he entered a bar in downtown El Paso and befriended Oklahoma City inventor and manufacturer Lester O. Thompson. Posing as a convention attendee, Jack accompanied the visitor to the Hotel Paso del Norte, where he punched Thompson in the face and patted him down, pocketing Thompson's wallet, which contained $800. On July 31, 1937, Jack Purvis was convicted of robbery and sentenced to five years in the Texas state penitentiary. Staring down half a decade behind steel bars, once inside the Huntsville unit, Jack Purvis did what he did best—he worked the situation to his advantage.

In October 1938, *Down Beat* magazine, which is still around today, reported on the notorious trumpet player's activities behind those steel bars:

> *Jack Purvis, pipe in full steam, prepares to give the down beat to his orchestra for a Texas Penitentiary broadcast. Formerly with several top-notchers, Jack ran into a little difficulty which has "taught me a lot," he says. Heretofore billed as one of the land's hottest trumpet tooters, Jack has learned to play the piano and several other musical instruments while in Huntsville prison. "I'll soon be out in the free world and seeking a break," Jack says.*[72]

Jack Purvis is arguably one of the most interesting characters in the Texas prison band stories. Perhaps unwittingly, he was a prime example of how the music of *Thirty Minutes* could help rehabilitate an inmate. He was, of course, the most professional musician among the inmates; he served as the original music director for *Thirty Minutes* and wrote the show's theme song, "Twilight and You," as well as many other swing and instrumental compositions. He did the musical arrangements, led the musicians for their on-air performances and played a number of instruments, allowing him to better train the less-skilled participants on their instruments. A May 1939 article in *Rural Radio* magazine spoke of Purvis's skills: "Jack Purvis, an inmate, teaches music to any prisoner who wants to learn. Most of his pupils are exceedingly anxious to improve their talents as they live with the constant vision of the day when they will be released."

The trouble with Purvis was that he suffered from alcoholism and mental illness. All who worked with him in the premier jazz bands of the 1920s and '30s attested to his accuracy, talent and genius, yet they all categorically emphasized his lack of discipline and his penchant for self-destruction. Such diligence and accomplishment as he exhibited on *Thirty Minutes* was only achieved through the stringent structure of prison life; in other words, he had no choice but to do his best. According to his convict records, Governor O'Daniel granted Jack Purvis a six-month reprieve on June 7, 1939, for military purposes, noted simply: "Army."

Not surprisingly, military records don't indicate that this particular Jack Purvis ever registered with the military. Even with a reprieve, he was required to make regular reports in order to keep his pardon in good standing, but in characteristic Purvis fashion, he couldn't stay in one spot. After December 1939, Jack Purvis successfully disappeared—for seven years. His conditional release was revoked, and eventually, officials caught up with him in Florida and sent him back to Texas as a conditional parole violator. In 1946, he went back to prison—a mess all over again—to finish out his five-year term for the 1937 El Paso robbery. According to some reports, once he was back behind the Walls, he told people that he went back intentionally because he missed the prison band.

Such a statement was, in all likelihood, just his typical bluster, but nonetheless, it tells of the significance of music to the inmates—especially one like Jack Purvis, who'd achieved quite a bit of musical fulfillment when he was in prison the first time around. However, even if Jack did allow himself to be captured in Florida—for he was quite wily according to all parties, so it's not out of the realm of possibility—he was still out of luck.

Records and photos of the Texas prison bands in the mid-1940s don't show Jack Purvis's involvement in any way, and his prisoner classification shows him categorized into "2B," which was the recidivist population. The last stint of his sentence relegated him to the Retrieve unit of the prison system, not Huntsville where he was previously incarcerated. And in Retrieve, he was forgotten about until the officials finally decided he'd fulfilled his sentence and let him go on September 20, 1947.

After release from the penitentiary in 1947, the trail becomes less distinct. Reports have surfaced that show Jack Purvis as returning briefly to Indiana, where he'd kept intermittent touch with his daughter, Betty Lou Purvis (who was born in the late 1920s during a short-lived marriage in Pennsylvania). Although he talked frequently of playing music with other bands following his release from the Texas prison, the offers never panned out. Therefore, serving as the prison band director on *Thirty Minutes Behind the Walls* was the last time Jack Purvis made any music on a regular basis.

Thirty Minutes Behind the Walls

On March 23, 1938, a rehearse-weary orchestra, a string band, a harmonica player, and a guitar duo nervously awaited the control engineer's signal to go on the air. But the listeners heard only the now familiar four chimes strike in WBAP's Fort Worth studio and the announcement: "We take you now to the main unit of the Texas Prison System"—the popping knuckles of the taut inmate performers were drowned in the theme song that took out into radio land the hopes and dreams of the entertainers, the officials of the Prison System, and the technicians of WBAP's staff.

The boys and girls in white who took part in that first performance were encouraged by the blessing of the then governor, James V. Allred, and the nine Prison Board members, but their nervousness was fanned by doubt until the first fan letters were opened. From the first performance, Thirty Minutes Behind the Walls *caught public fancy and swelled the high tide under the pull of popular favor.*[73]

On that very first episode, the four cowbell chimes ushered in the opening theme song, Jack Purvis's composition entitled "Twilight and You." Nelson Olmsted—WBAP announcer who would later become a popular horror host on the radio and television with shows such as *Lights Out* and *Sleep No More*—then gave a short speech, followed by an inmate announcer. The inmate announcer introduced the prison orchestra with "You Can't Stop Me from Dreaming." From there, a prison official introduced Governor Allred, who gave a long speech, punctuated by the string band's rousing rendition of "Ragtime Annie." Then came WBAP head honcho and chief cowbell-clanger Harold "Hired Hand" Hough, who spoke hopefully of the station's role in the radio show's future. After his speech, the "Negro Choir" hummed in the background as the inmate announcer made their introduction. The introduction itself is embarrassingly telling of how the radio show displayed its "progressive" intent to racially integrate the performers.

> *Song is the Negroes' heritage. Wherever they are, whatever they do, they're happy whenever they sing. Prison is no exception. As an example we've gathered together from the rolling cotton fields of the prison system eleven Negro singers. They give you now a Spiritual that has echoed for ages across the deltas of Darkyland—"Come Along, Come Along."*[74]

Immediately after "Come Along, Come Along," the prison orchestra jumped in with "You're a Sweetheart." Then came a "smiling Colored boy" who laid forth into radio land a novelty harmonica instrumental called "Rabbit, Get Up in the Hollow." The guitar duo followed and then more official speeches, and so on, until one last song from the prison orchestra closed out those first thirty revelatory minutes behind Texas prison walls.

On the Radio

Prisons and Prisoners

Although a unique, effective and award-winning radio show, *Thirty Minutes Behind the Walls* was not the first of its kind. Prior to its first episode in 1938, similar radio programs had aired in other states, to great acclaim. In the years between the stock market crash of 1929 and the end of World War II, radio campaigns abounded throughout the nation, aimed to raise public awareness of social issues, appealing to the listening public and encouraging virtues such as compassion, empathy and good citizenship. Publications in the radio industry reported an increasing number of shows throughout the United States that utilized a prison setting, from officials discussing prison reform to inmates discussing their crimes, their surroundings and sometimes even serving as pundits, of sorts, for prison reform discussions.

These trade publications reported regularly on such shows, highlighting their importance and their popularity with the public. The heavily positive public response was perhaps an indication of listeners' sympathy for the average American who might have fallen on hard times—even those who made immoral or illegal choices in order to keep themselves or their families alive.

One reference to a strikingly similar precursor to *Thirty Minutes* was published in the August 1937 issue of *Broadcasting* magazine. *Broadcasting* devoted a glowing two-page spread, in color no less, to the enormous success of a live floor show/radio program that took place at the McAlester unit of the Oklahoma State Penitentiary and was broadcast live through WKY in Oklahoma City:

> *Booked for a one-night stand on June 12th, WKY's one-hour broadcast from behind the walls of Oklahoma's state penitentiary turned into a complete, all-around click. Another was promptly scheduled for July 10th; still another is set for August 7th. From a seat in the air audience, the shows were tops in entertainment and showmanship.*

> *As a vehicle for acquainting Oklahoma with the earnest rehabilitation efforts being carried on in its penal institutions, the programs were high in public interest. Most notable, yet unexpected, was the striking morale-building effect of the programs on the entire prison population, a subject of enthusiastic commendation from prison and state officials.*
>
> *Here is another sample of how WKY goes out of its way, turns off the beaten path, to serve public interest and give its audience something fresh and novel in entertainment. Such are the accents in programming that keep WKY the most listened-to station in Oklahoma and make it the station on which your sales story gets the most attention and the best hearing.*[75]

The uncanny similarity of the July 1937 WKY broadcast to the theme of *Thirty Minutes Behind the Walls* indicates that it may have been the direct source on which to pattern the Texas radio show. After all, WBAP was a clear-channel radio station that not only frequented the pages of *Broadcasting* magazine throughout the 1930s but also bordered the state from which the WKY broadcast was made. Officials of the prison or the radio stations could no doubt tune in to the show; all the announcers knew one another and, in Texas at least, had ties with government officials who might be able to make such a show become a reality in Texas. Whether speculation or not, just seven months after this article came out, WBAP in Fort Worth aired its first weekly broadcast of *Thirty Minutes Behind the Walls* from the Huntsville unit of the Texas state penitentiary.

After *Thirty Minutes Behind the Walls* became an immense hit with the listening public, other similarly formatted radio shows followed suit. In California, *San Quentin on the Air* aired as early as 1942 and consistently made national news while it existed. On the East Coast, other penitentiaries also jumped on the "prison variety show" bandwagon. In 1940, *Broadcasting* magazine published a lengthy feature on Central Prison in North Carolina:

> *A new angle in success stories comes from the Central Prison Varieties, originated by WRAL, Raleigh, N.C., and relayed to Carolina Network stations WFTC, Kinston, WGTM, Wilson. The weekly half-hour, broadcast direct from the auditorium of Central Prison, the State penitentiary just outside Raleigh, has become a popular feature for listeners. But prison officials comment that its effect on participating prisoners has been even more remarkable…*
>
> *Music is the backbone of the program, with vocal and instrumental soloists drawn both from the men's and the women's prison. In addition to*

> *specialties by the String Band, the Four Walls, the Negro chorus, hillbilly crooners and blues singers, the feature incorporates prison news commentaries by another prisoner, a young forger who upon completing his sentence plans to seek employment in radio.*
>
> *Proof of the good effects of the program are best drawn from examples cited by prison authorities. One prisoner, condemned to death for murder, became a particular problem for the officials after his sentence was commuted to life imprisonment. During the year before the WRAL series started, he spent nine of the 12 months in solitary confinement, all with no placating effect on him. Fred Fletcher, WRAL program director, about that time spoke to the warden and other officials about starting the program. The prisoner expressed a desire to participate, so the warden secured an electric guitar for him. For the last 10 months he has been a model prisoner, has not missed a single broadcast, and has not spent a day in solitary confinement.*
>
> *The prison news commentator, a forger, is another case in point. Participation in the program has revealed his gift for terse, discerning and witty comment and has prompted him to look to radio as a profession when he leaves prison. Another star of the series is a 19-year-old girl singer who was imprisoned for bigamy. She was one of the first women to appear on the program after participation was extended to include the women's prison…*
>
> *The beneficial results of the program are indicated by the officials' efforts to buy more instruments for the prisoners, secure a musical director and in general to further this means of expression. WRAL takes particular pride in the program as a public service, flatly ruling out all offers for sponsorship. Station officials emphasize that the program better serves its purpose by merely acting as a working example of the place of radio in the world today. The station reports even that in several cases inmates of other prisons in the State have asked to be transferred to the Raleigh prisons so they can participate in the programs.*[76]

Industry magazine reports of other states' prison radio shows from the 1930s, when compared with *Thirty Minutes Behind the Walls*, show one consistent message: playing music was a transformative experience for the convicts. As for the listeners, how could they *not* tune in? These were the reality shows of the era—especially when they had a dynamic format similar to many popular non-prison radio shows of the 1930s.

On the surface, the radio shows resembled the popular barn dance programs like Chicago-based station WLS's *National Barn Dance* and amateur variety hours such as *Major Bowes' the Original Amateur Hour*. Under that surface, these programs were carefully orchestrated—at times, even more so than the bands that played on them—serving as wide-reaching platforms for the image rehabilitation of various government programs.

In Texas, the advertisements of *Thirty Minutes* were government programs and the advertisers government officials who spoke eloquently of modernization, rehabilitation and the plight of the unfortunate "boys and girls in white." These "boys and girls"—who in Texas were seldom publicly referred to, collectively or separately, as "men" or "women"—were entirely responsible for the broadcast, from preparation to publicity to production to performance, just as the 1937 WKY broadcast from Oklahoma had been.

Showtime at Huntsville

Thirty Minutes Behind the Walls first aired on March 23, 1938, and operated as a live radio broadcast from inside the prison grounds for close to a decade. Through the performance of popular music, comedic moments and human-interest interviews with inmate participants, government entities could focus on their platforms for rehabilitation by making themselves and their diversely talented inmates relatable to the public.

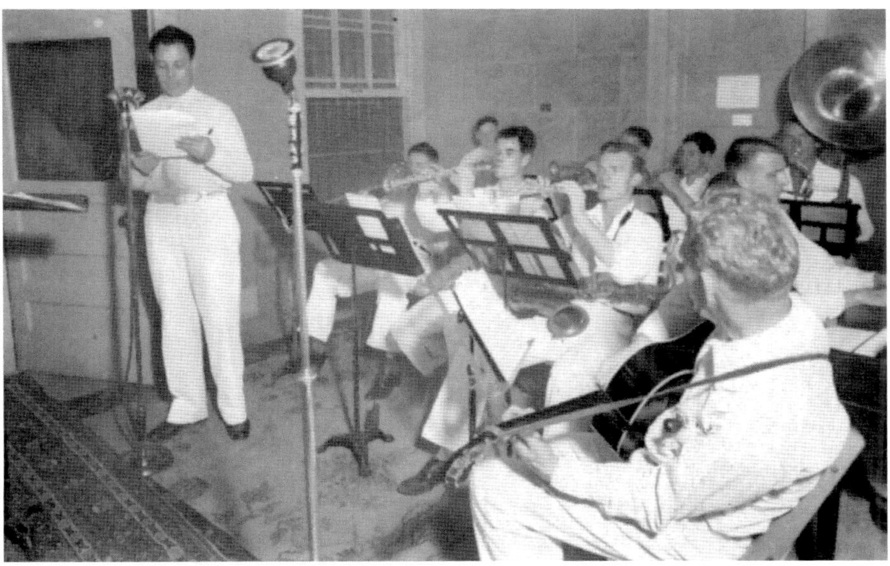

The first broadcast of *Thirty Minutes Behind the Walls*, on March 23, 1938. *Texas Prison Museum.*

Due to curiosity, a sense of solidarity or perhaps simply the quality of the music, *Thirty Minutes* was enormously popular with the listening public. As a clear-channel radio station, WBAP aired the show throughout most of North America and received more than 1,000 cards and letters after its inaugural broadcast. At its peak, *Thirty Minutes* had an estimated audience of five million listeners. Thousands of fan letters and requests poured in each week for its duration. In honor of one early anniversary episode, the announcers challenged the audience to write and request that *Thirty Minutes* be extended to a full hour broadcast. They received 220,000 letters the following week in support of this proposal.

The inmate cast of the radio show worked extremely hard to make *Thirty Minutes* a hit. They already rehearsed nightly after their ten-hour work days were completed, but on Wednesdays, they were permitted to rehearse most of the day in preparation for that evening's performances. For not only was *Thirty Minutes* a radio show, it was also a stage performance. Each week, hundreds of curious outsiders walked through the prison walls to watch the inmates sing and play in person before *Thirty Minutes* was broadcast on the radio.

Shortly before each Wednesday's regularly scheduled broadcast time of 10:30 p.m., the prison auditorium doors swung open. At 9:30 p.m., the audience

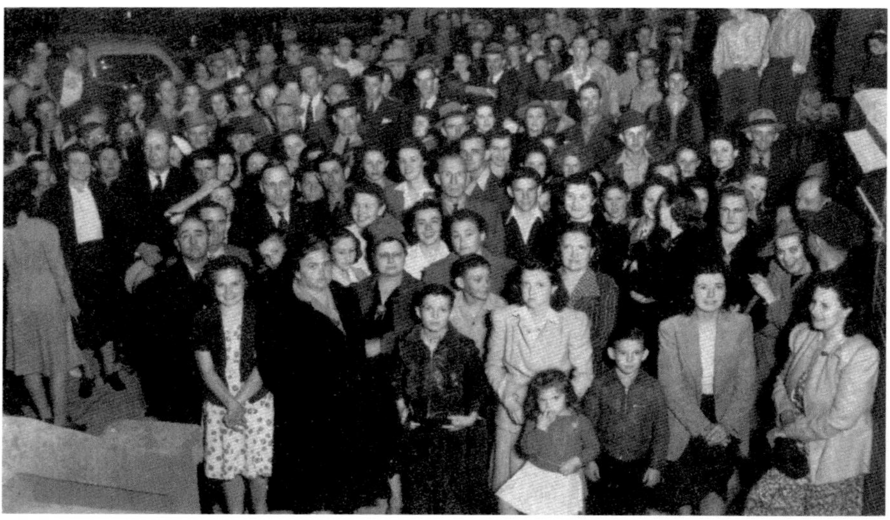

A crowd waits outside the Walls anticipating entrance to a live floorshow of *Thirty Minutes Behind the Walls*. Audience members flocked by the hundreds for each week's live performance. *Texas Prison Museum.*

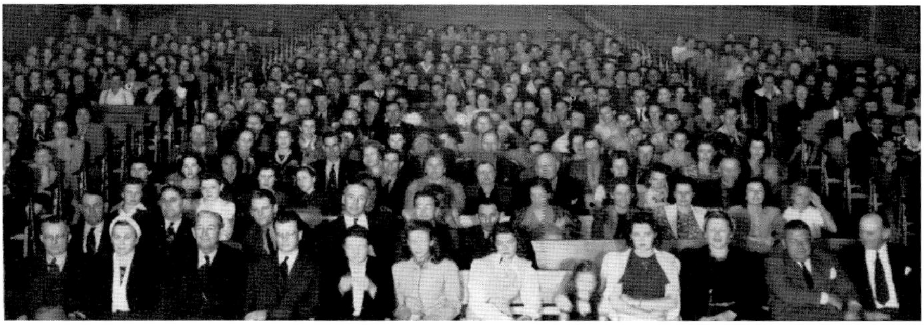

A photograph of the 1942 audience for *Thirty Minutes Behind the Walls*' fourth anniversary performance. *Texas Prison Museum.*

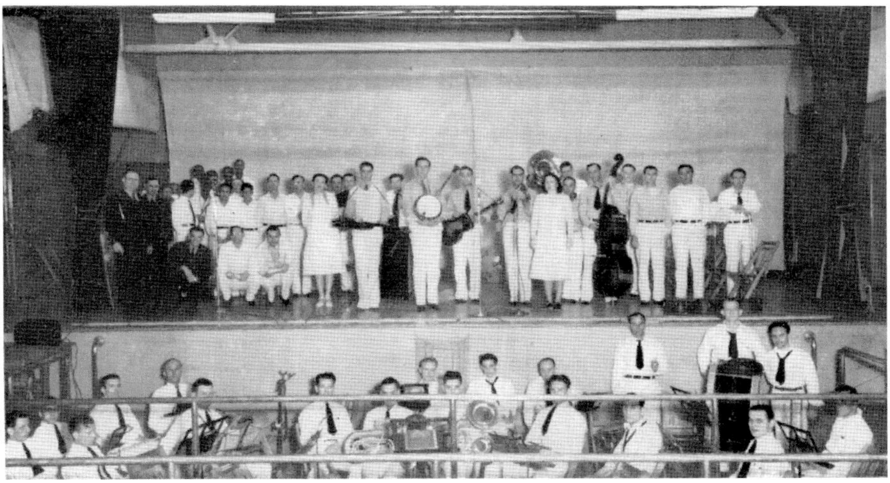

The full cast of *Thirty Minutes Behind the Walls* poses onstage. *Texas Prison Museum.*

streamed in, and the live floor show started at 10:00 p.m. The live floor shows featured many of the inmates who would perform on that night's broadcast. The in-person attendance at these live performances averaged three hundred to four hundred attendees and had as many as nine hundred for some shows. Like the Texas Prison Rodeo, the *Thirty Minutes* floor show was a big attraction in east Texas and beyond. Some attendees traveled for hundreds of miles to the Huntsville prison to get a glimpse of the performers they heard on the air each week and satisfy their curiosity about life inside penitentiary walls.

The radio show's broad variety in content expanded the listening audience, allowing inmates of varying genders and races to participate—as

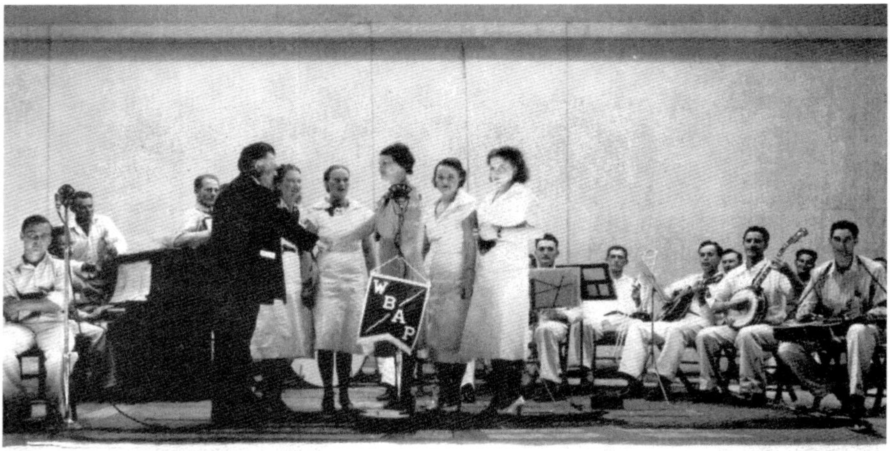

Onstage during a live floor show, the *Thirty Minutes* cast looks on as Mrs. Heath, surrounded by the Goree Girls, shakes the hand of WBAP station official Harold Hough. *Texas Department of Criminal Justice.*

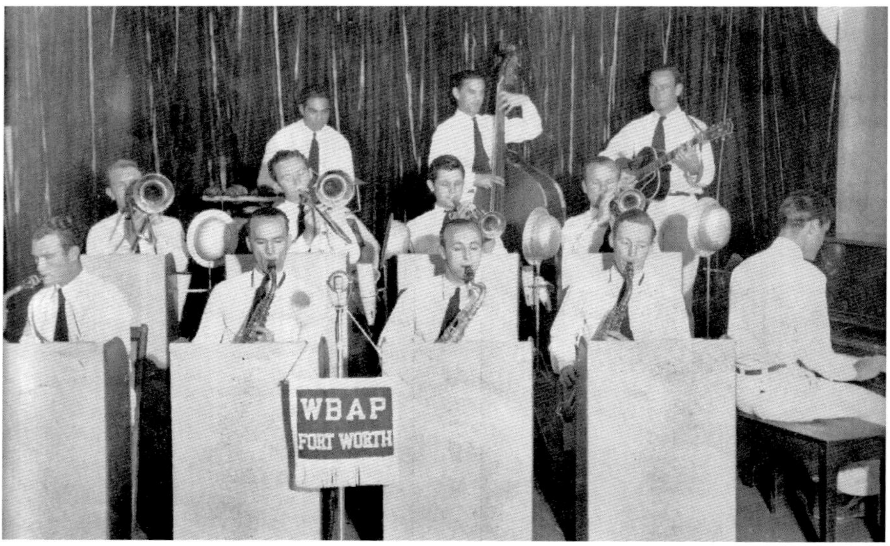

The Serenaders, a jazz ensemble, play on *Thirty Minutes Behind the Walls*. *Texas Prison Museum.*

long as they adhered to the institution's expectations for good behavior. For above all, the radio show was still a rehabilitative program. Radio transcripts document the first three years of *Thirty Minutes* and were printed and bound into book format at the prison print shop.

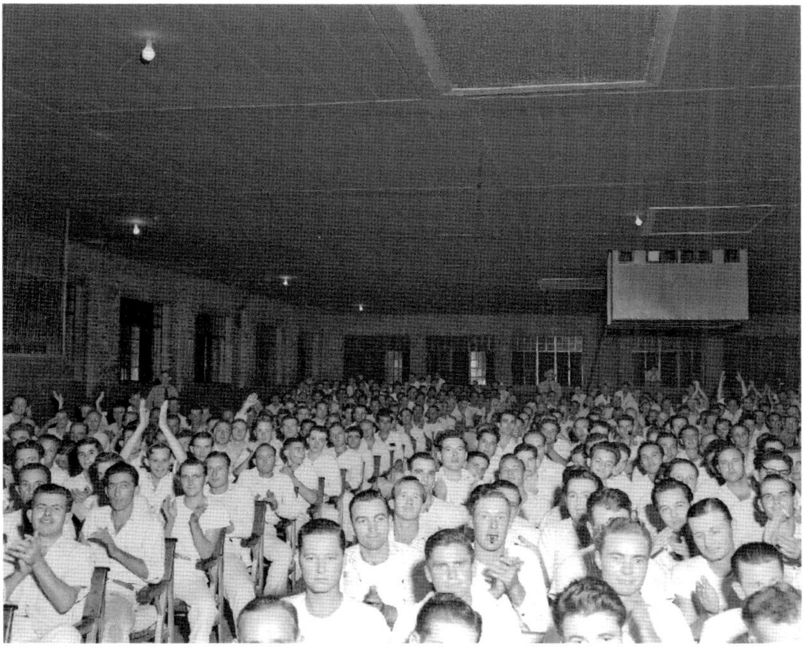

An inmate audience watches the *Thirty Minutes* floor show in the mid-1940s. *Texas Prison Museum.*

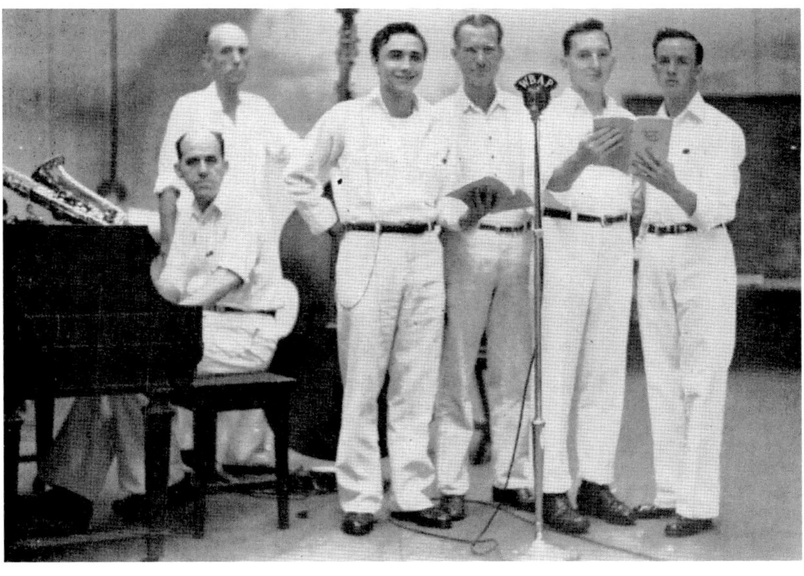

Male inmates perform on the *Thirty Minutes* stage. *Texas Prison Museum.*

Only a couple of the bound transcripts survive, but existing copies provide tremendous insight into the radio show's format, style and tone. Each episode featured a grab bag of hits from a number of popular musical genres; country and western, patriotic, hymns, blues, swing, jazz, pop and Hawaiian music were part of the typical rotation, as well as instrumentals of any genre. Except for several unique broadcasts in its later years, which featured the inmates' own compositions, most of the songs were popular radio hits, supplemented by sheet music that was made available to the inmates and stored in the prison's song library, which the *Prison Echo* reported as being up to the standards of many radio station libraries in the United States. In 1942, the *Prison Echo* boasted, "Twelve hundred songs, orchestrations and copies of sheet music have been catalogued in the past few weeks.[77]

Convict #75552

In addition to performing all the music on the show, inmate announcers made valuable contributions to the show, often helping out the WBAP officials and kicking off the band performances. One inmate who appeared regularly on *Thirty Minutes* was a former death row inmate named Paul Mitchell. He was interviewed several times on the radio show and acted as an occasional inmate announcer. The interview he gave to WBAP official Harold Hough on an early episode depicted a little thrilling, chilling portrait of the death row experience:

> *HOUGH: Do you remember how you felt when you received your sentence?*
> *MITCHELL: Yes, I do. But my feelings were so mixed, it would be hard to tell you exactly. It was kind of like getting an arm cut off, or something. I knew what it meant, but I couldn't grasp the magnitude of the thing.*
> *HOUGH: I believe I understand. Now, tell me, Paul—what did you think when you were ushered into the Death House?*
> *MITCHELL: Mister, I can't begin to do it! It was the strangest, most lonesome feeling I've ever experienced...like a horrible nightmare—like floating away into space. I haven't the power to describe it, that's all...*
> *HOUGH: Paul, I understand you came within hours of your death on two occasions; that you ate two "last supers"* [sic]*—is this correct?*
> *MITCHELL: Yes. You always get what is called a "last supper" before you go down at midnight. I had two of them.*

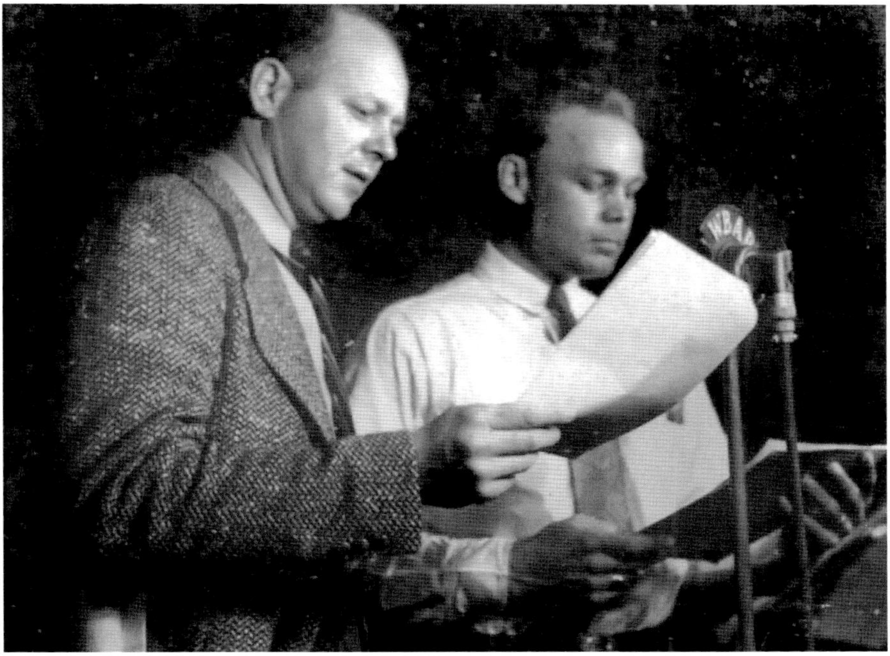

Paul Mitchell, *right*, works with WBAP station announcer Dave Byrn on *Thirty Minutes*. *Gayle Royer.*

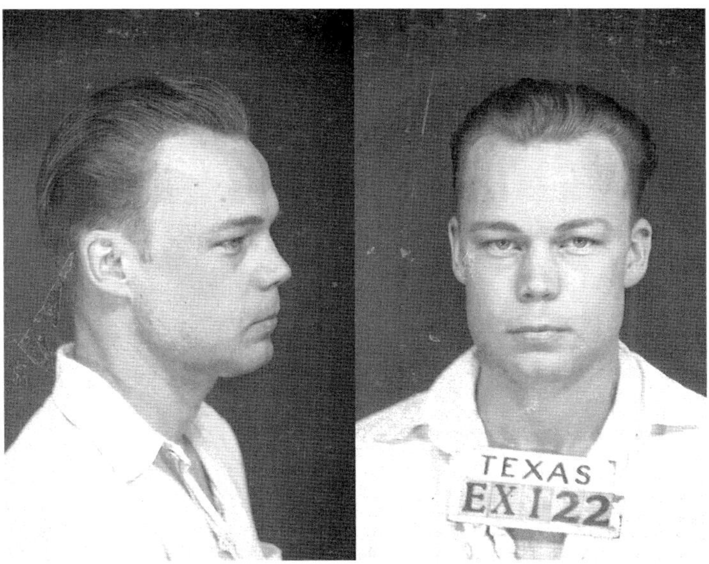

Mug shot of death row inmate 122, Paul Mitchell. *Texas Department of Criminal Justice.*

> *HOUGH: And you were reprieved during the final few hours—tell me…how did you feel so close to death, knowing you were helpless to do anything about it?*
> *MITCHELL: Well, the closer I got to the chair, the faster I tried to think. And though it may seem odd, I wasn't thinking about ways to miss paying the penalty, either. I was just trying to recall as many of the enjoyable moments of my life as possible—trying to relive them all over again while there was time…*
> *HOUGH: Now, Paul—you must have seen and heard some strange things while you were on Death Row—what* [would] *you term the most unusual in this regard?*
> *MITCHELL: It would be a request one of the men made from me. I played a mouth organ quite a bit then, and one of the men took a fancy to "Chicken Reel." He asked me to play it for him when his time came—said he wanted to go down with that tune ringing in his ears. I thought it would be easy, but…well, at midnight he came by and shook hands with me. I had the harmonica in my hand. He tried to say goodbye—but he just kind of choked up. Then he pointed to my mouth organ and I began playing…and he began walking toward that little gray door. Mister, that was the hardest piece I ever played in my life! And it kept getting harder! Then, when it was all over, I threw my harmonica in the corner and both sides flew off of it. Now I never play "Chicken Reel" anymore.*[78]

Mitchell's death sentence was the result of an October 1932 robbery during which Lubbock grocery store worker Robert Tharp, a former football star, was shot and killed.[79] Each time Mitchell's death date loomed, he received a reprieve. Newspapers covered the last-minute reprieves in detail, noting the tireless efforts of Mitchell's mother; eventually, his death sentence was commuted to life in prison.

After the commutation, the tall, friendly, articulate inmate began to impress the prison officials and became a trusty and a frequent chauffeur for the prison officials, sometimes on long, out-of-state journeys. He enjoyed working with the radio show in particular, in part because he seemed to be, along with many fellow male inmates, smitten with pretty inmate Reable Childs.

For Mitchell, Purvis and countless other inmates, participating in the *Thirty Minutes* broadcasts proved a transformative experience. Issues of the *Texas Prison Echo* from that time burst with praise, pride, joy and hope in the inmate-written articles and columns. Many of these call out the praise for particular inmates but also of the radio show's importance in their lives and of its many possibilities for rehabilitation.

5

COWBOYS, SONGSTERS AND FIDDLERS

The Rhythmic Stringsters

Many of the convicts spend their leisure composing, hoping that a tune, born in the gloom of a prison cell, may click and provide funds to finance pleas for clemency. Many of the songs played on the program are prison born. The lyrics yearn for home and fireside, the sweet face and gray hair of mother, the thrill of riding down a mountain trail with the sun in your face and a surefooted pony under your creaking saddle.[80]

—*Don Hinga,* Baltimore Sun

Country Music and Prison

Of all the popular tunes and current radio hits performed at the Texas Prison Rodeo and on *Thirty Minutes Behind the Walls*, country and western songs were the mainstay. Represented in the 1930s as "western," "string band" or "hillbilly" music, country music developed into an extremely popular musical genre, starting about fifteen years before *Thirty Minutes Behind the Walls* began in 1938.

From its humble beginnings in the farm homes and mountain shacks of American migrants, country music emphasized the plight of the outsider and the renegade. Similarly, western and cowboy music featured themes of an open trail, freedom and a hard but simple life, unfettered by the shackles of society's expectations. Holding an undeniable appeal for the public as well as the prisoner, country and western music made for a perfect fit at the prison rodeo and, later, *Thirty Minutes Behind the Walls*. According to eminent country music scholar Bill Malone, country and western music appealed to the masses in part because it satisfied the "preoccupation with the mythic common man that touched every realm of art during the Depression years."[81]

Even as early as 1922, Victor Records released a number of longtime American folk songs, including fiddle favorites "Arkansas Traveler" and "Turkey in the Straw," recorded for Victor Records by champion Texas old-time fiddlers Eck Robertson and Henry Gilliland. In the mid-1920s, popular songster Vernon Dalhart, also from Texas, had one of country music's earliest smash hits, "Wreck of the Old '97." The record sold millions, and its B-side had almost equal success with "The Prisoner's Song." "The Prisoner's Song" is generally considered to be the very first prison song associated with country music.

By the late 1920s, country music had solidified into a viable commercial genre, in large part due to the success of Jimmie Rodgers, also known as "The Singing Brakeman," who was later heralded as the "Father of Country Music." Rodgers's songs of the rounder, the loner, the prisoner and the haunted—in other words, the common man—captivated America. His commercial success spawned dozens of imitators whose contributions further developed the country music identity and helped define the genre.

The growth of country music as a commercial musical genre was also aided exponentially by barn dance radio. Proving that its roots of country music are deep indeed, in January 1923, WBAP itself aired one of the first ever barn dance radio shows. Known simply as *The Barn Dance*, the ninety-minute radio show featured local musicians, such as another champion Texas fiddler, Captain Moses "M.J." Bonner. Other barn dance radio shows followed suit, most notably Chicago's WLS *National Barn Dance* and, of course, the most famous radio barn dance, lasting until the present day, WSM's *Grand Ole Opry* in Nashville.

The barn dance radio shows presented an idealized homeland, a mythical, close-knit, farm community from which the outsider was excluded. It also provided for the listening public a definition of what country music represented—home and hearth, church and field, mother and daddy, labor and land—and ingrained a nostalgia of sorts for a world that no longer exists. At the same time, Hollywood capitalized on America's fascination with the cowboy and the western frontier, taking a historically gritty, unglamorous American tradition and sanitizing it by making stars of its "cowboys": actors and singers with clean-shaven square jaws, wavy hair and melodious singing voices who were usually clad in high-quality, starched outfits and crisp, perfectly cocked cowboy hats.

With country and western music firmly ensconced in the American consciousness, country music played a central role in the Texas Prison Rodeo musical festivities throughout its decades-long existence. Country music was also the most frequently performed genre on *Thirty Minutes Behind the Walls*, beginning with the prison system's all-male string band: the Rhythmic Stringsters.

The "Boys in White"

It was a typically Texas July afternoon. Twelve perspiring musicians, clad in cheap cotton work clothes, laid aside somewhat battered instruments and mopped their brows with cheap cotton handkerchiefs. Had the group been dressed in ordinary street apparel they would not have differed from the appearance of other big name bands. This orchestra, however, was the musical combination now attracting fame via the WBAP–Texas Prison System series, known as the "Thirty Minutes Behind the Walls" *program.*[82]

Composed of approximately a half-dozen incarcerated men, the inmate musical group called the Rhythmic Stringsters formed years before the advent of *Thirty Minutes*. Beginning with two inmates on string instruments—most likely guitar and banjo, or possibly fiddle—the Rhythmic Stringsters provided vaudeville-style entertainment at special events held within the prison system. The group soon expanded in members and instruments, learning myriad different musical genres that could be performed on their string instruments. By the early 1930s, the Rhythmic Stringsters provided popular and string band music, even some hot string jazz, for the audiences that arrived in droves to watch the Texas Prison Rodeo. A 1941 issue of the *Thirty Minutes* souvenir program that was sold to the live audience members each week detailed the band's history, explaining, "The wide demands for particular numbers resulted in the building of an unusual catalogue of music, and as fast as one musician replaced another, he learned the catalogue."[83]

The *Thirty Minutes* radio show transcripts indeed reveal a varied and comprehensive repertoire performed by the Rhythmic Stringsters. In addition to the show's closing theme, "We Gotta Go," the Stringsters

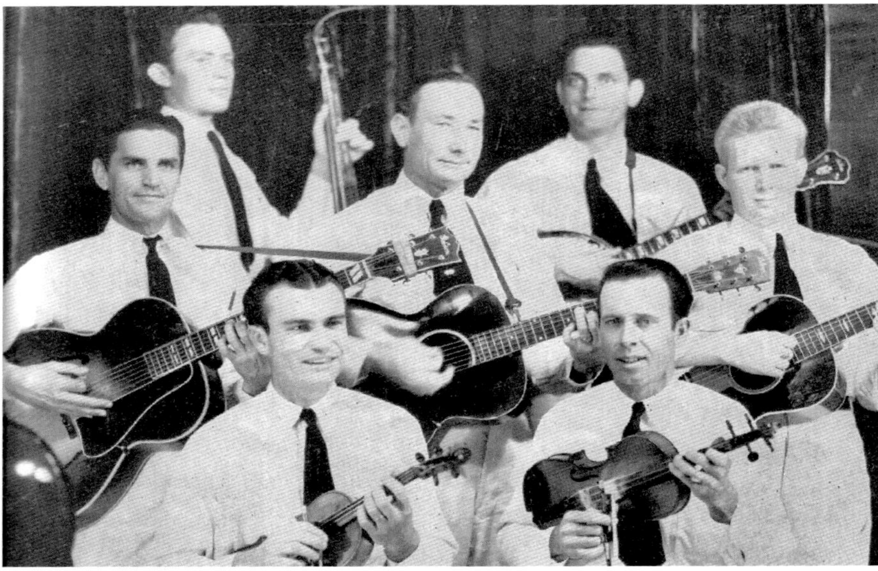

An early photograph of the Rhythmic Stringsters, around 1938 or 1939. *Texas Prison Museum.*

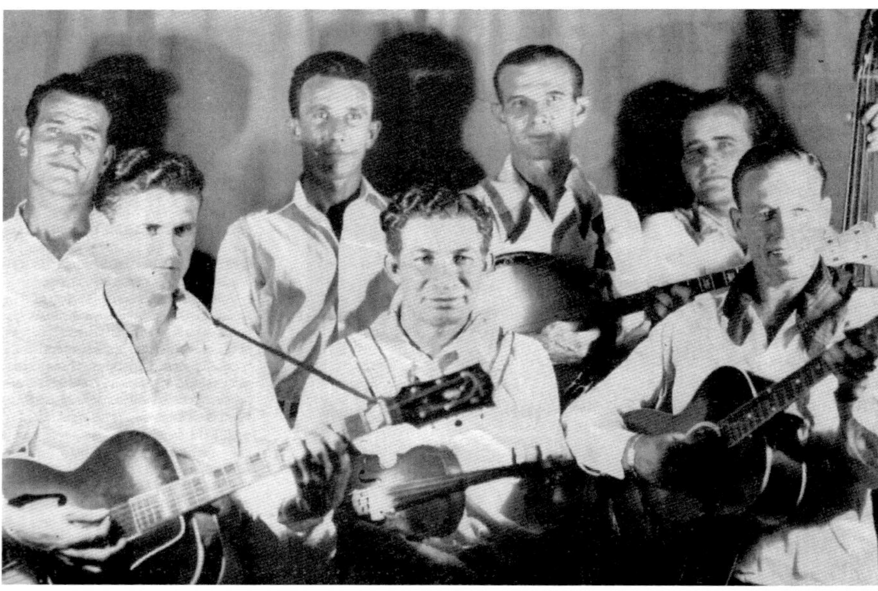

A promotional photograph of the Rhythmic Stringsters, circa 1944. *Texas Prison Museum.*

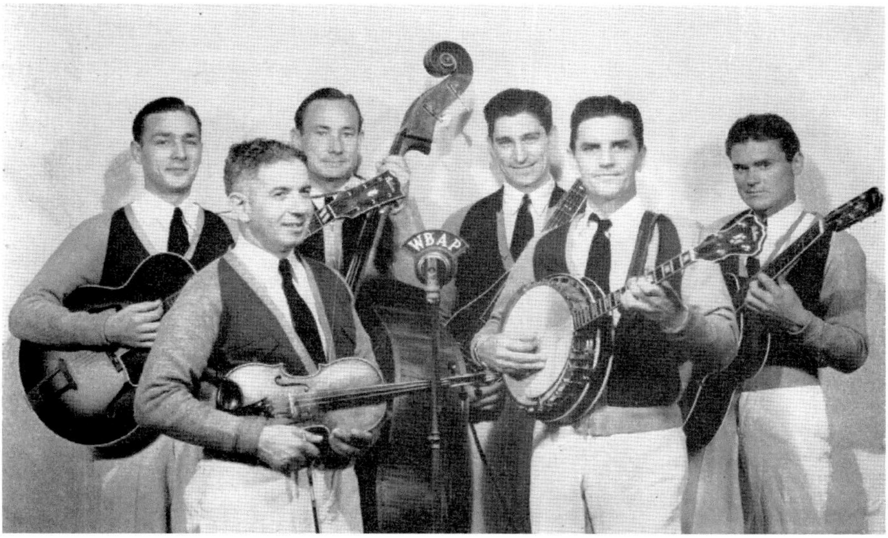

A promotional photograph of the Rhythmic Stringsters, circa 1942. *Texas Prison Museum.*

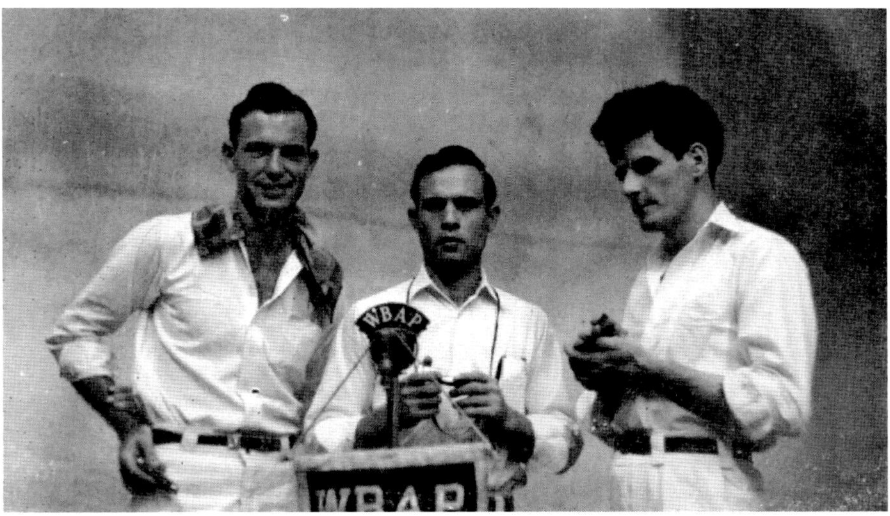

A male trio performs on *Thirty Minutes Behind the Walls*. *Texas Prison Museum.*

performed traditional old-time tunes such as "The Ozark Stomp" and "Ragtime Annie" during the first episodes. As country and western music strengthened its hold on American culture, their repertoire followed suit, with songs made famous by a number of current radio stars like Jimmie

Rodgers, Bob Wills and Stuart Hamblen. Between 1938 and 1941, the Rhythmic Stringsters performed dozens of popular old-time and country and western songs on *Thirty Minutes Behind the Walls*, a small selection of which is listed below, along with the artist—or artists—who originally made the songs famous.

"I Only Want a Buddy, Not a Sweetheart"—Bing Crosby, Patsy Montana
"The One Rose"—Gene Autry
"I'll Keep On Loving You"—Floyd Tillman, Cliff Bruner
"Little Old Rag Doll"—Stuart Hamblen
"Out on the Texas Plains"—Stuart Hamblen
"Osage Stomp"—Bob Wills and His Texas Playboys
"Devil's Dream"—traditional
"Sweet Sue"—Bing Crosby, Mills Brothers, Tommy Dorsey

Even early in the series, the Rhythmic Stringsters also introduced their own original compositions to the musical mix. On May 18, 1938, the ninth episode of *Thirty Minutes*, such a song made its debut, written by inmate J.D. Roe and entitled "Back Home Again in Texas." While in no way diminishing the value of their original contributions, some assumption can be made that many purportedly "original" inmate compositions were heavily derivative, if not straightforward variations of, current popular hits. For example, the title alone of "Back Home Again in Texas" sounds markedly similar to a 1937 song recorded by Bob Wills and His Texas Playboys called "Back Home Again in Indiana." Since no extant recordings of *Thirty Minutes Behind the Walls* have been located, this is as yet an unproven theory, but a nonetheless likely one, given the number of songs the bands needed to learn or compose for some of the occasional "all original compositions" broadcasts of *Thirty Minutes*.

Note-able Stringsters

Individual members of the Rhythmic Stringsters changed frequently, but a few inmates stand out within the earlier incarnations of the band for their talent and, sometimes, for their antics. As the series progressed and the show became increasingly newsworthy, some even made the industry rags. One such instance was Woodrow Wilson (W.W.) "Woody" Stansberry, a tall, young guitar picker serving a five-year sentence for theft.

Stansberry played guitar in the Rhythmic Stringsters for the first few episodes of *Thirty Minutes*. His musical talent was lauded, but unfortunately, it was short-lived. *Broadcasting* magazine reported:

> *The fifth broadcast of* Thirty Minutes Behind the Walls *on WBAP, Fort Worth, originating at the Texas Prison, Huntsville, made headlines when W.W. Stansberry, featured guitar playing inmate slated for duty on April 20, escaped the night previous to the broadcast. Although recaptured, the erstwhile radio star will be denied the privilege of appearing on the already famous WBAP half-hour produced and presented entirely by prison inmates. On the WBAP newscast previous to the broadcast it was announced that "Since Mr. W.W. Stansberry, prison radio star, took the air last night he will not apppear* [sic] *on the air tonight."*[84]

According to several newspapers, the night before the *Thirty Minutes* broadcast, Stansberry acquired a suit of clothes from the warden's offices. He walked out of the prison gates, having been mistaken for one of several members of the press who were leaving the prison grounds at the same time. Stansberry managed to obtain a getaway car while on the lam but was found by officials—drunk in a ditch near the vehicle—the very next day.[85] However, during the brief time he appeared on *Thirty Minutes*, he managed to entrance the radio audience with his jazzy electric guitar. Although the inmate's name was not mentioned, by the November 1938 issue of *Down Beat* magazine, prison officials painted the story with a humorous hue for the reporter, commenting, "It seems that the escaper also had mike fright because he had been slated to play a guitar solo on the program the following evening."[86]

Another well-known *Thirty Minutes* performer was "Cowboy" Jack Ramsey. Ramsey, an "ex-cowpuncher," played acoustic guitar and sang the cowboy and western songs the audience loved. He is significant in the story of *Thirty Minutes* because his simple rhythm guitar served accompaniment to Hattie Ellis in the John Lomax recordings. His vocals were highly anticipated on the radio show, but even more importantly, his acoustic guitar work behind Hattie Ellis—however simple—still stands within the only extant recordings of the *Thirty Minutes* cast from that era.

Cowboy crooner Wyoming "Red" Stammitz also had a big part in the *Thirty Minutes* stories. As the director of the fifty-piece military band and reportedly possessed of swoon-worthy vocals, sung over the Rhythmic Stringsters' instrumentation, Stammitz was one of the most frequent features of the radio show and a fan favorite as well.[87] Another Stringster, Herman "Mexico" Brown, wrote of Stammitz in the *Echo*:

> *"Wyoming Red" Stammitz can be heard practicing on his cowboy numbers with much gusto. His voice is above par and is expected to be even better by October. He can be seen shining his boots in preparation to looking like a "drugstore cowboy" as he renders his western songs, such as "Riding Old Paint" and "Leading Old Bald."*[88]

Fiddle duets were also featured on many of the earlier *Thirty Minutes* episodes. During the first few years, one frequently mentioned inmate was Delmar Clayton, whose occupation was listed as "musician" in his entry log for the Texas prison system. Clayton, serving a six-year sentence for assault and robbery, was frequently announced to play a "hot fiddle." With such a positive musical reputation in the prison, it would have been interesting to see Clayton go up against "Pappy" Franklin, another fiddle-playing inmate who occasionally played with the Stringsters. Franklin's story makes for yet another sensational anecdote in the history of Texas prison bands.

Convict #87043

> *"I had a wonderful time." That was the expression commonly heard after the Old Fiddlers contests at the Municipal auditorium last night under the auspices of the Tri-State fair. With 2,000 persons present for the first contest it is believed that plans for two other contests will be completed. One of these contests will be open to the world.*
>
> *Louis* [sic] *Franklin, left-handed fiddler from Vernon, Wilbarger county, won first place in a play-off with Milt Trout, Dimmitt, Castro county, second place and H.E. Wetchell* [sic], *Amarillo, third place. Franklin, a veteran at the game, did some wonderful playing. Trout, elongated Castro pioneer, while not the finished fiddler that Franklin is had more volume and a more striking appearance, than the chubby musician.*[89]

Lewis Franklin, a rare left-handed fiddler born in Bonham, Texas, in 1874, seemed on top of the world in 1928. As an instrument, the fiddle—which is the same as a violin, only different in name and style in which it is played—has strong roots in most families of Anglo descent who immigrated to America in the eighteenth and nineteenth centuries. Franklin

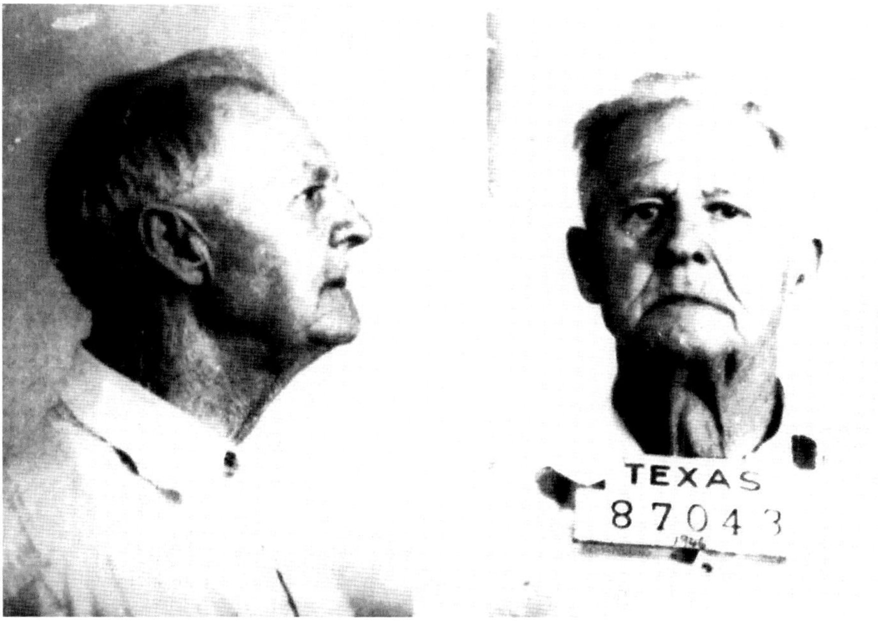

Mug shot of Lewis "Lefty" Franklin. *Texas Department of Criminal Justice.*

learned to play the fiddle at an early age and won his first fiddling contest at age thirteen; the prize for his triumph was a bottle of sorghum syrup.

As an American entertainment tradition, fiddle contests began to proliferate in the 1880s, originally popularized by Civil War veteran reunions throughout the nation. In Texas, fiddling contests became enormously popular, family-friendly events that continue to the present day. Eck Robertson, "Victor recording artist, known as the world's champion fiddler," was already a luminary in the Texas fiddle tradition by the time he made his recordings in the early 1920s. Through his seminal old-time fiddle recordings with Henry Gilliland, Eck Robertson is heralded as a country music pioneer and fiddling legend.[90] But even as early as World War I, Robertson went up against Lewis Franklin, along with another champion fiddler, A.P. Howard (known for his group Doctor Howard's Dixie Fiddlers). The three were each champion fiddlers in their own right—competitors to one another—but they also used their respective reputations to form a "champion fiddler" trio that worked together for the greater good. The Robertson-Howard-Franklin trio often traveled together and played against one another to garner support for the war effort and, later, to honor veterans. Even a decade after the end of World War I, an article appeared in the *Vernon Daily Record* boasting of their fiddlers' good turn.

> *"Eck" is known far and near as the world famous cowboy fiddler and began his fiddling path to fame here in Vernon. During the* [First World] *War, for the benefit of the Red Cross, Eck Robertson, Dr. A.P. Howard, Louis* [sic] *Franklin and others staged a three-day fiddling bout, playing to packed houses. After that the trio went to Tennessee and fiddled with Ex-Governor Taylor, "fiddling governor" of that state, by request.*[91]

In keeping with established traditions from the Civil War veteran reunions, fiddle music played an integral part of American culture well into the 1920s. A 1921 article described the celebration—including a detailed account of the fiddlers' competition—when seeing Wilbarger County's own "veterans of gray" off to Chattanooga, Tennessee, for a national Civil War veterans' reunion:

> *There were good-bye kisses from wives and daughters, hand-clasps from sons and friends, and hearty claps on the shoulder as the 1 o'clock Denver affed* [sic] *its way into the local yard Saturday afternoon. "God speed, take care of yourself," rang out on every hand, and yes, there were a few wet eyes as grey coated figures clambered aboard. Veterans they were—wrinkled, white headed and seasoned—bound not for the gory fields of battle but nevertheless to join the ranks of an army assembling from every point in the nation…*
>
> *Music was not omitted from the formality of departing, for three fiddlers, gorgeously attired in wondrous hued silk shirts, leather collars, flowing ties, and cowpuncher boots performed grandly to the great satisfaction of all in the waiting room. Dr. A.P. Howard, Lewis Franklin, and A.C. (Eck) Robertson "pulled a mean bow" while the crowd clapped and whistled its approval of their efforts.*[92]

Such press shows that Lewis Franklin achieved legendary status in the world of old-time fiddling and in his association with Eck Robertson. Competing in dozens of contests in his lifetime—often accompanied by his brother, banjo player M.H. Franklin—the left-handed fiddler won prize after prize. Sometimes the prizes were cash, sometimes dry goods, but no matter the form, the prize for championship fiddling didn't always pay the bills or buy Franklin bow strings, silk shirts and leather collars—especially after the advent of the Great Depression. In between his fiddling competitions and other music gigs, Franklin bolstered his income by doing odd jobs and generally working as a laborer.

On July 5, 1937, an enormous celebration marked not only Independence Day but also the opening of a fancy new bridge spanning 1,900 feet across the Pease River. Thousands of Oklahoma and Texas residents attended the celebration, which included fireworks, speeches by state officials, baseball and square dances and even an automotive show. Lewis Franklin was an acclaimed special guest, booked to display his left-handed championship fiddling skills alongside the musical group arranged for the square dances.[93]

A few weeks after the landmark joint celebration, Lewis Franklin arrived back at the rooming house in Chillicothe, Texas, where he'd lived for the past several years. Accompanying him was Sam Hysmith, another resident of the house and a fellow fiddling contest competitor. Soon after their arrival on that Sunday evening in early August, Lewis Franklin engaged in a heated dispute with Cora Houston, his landlady, over the car he'd just come back in—her car. Incensed by the argument, Lewis went back to his room and grabbed a .32-caliber pistol. He found Mrs. Houston and, without further ado, shot her in the right side of her body. The bullet's trajectory tore straight through her entire torso and lodged itself in her left arm, killing her straightaway.[94]

Hysmith and several other residents were in the rooming house when the murder occurred, but none witnessed the shooting. Upon the arrival of law enforcement officials, Franklin didn't try to escape or claim he hadn't shot Cora Houston. He simply surrendered and was arrested that evening. The next day, the *Vernon Daily Record* blazed a new and different headline for its celebrated hometown fiddler: "Lewis Franklin Charged in Chillcothe Slaying: Widely Known Musician Is Held in Case."

Although the insanity plea was considered for Franklin, it was eventually abandoned. After some delay, his trial was held two months later. On October 15, 1937, Lewis Franklin, the renowned sixty-three-year-old left-handed champion fiddler, was given a life sentence in the Texas state prison for murder with malice.

Even with a life sentence, Franklin found himself in a prime position to showcase his talent after his entry into the penitentiary in October 1937. *Thirty Minutes Behind the Walls* began in March 1938, and with a newly added prison moniker of "Pappy" Franklin, he was regularly mentioned among its ranks as fiddle player for the Rhythmic Stringsters.

Although often noted as a champion left-handed fiddler, Franklin's earlier accomplishments—such as his work with Eck Robertson or his general prominence in the fiddling world—were not expounded upon in any further detail while he was in prison. It's possible that Franklin did not care to share the details for public consumption or in any way publicize that area of his life. Downplaying his fiddling champion status while incarcerated probably helped him later because then he could—and did—participate in more old-time Texas fiddling competitions before his death in 1956, at age eighty-two.

An interesting aspect of the Texas old-time fiddle tradition, especially in the heyday of the fiddling contests and veteran reunions popular from the 1880s to the 1920s, was that they were known as a chance for the "tough old man" to shine. Old-time fiddling contests were an old man's game, a rare opportunity for these tough old men to "show the youngsters how it's done." Competitors were surely assessed for fiddling talent; but also considered—if unofficially—were the competitors' age, veteran status, stamina, showmanship and even physical appearance, as evidenced in the earlier quote about Franklin's "chubby" physique.

Although they were highly prized attributes when it came to the Texas old-time fiddling tradition, other valued qualities in the competitions were displays of valor and gentility, if not discretion. Perhaps that is why when Franklin was granted a full pardon in August 1949 he rejoined the competitors' circle at many Texas fiddling contests with nary a mention of his decade-long incarceration in the Texas penitentiary. His name appeared frequently in the newspapers, but once again, his name was only linked with fiddling competitions. Franklin's life was fiddling; he fiddled his way to legend until 1937, and after he was released, he just went back to it as if nothing had happened. This may not be surprising, but what is curious is that the newspapers, when mentioning his name after 1949, made no mention of the ten-year stint he did for murder. Lewis Franklin was treated as well as any well-respected elder statesman in the Texas fiddling tradition. The strange 1937 deviation Franklin made from the usual path of his life was not mentioned again.

By coincidence, beginning in the mid-1940s, another Texas fiddler named Lewis Franklin—a much younger (and unrelated) Lewis Franklin—began to take the old-time Texas fiddling contest circuit by storm. Eventually, this Lewis Franklin, and members of his family, made considerable contributions to the Texas fiddle tradition and gained a prominent place in the annals of Texas old-time fiddling lore. However, the earlier Franklin's work with Eck Robertson and Doctor Howard's Dixie Fiddlers has largely remained a mystery, and the full story of Lewis "Lefty" Franklin, the left-handed fiddler and murderous convict—who, by the way, ran with bona fide country music pioneers—has not been fully brought to light.

Franklin's story is not the only one that concerns the often-unheralded musical contributions of a Texas prisoner. While the story of Lewis "Lefty"

Franklin is perhaps the most unexplored in the Texas prison tales, another inmate from the 1920s and '30s also made important contributions to the country music tradition—this time through the songs that he wrote.

Convict #60339

Raymond E. Hall, Eastham One Farm Correspondent of long standing, has recently gained recognition by the publishers of Who's Who in Poetry in America. *The Who's Who Publishing Company…is running a short biography of Hall, one of his poems titled "The Voice of Conscience," along with his photograph.*

The Echo *Staff and Raymond's many friends in the Walls, are glad his untiring efforts in the various fields of literature have gained him recognition. He has come up the hard way if ever a writer did.*[95]

The *Echo* then reprinted the blurb and biography from the *Who's Who* publication. Here is one stanza of the esteemed poem:

Ah, my great and sleeping people, awake from lethargy!
Do you not hear the trumpets of the pagan god?
His clamor and ruthless march is not far distant.
Even now a Congress wrangles, some to bask in the limelight,
The fullness of liberty's glory is shadowed
With the menacing approach of a heavy hand, not peace.[96]

On June 1, 1938, convict #60339—Raymond E. Hall—played in the prison string band at the Eastham unit, from which the show was broadcast that evening. The Eastham unit was one of the roughest and most brutal in the Texas prison system, reserved for secondary and tertiary classifications of mostly white inmates: recidivists, hardened criminals and violent convicts. Eastham also held notorious prisoners Clyde Barrow (in 1930) and, later, Ray Hamilton, who escaped from the unit on January 16, 1934, only to be recaptured a few months later. This escape landed him on death row—where he made his second, famed escape with Barrow's assistance in July 1934 and managed to stay out until recapture in April 1935. A few weeks later, on May 10, Hamilton became "Execution #147" of the Texas prison system.

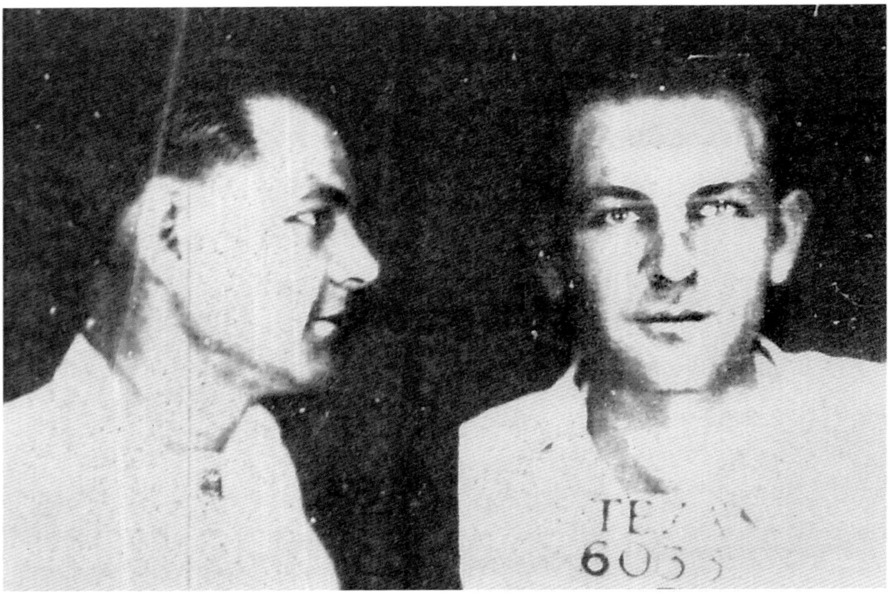

Mug shot of Raymond E. Hall. *Texas Department of Criminal Justice.*

Hall was in the Eastham unit as a violent offender with multiple life sentences attached to his name. He was also an accomplished songwriter and poet—as the above excerpt from the *Texas Prison Echo* shows—with an unassailable gift for rhetoric.

Born around 1904 in Oklahoma, Hall's early life is difficult to pinpoint through public record, except for documentation that he was a reform school recidivist—albeit a highly intelligent and well-educated recidivist. By his early adulthood, he was a vagabond, thief and volatile insurrectionist with an ear for music and an eye for opportunity who desperately grasped at any small break he thought he could get. However, Hall's biggest break, out of which arose his most important contributions, occurred through a happenstance meeting when he was working the railroads in the mid-1920s.

Jimmie Rodgers, the future "Father of Country Music," met the peripatetic young Hall at a speakeasy on Reno Avenue, a derelict area of Oklahoma City, in 1925. The two hit it off, communing for an hour or two about music as well as life on the rails. Rodgers was not yet a country music hit-maker; at the time he encountered Hall, he'd only recently quit his own career as a railroad worker. Traveling with a band, Rodgers was doggedly trying to maneuver his life into that of a successful full-time musician, despite the tuberculosis that plagued him. Their conversation eventually led to an exchange of songs, during which Hall sang one of his own compositions, "Take Me Back Again," for Rodgers. Hall told Rodgers he'd written the song during one of his (numerous) stints in the Oklahoma state reformatory.[97]

Rodgers—no stranger to hard times himself—saw something that spoke to him both in the song and in the writer. After about an hour, Rodgers took his leave, making sure to write his address on some scrap paper, which read "J.C. Rodgers, c/o Billboard, Cincinnati, OH." Rodgers also reinforced his belief in Hall's talent by telling him, "Look me up if you ever write any more songs like that. Get in touch if you ever need anything."[98] This companionable chance encounter later turned into a historically significant musical alliance when Rodgers became famous just a couple of years later. Unfortunately, in 1933, when tuberculosis ended Rodgers's life, Hall was unable to attend his friend's funeral. By that time, he was permanently established at the one residence from which he could not (legally) depart: the Texas state penitentiary.

Hall's convict number upon entry into the system was #58523—not #60339, as he was later assigned. This is an intriguing deviation, because the prison system only issued a prison record number if an individual was convicted and sentenced for a separate, unrelated offense than the one for which he or she had originally served time.

Newspapers from Texas and Oklahoma relay a whopper of a story in explanation, one that serves as yet another intriguing insight into the modus operandi of Raymond E. Hall:

> *One of the slickest prison escapes ever devised by prisoners anywhere would have worked perfectly, and two prisoners would soon be free men if Raymond Hall hadn't let his impatience get the better of him. Hall couldn't wait. So instead of being free, he is continued on a charge of first degree murder, and may die in the electric chair.*
>
> *Hall, who has a long criminal record, was sentenced to 99 years last winter for a holdup. He was tried at Wichita Falls and was ordered confined in the farm prison at Huntsville, near Houston. When he was sent to prison there* [was] *another convict sent with him—a young chap named Raymond Tucker, who was due to serve one year for violating the liquor laws. On the train the two got acquainted and cooked up this scheme:*
>
> *"They traded names and papers. At the end of one year Hall, posing as Tucker, would be released. Then, when Hall had enough time to get out of Texas, Tucker would reveal his real identity; and while he undoubtedly would be punished for aiding in Hall's escape, the punishment would not be very heavy and, having served his year, he, too, would be freed shortly afterward.*

> *It probably would have worked perfectly if Hall hadn't got impatient. Huntsville prison officials never discovered the hoax; they listed Hall as Tucker, serving a one-year sentence, and put Tucker down as Hall, with 99 years to go. His year would have been out in December.*
>
> *But Hall couldn't even wait to serve out his one year. One day recently Hall and some other convicts were working in a field under the direction of guards. Catching a guard by surprise, Hall overpowered him and took away his pistol and shotgun. He and six other prisoners made a break for freedom. Sergeant Henry Ward ordered them to halt and Hall shot him dead. The seven ran to the road, commandeered a passing auto and made the driver speed toward the town of Richmond, but were captured by a posse after a gun battle. So now Hall faces a charge of first degree murder.*
>
> *When he was caught, however, he was put down on the books as Raymond Tucker. This was too much for the real Tucker and he promptly revealed the hoax. As a result, the entire prison system is being investigated. Meanwhile, however, Raymond Hall awaits almost certain death in the electric chair. And all because he couldn't wait for four more months to pass!*[99]

Pioneering country music scholar Nolan Porterfield visited Raymond Hall at the penitentiary during the spring of 1975, while working on his seminal biography of Jimmie Rodgers. During his interview with Porterfield, Hall mentioned the identity swap but appeared to conceal the full story. In the version he laid out for Porterfield, Hall painted himself a victim of happenstance who "was mistakenly given another convict's identity and found himself serving not one but two life sentences."[100]

In 1929, Hall wrote to his old railroad buddy Jimmie Rodgers from the Huntsville unit of the prison, asking for support. Rodgers—by then a major star—wired him back quickly with a promise to assist if he could, and by the way, had Hall produced any song material he could use? Hall sent Rodgers "Moonlight and Skies" in response. After a couple of versions, "Moonlight and Skies" evolved into a bona fide prison song—half truth, half embellishment—about the crime for which Hall was first convicted. In the song, two men carry out an armed robbery, during which one man, Blackie, is shot and killed; the other is captured and sent to prison. "Moonlight and Skies" was just what Rodgers wanted: a "convict song, like the one Dalhart did."[101] Rodgers was almost surely wishing for a viable successor to Texas musician Vernon Dalhart's titanic hit "The Prisoner's Song" a few years prior.

Thus began a short-lived but prolific collaboration during which Hall penned "99 Years Blues" and "Gambling Polka Dot Blues" and contributed to the writing of one of Rodgers's most notable songs, "T.B. Blues." Rodgers's own tuberculosis was steadily worsening by 1930, and he moved to Kerrville, Texas, for a time, in hopes the drier climate would subdue his disease. On June 5, 1931, Rodgers went to Huntsville to visit Raymond Hall and conduct some songwriting credit business for "Moonlight and Skies," which turned out to be a modest hit, and discuss Hall's plight. Although Rodgers was sympathetic and supported his release in general, Hall was not about to be let go anytime soon. Hall's conduct registers are bursting with notes on numerous infractions and attempted escapes.

March 13, 1929	"500 hours solitary, fighting officers and disobeying orders"
July 17, 1929	"22 days solitary—attempting to escape and to kill inmate"
September 6, 1929	"30 days solitary. Refusing to work"
March 22, 1931	"Rec[eived] 16 reg[ular] strap for fighting and assaulting Harry Burger, an inmate"
September 8, 1931	"6 hrs on Brl [barrel] for laziness"
September 17, 1931	"20 lashes reg Strap for agitating and trying to instigate a Buck" and "9 hrs on Brl for not picking cotton as he should"
July 27, 1932	"6 hrs brl for laziness"
March 9, 1935	"Attempted to escape from Guard at Retrieve State Farm. Lost all [good hours accrued]"
May 7, 1935	"Issued 20 lashes for inflicting injuries to self to avoid work"
May 11, 1935	"Above order executed; 20 lashes"

Hall was clearly a frequent recipient of harsh punitive actions, even making the news in April 1935, when one hard-hitting newspaper article described extensive punishment of inmates—and him in particular. Sometime that spring, several prison board members drove into the gates of the Retrieve prison unit in response to inmate letters reporting extreme brutality at the unit. Upon the board members' arrival at the unit, two inmates were discovered in the act of mutilating each other with axes, reportedly to avoid further punishment from the guards. An official named T.K. Kelley refuted all claims of cruel and unusual punishment, even going so far as to preposterously declare that the Retrieve prison guards never got closer to an inmate than ten feet. According to the article, the prison board members were in possession of a convict letter reporting details of the guards' behavior and remained unconvinced.

> *"The farm is hot and on fire," the* [convict] *letter said... "They started in again by whipping Raymond Hall in the building with handcuffs and spurred him with spurs and boot heels. They told him they would kill him when he came out to work, and they put him in the hoe squad."* [Texas Prison Board members] *Dulaney and Boyett discovered Hall's head was badly lacerated, the* Press *said. Hall had tried to escape and was shot when he appeared in the field with a pistol which was smuggled in.*[102]

Just one month later, Hall became involved in yet another violent incident at the Retrieve State Farm, during which a fellow convict named Everett Melvin was stabbed and killed. Hall was a frequent recipient of punishment at the prison, and reportedly, he was present at the time of the stabbing. The extent of his involvement was unclear, however, and most eyewitness accounts attributed Melvin's murder to another convict: Clyde Thompson. Dubbed with several fearful nicknames such as the "thrill killer" and "the meanest man in Texas," Clyde Thompson was already infamous for several other murders both in and out of prison.

Due to his alleged involvement in the slaying of Everett Melvin, Hall made headlines once more. This time, however, Hall's trial gained notoriety for another reason than his—and even Clyde Thompson's—actions. District Judge M.S. Munson was concerned about jury bias regarding Thompson's dastardly reputation and vehemently disallowed any media coverage of the event in advance of the court trials. All violators, he threatened, would be punished to the fullest extent of the law. Several newspapers published coverage anyway, resulting in "contempt of court" citations filed against six editors and reporters for several Houston newspapers. The new case caused hot debate among Texas lawmen, essentially pitting freedom of speech against the right to a fair trial. In part due to the kerfuffle, Hall's criminal trial regarding his role in Melvin's murder was delayed, and no conviction of the additional crime was found in his prison records—however, he was already serving two life sentences at the time, so any further sentencing might have been redundant. Clyde Thompson, "the meanest man in Texas," remained in the penitentiary until the mid-1950s and was granted a full pardon in 1963—almost fifteen years before Raymond Hall would achieve his own freedom.

For his many misdeeds, Hall spent very close to the remainder of his entire adult life behind bars, shuffled between the Eastham, Huntsville and Retrieve units. He was granted parole in January 1976, and a full pardon was extended to him on June 3, 1977. His markedly bitter views of prison authority and often violent refusal to abide by establishment rules show through his convict records and news articles written during the first ten years of his incarceration. Contrastingly, his written criticisms of the system and introspective approach to his creative life make for a compelling polarity, one in which Raymond Hall arguably represents the quintessential anti-hero.

Despite his incalculable and sometimes unforgivable transgressions, Hall was well respected and supported by not only Jimmie Rodgers but also by many inmates and officials within the prison system, as evidenced in the earlier article that outlined his accomplishments for the 1941 *Who's Who in Poetry in America*. Raymond Hall was a shrewd, if unconscionable, individual in a powerless situation, so he regained what little power he felt he had lost by retaliating with words—words that could be written, spoken or sung.

If handled diplomatically, *Thirty Minutes* could become a venue for its inmates' thinly veiled criticisms of public perception of them—if not the entire penal system. Hall skillfully employed his gift for rhetoric on an early episode of *Thirty Minutes* when Nelson Olmsted, a WBAP announcer—and an "outsider," whom Hall may well have perceived as condescending—asked him how he felt about being committed to the Eastham farm. The exchange that follows shows something of Hall's keen intellect and adroit double-speak:

> *HALL: In my opinion, no man is without hope, regardless of how he may be classified. It might be that one may say of another whether he has or has not hope—whether he has or has not some good left within him. But I see that as emulating the powers of God.*
> *OMSTEAD: I see you've thought the question over pretty thoroughly, whatever your position. And now, Raymond, I'd like you to tell us something about the men in your building. The Law* [sic] *sees them as hardened criminals—dangerous—difficult to handle…tell me in your own way just how you see them.*
> *HALL: I won't attempt to judge my fellowmen* [sic]*—I'll just say this: There are 26 of them in there. They're human, for all their lawlessness. They live and breathe and love freedom—like you—like all men—like the beasts of field and forest. That's as natural as day and night. They're all long-termers; most of them lifers or 99-year men. The fact that they're*

> *daring, difficult to handle, is because most of them see only a life of living in a stone and steel-barred world. Almost anyone except the most craven coward would be the same way under similar circumstances. Hope, to us, is the stuff of life. Take it, and we have nothing left.*[103]

A minute later, Raymond Hall sang "Life's Weary Way," his own composition, on the air. This was the only time Hall has ben confirmed to play in the prison band or appear on *Thirty Minutes Behind the Walls*; at least, it's the only one on record. The WBAP radio show rarely conducted broadcasts at the Eastham unit, and any *Thirty Minutes* transcripts after March 1941 have never been located, so this date remains the only confirmed appearance of the man whose songs made unlikely partners of country music and prisons.

Although no recordings exist of that evening's original composition, "Life's Weary Way," many recordings of Raymond Hall's songs exist today through the music of Jimmie Rodgers. In turn, Rodgers had an incalculable influence on country music, and his numerous songs about the lonely prisoner, the forgotten man, touched dozens of future country stars, including Jimmie Davis, Lefty Frizzell and more. Collectively, their associations with the prison song set a precedent for later country music legends, such as Johnny Cash, Johnny Paycheck and Merle Haggard, who redefined the country music prison song for newer generations. Raymond Hall's creative contributions from his Texas prison cell represent something of a missing link for why the prison song is one of country music's defining themes.

6

THE GOREE GIRLS

Songbirds of Texas Prisons

We glowed with pride when we remind you that some of the outstanding talent comes from this unit: Helen Rogers, Ella Ray, Ruby Morace, Eleanor Dale, and our blues-crooning colored girl, Hattie. They're so unassuming in our midst that we pass them unconcernedly at least six days a week, but when we hear them on the air it's different. They are stars then, shining in our own little sky above our backyard, and we clasp hands on the back porch to dream little dreams that are made of stardust.[104]

—*Reable Childs, "Across the Back Fence,"* Texas Prison Echo

Who Were the Goree Girls?

In the 1930s, when the Texas Prison Rodeo and *Thirty Minutes Behind the Walls* made the world aware of the wealth of inmate talent housed in the Texas prison system, female inmates of the system played a minor role in the festivities. At times, the residents of Goree State Farm for Women were even excluded from participation. However, as the 1930s drew to a close, female roles in the rodeo musical performances became indispensable—the crowds whooped and hollered for more. When the Goree All-Girl String Band debuted on *Thirty Minutes* in 1940, their enormous and immediate popularity ratcheted the already impressive radio show up to another level, one of unforeseen success.

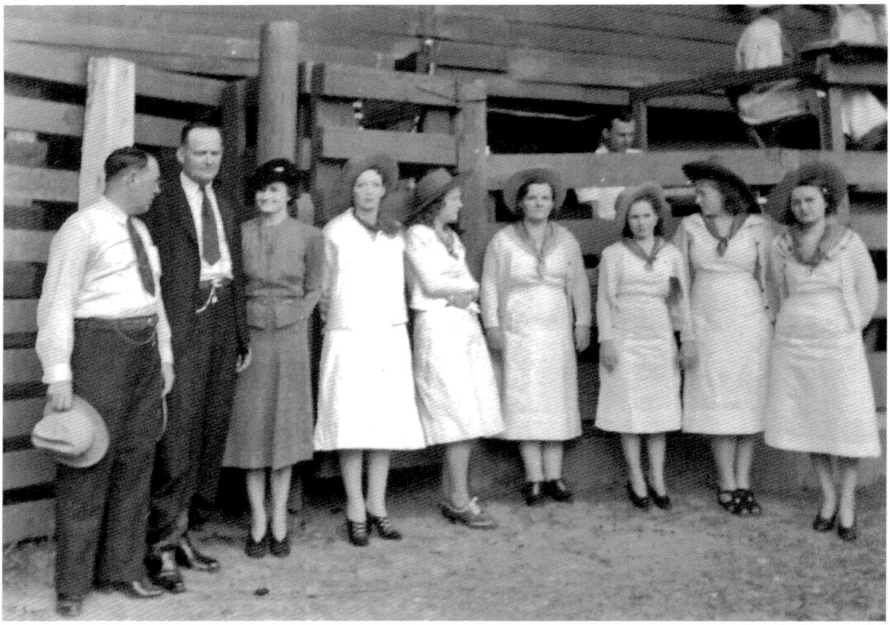

Rodeo performers from Goree await their turn on the Texas Prison Rodeo stage. *Left to right*: unidentified, Captain Heath, Mrs. Heath, Mozelle McDaniel, unidentified (possibly Georgia Fay Collins), unidentified (possibly Patsy Hutchings), Burma Harris, unidentified (possibly Jerry Lee Norris) and Reable Childs. *Texas State Library and Archives Commission.*

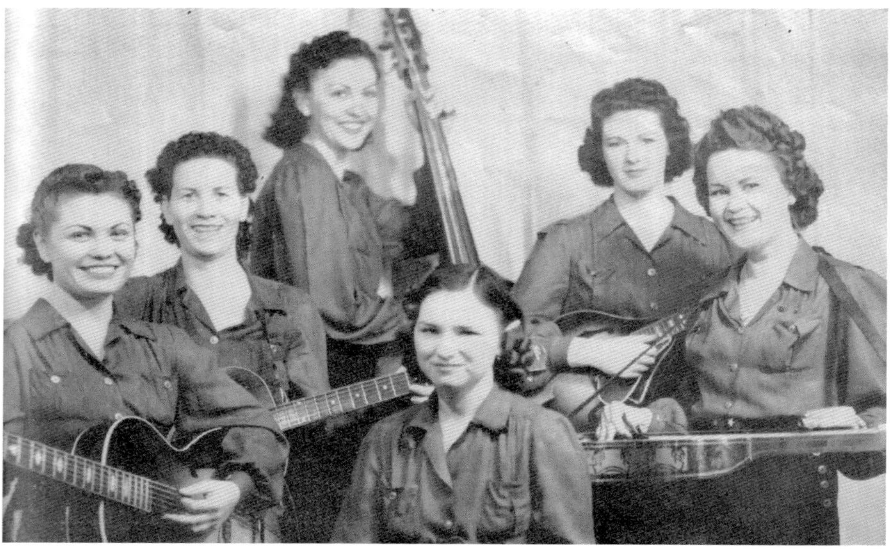

The Goree All-Girl String Band, circa 1943. *Left to right*: Georgia W., Barbara A., Bonnie Scott, Georgia H., Clomer J. and Reable Childs. *Texas Prison Museum.*

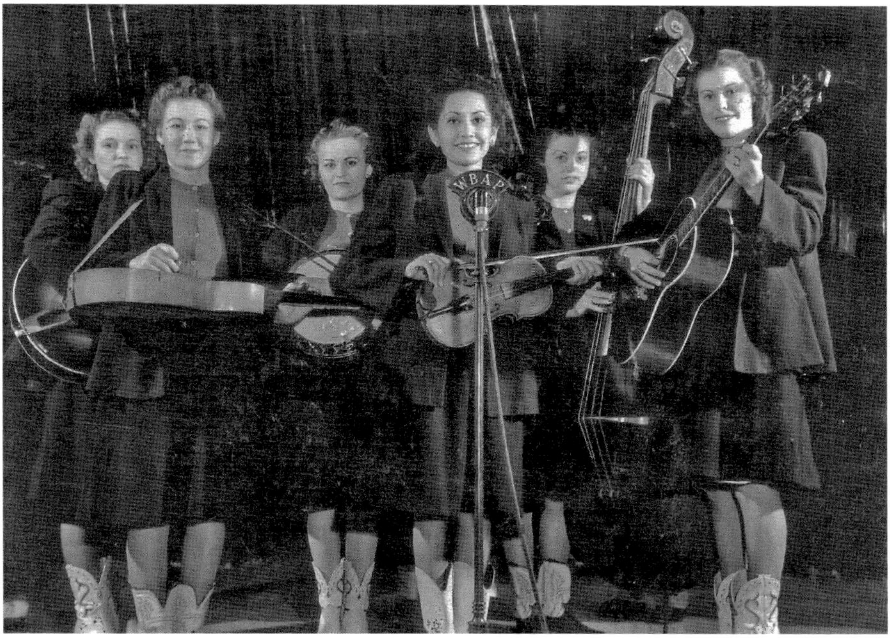

The Goree All-Girl String Band, circa 1942. *Left to right*: unidentified, Winonna Shirey, Reable Childs, Eva Vigil, unidentified and Ruby Dell Guyton. *Texas Prison Museum.*

The compelling story of the female prisoners who performed on the Texas-based radio show *Thirty Minutes Behind the Walls* offers a unique example of music's transformational possibilities within a gray, barred world. For these marginalized women, the music they made became a vehicle for challenging and redefining the public's understandings of their lives. Their performances at the rodeo and on *Thirty Minutes* changed the way they were treated, both as prisoners and in society at large. In some cases, their musical accomplishments eventually allowed them to maneuver themselves out of a bleak and literally confining existence.

To the public, the female inmates of the Texas prison system were generally thought to have fallen from grace. In no way did an incarcerated woman fit the stereotypical image of the innocent farm girl of country music or that of the benevolent, sentimental mother figure that were so common on the country music radio barn dances of the era. Even so, the music and image presented by the women of the Goree State Farm shifted the public's perception of who they were, humanizing them and, ultimately, allowing these not-so-wholesome women to resurrect themselves in the eyes of the public, the prison system and, perhaps, themselves.

The image the Goree performers presented through their music and its resultant publicity was a jarring contrast with their existence in an oppressive—and sometimes violent—environment, as well as the reality that they were serving heavy prison sentences for crimes such as cattle rustling, robbery, assault, heroin possession and murder. Like Hattie Ellis and Raymond E. Hall, however, the Goree Girls nonetheless navigated the equally heavy expectations of non-inmate radio officials, the conventions of commercial music and the popular perceptions of prison inmates in an effort to change how others might view them. Projecting a sense of penitence, coupled with valiant gaiety and quiet femininity—in addition to a fashionable visual image—helped the Goree women achieve the compassion and respectability they needed in order to change the course of their lives.

Thirty Minutes certainly aired female performances during its first couple of years, but for the most part, the women were relegated to a sentimental or western song or two out of every two or three shows. One notable exception to this rule was Hattie Ellis, whose raw talent came into being on the radio show in 1938 and galvanized the public, garnering much admiration for a strikingly gifted woman who was often condescendingly referred to as a "blues-singing Negress" or a "dusky songstress." She appeared on most episodes of *Thirty Minutes* from 1938 to 1940, singing popular songs like "Over the Rainbow" and "Heart and Soul," with an occasional blues or jazz number thrown in.

Although the Goree unit band changed members frequently because of paroles or other clemencies, until her 1943 parole, the one constant in the group was Reable Childs. Just a few months after their first public performance, in December 1940, a *Thirty Minutes* inmate interview identified members of the Goree All-Girl String Band as Reable Childs on the banjo, Lillie Mae Dudley on bass fiddle, Ruby Guyton and Bonnie Scott on acoustic guitars and Burma Harris on fiddle. Vocals were shared between Ruby Morace, Reable Childs, Mozelle McDaniel and Fay Woodard (possibly referring to Georgia Fay Collins).[105]

Although the best-known story of the Goree Girls is that of Reable Childs, every inmate had her own tale to tell. While public documentation is scarce for most later members of the Goree band and other female performers on *Thirty Minutes*—and even more so for their male counterparts—there is a story behind nearly all of them. For the original members of the Goree Girls, as well as one or two other women appearing on *Thirty Minutes*, a little more information is available.

Convict #83156

Elizabeth Helen "Patsy" Hutchings was one of the first female inmates who appeared on *Thirty Minutes*, known for her sweet voice and penchant for sentimental love songs. Listed as a "singer" for her occupation, convict ledgers show that the twenty-five-year-old St. Louis native did some time in the Illinois Reformatory for Women before receiving a five-year sentence in March 1936 for an El Paso robbery. Hutchings was a trusted inmate during her incarceration; she was featured heavily on the early episodes of *Thirty Minutes*, no doubt due to her background as a singer. Hutchings also wrote the Goree unit's newspaper column, "Across the Back Fence," for the *Texas Prison Echo*. After Hutchings's conditional pardon in October 1938, Reable Childs took over as Goree's columnist for the *Echo* and continued singing on *Thirty Minutes* as a vocal soloist and, later, as star performer of the Goree All-Girl String Band.

Convict #89894

Another early singer of *Thirty Minutes* was a fellow Missourian to Hutchings: Jerry Lee Norris. Born in Arkansas and residing in Joplin, Missouri, Norris was convicted—along with her husband—of an El Paso robbery and sentenced to two and a half years at Goree. In an interview on *Thirty Minutes*, Norris stated that her husband was in the Huntsville unit and worked in the shoe shop. Nelson Olmsted, WBAP announcer, responded:

> *OLMSTED: And I'm certain he will enjoy the number you are going to sing tonight. But listen—except for your first number several weeks ago, you've sang only Hawaiian songs. I just wondered why this is.*
> *JERRY LEE: I don't know…I'm especially fond of Hawaiian music. Perhaps that explains it.*
> *OLMSTED: Well, have you ever been to Hawaii?*
> *JERRY LEE: No, but someday I'd liks* [sic] *to go there.*
> *OLMSTED: Tell me, Jerry Lee—have you ever appeared outside as a professional entertainer?*
> *JERRY LEE: No, all the singing I've ever done has been just for my own amusement.*

> *OLMSTED: What was your occupation outside?*
> *JERRY LEE: Keeping house for my husband.*
> *OLMSTED: And of course you want to get back to that as quickly as possible?*
> *JERRY LEE: You bet I do! And the sooner that day comes around the better it will suit me.*[106]

Convict #89363

Although the male inmates of *Thirty Minutes* occasionally worked as musicians prior to entering the prisons, this did not hold true for the majority of women in the early Goree string band. Only one of the inmates in the Goree Girls had any type of musical career prior to her incarceration. On *Thirty Minutes*, Louisiana native Ruby Mae Morace told her story to that evening's announcer:

> *RUBY: I went to school in Ferriday, Louisiana…that's my home.*
> *BYRNE: Did you finish school there?*
> *RUBY: No, sir…my daddy went blind about eleven years ago…Mother had to go to work—When I was 15 I had to find a job, too, because I had little sisters—so I got a job singing in a night club.*
> *BYRNE: How old are you?*
> *RUBY: I'm 21—I was about 18½ when I got into trouble.*
> *BYRNE: Have you been on the program continuously?*
> *RUBY: No, sir…I missed three months last year…I underwent an operation, and I almost went under…But Mrs. Heath and the prison doctors were so wonderful to me, I came out of it—singing.*
> *BYRNE: I'll say you did.*[107]

Although she hailed from Louisiana, Ruby Mae Morace was clear on the other side of Texas when she "got into trouble" at age eighteen. Ruby and her boyfriend—tall, fair-haired Ruffin G. Matthews—flagged down El Paso salesman W.T. Woodward near Finlay, an old West Texas ghost town in Hudspeth County, just northeast of the Mexican border. Once Woodward stopped, Matthews hit him four times with the handle of his pistol, "until the handle were broken off."[108] Morace reported that she was "too scared to do anything." The pair then tied Woodward to a tree and left in his vehicle. All told, they took forty-four dollars from Woodward for their trouble. They received twenty-five years each for robbery and assault with a deadly weapon.

Once in the prison, Ruby worked as assistant bookkeeper to Mrs. Heath and sang alone in her cell until a guard took notice and let the radio show officials know that they had quite a songbird behind the walls of the women's unit. From then until her conditional pardon in the spring of 1942, Morace was one of the primary vocalists for the Goree Girls, in addition to playing acoustic guitar and mandolin. Her songs were in high demand on the radio show, receiving gifts of money and accolades from faraway listeners. In 1941, she told the *Thirty Minutes* announcer, "The biggest thrill I ever got was when a gentleman in Waco wired me $50.00 after hearing me sing on this program."[109]

"The Little Blue and Gold Songbird"—with her fair hair and blue eyes—received a conditional pardon in 1942. After she left, the *Echo* said of her departure, "We miss Ruby's wistful singing of sentimental songs, and we wish to say that the little blue and gold songbird, Ruby, that your memory lingers on."[110] After Morace's release, she left for Arkansas, telling her family that she was going to live with "Lillian from prison," most likely referring to fellow Goree band member Lillie Mae Dudley. Morace also kept in touch with her old boyfriend and partner in crime, Ruffin G. Matthews. Matthews was granted a conditional pardon in 1943, and at some point after his release, he and Morace reunited and married, or simply listed themselves as living together as husband and wife for the public directories of Hot Springs, Arkansas, in 1946.[111]

Eventually, however, Morace made her way back to her hometown of Ferriday, Louisiana. She married again, this time to a former U.S. Army Air Corps pilot named Burl N. Poole. After he died in 1956, Morace started a beauty salon in Ferriday using the skills she'd gained in the prison's beauty shop. She also began to spell her name as "Rubye." Public records show that Ruby Mae Morace had at least four to six marriages during her lifetime, although she never had children (for reasons that will be discussed later). As one of seven children born to Edward and Emma Roena Corley Morace, she did, however, have a large extended family. Later in life, she moved to Monterey, Louisiana, marrying former World War II and Korean War naval veteran Vanice Marley Osmon. Morace remained married to him until her death in May 1995. She is buried next to her former husband Burl Poole in Natchez, Mississippi.

Convict #87351

Blonde Mozelle McDaniel, 18, and pretty, was under a seven-year prison sentence today because she shot and killed her stepfather after he threatened to whip her and told her mother to keep her mouth shut or he'd "beat her brains out." A jury before which Mozelle was tried for murder returned a verdict of guilty after hearing her describe how she killed her stepfather, Jack Watkins, 38, and oil field worker, last Aug. 14.

Mozelle said that her stepfather, who was drunk at the time, threatened to beat her because she went riding with her 16-year-old sister, Emma, and two boy friends after going to town for a sack of potatoes, and did not get home before dark.

Mozelle's mother became hysterical when the verdict was read and was placed under a doctor's care. Mozelle, weeping softly, tried to comfort her mother.[112]

As had occurred with Reable Childs, Mozelle McDaniel received heavy newspaper coverage after she shot her stepfather. All over Texas, headlines like "Fearful of Spanking, Girl Shoots Father" portrayed her as an ungrateful teenager who demanded the family car and shot her family's caretaker and authoritarian in order to get what she wanted. They reported how the seventeen-year-old got into an argument with her stepfather and then went into the house, grabbed a rifle, came back out and fired sixteen shots at him, hitting him eleven times in the torso and even his face. McDaniel's mother was present for the argument and witnessed the shooting. Deputy Sheriff Carl Siebrecht later told a reporter, "I have never seen anyone so calm after killing a human." Other newspapers reported that after Mozelle McDaniel shot Jack Watkins, she drove off to get the nearest doctor. Charges were filed shortly afterward, with a $5,000 bond posted by her father, Moe McDaniel.[113]

As the story emerged during the trial, the press got a look at the defendant and the support she had from her family—in particular, her mother, who had witnessed the shooting—and it became apparent that the curly, blond-haired teenager was, just perhaps, not some callous ingrate of a girl. The back story was complicated, and the family dynamic was troubled. Certainly McDaniel's slaying of her stepfather was a reprehensible and irreversible act. Yet the jury seemed to believe her testimony, understanding that her criminal act was probably borne of an ill-advised, reckless and altogether immediate determination to end the suffering of herself, her mother and her siblings at the hands of an abusive alcoholic. As McDaniel told the jury, "I shot Papa Jack to protect the family."[114]

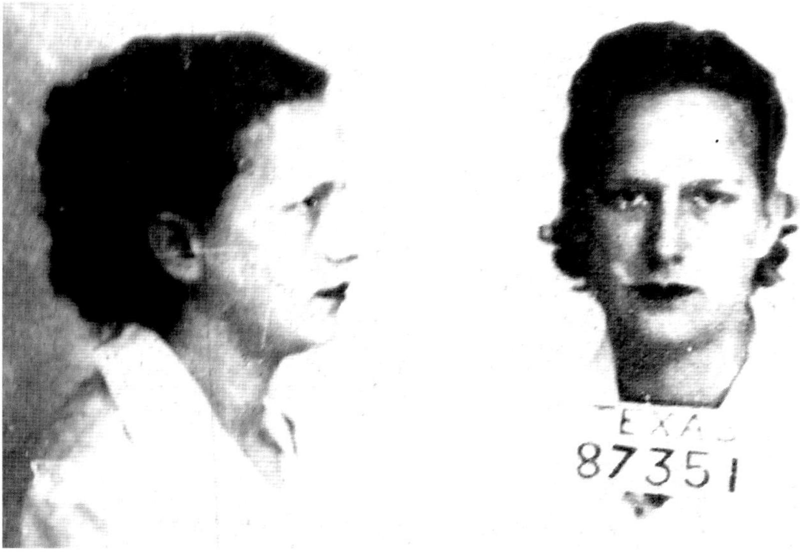

Mug shot of Mozelle McDaniel. *Texas Department of Criminal Justice.*

McDaniel entered the Goree prison on January 29, 1938, with seven years to serve. For a murder conviction in the state of Texas, seven years was a relatively light sentence; from this one can suppose that the jury believed McDaniel's crime had been one of passion or a desire to protect herself and her loved ones, committed under duress.

Just under eight weeks later, the first episode of *Thirty Minutes Behind the Walls* aired on WBAP. Another eight weeks after that, on May 25, 1938, McDaniel made her first appearance on the radio show—albeit as an interviewee, not a singer. Later, she became the radio show's own "yodeling sweetheart," much lauded for her talent in singing western songs such as "I Want to Be a Cowboy's Sweetheart," among other yodeling favorites. McDaniel's singing cowgirl performances with the Goree Girls were a highlight of many *Thirty Minutes* programs before she was released on a conditional pardon in December 1940.

After her time in the penitentiary, McDaniel lived out the rest of her quiet life in Texas. She was married several times, but no evidence exists of her having had children. She passed away in January 2003, but not before Skip Hollandsworth located her and visited the rest home where she resided. Although she did not speak in detail of her time in the prison, Hollandsworth was able to get an acknowledgment of her participation in the band and a few anecdotes.

> *I asked her why she had never told anyone that she had once been famous. Another long silence ensued. I wondered if she had heard my question. Then, out of the blue, she started speaking. "Didn't want to bring it all up," she said. "What I did. All that back then. What people said about me." I stared at Mozelle, amazed. Here she was, at the end of her life, her faltering mind still haunted by that one desperate act she committed when she was seventeen years old.*[115]

With the horrors of Jack Watkins's murder, the trial and her imprisonment long behind her, McDaniel was still unable—or perhaps somewhat unwilling—to discuss her time with the Goree Girls when asked. Sadly, she never witnessed the public's response to her work with the Goree Girls because she passed away just a few months before Hollandsworth's article was published. However, regarding her role in the band, she did relay a moment of pride in what they—those forgotten women behind bars—achieved with their music. "No one thought we could sing, but we did. We sure damn did. At least we did that."[116]

Convict #89669

The most diminutive of all the Goree All-Girl String Band members, Burma Harris stood under five feet tall. Her height, however, did not keep her from fiddling up a storm; in fact, she was often referred to as the leader of the Goree Girls. Reable wrote in August 1940, "I hear strains of a violin floating across the air from the direction of the chapel. It must be Goree's own little violinist. Atta girl, Burma. Keep up the good work, you are tops with us."[117]

Harris did not know how to play the fiddle prior to joining the band. However, alongside the other Goree Girls, she was taught by musically inclined inmates from the male unit. Sybil Heath, the daughter of Captain and Mrs. Heath, taught the women music theory and sight-reading. In the *Echo*, Reable wrote of their experiences learning from the male instructors:

> *Those three able instructors, Pat, Lucky and Kelly, of the Rhythmic Stringsters, have faithfully done their duty, but needless to say, it has sure kept the "All Girl Stringsters" on the run preparing new numbers for each Wednesday night broadcast and other programs…but we enjoy it a lot because we like plenty of action.*[118]

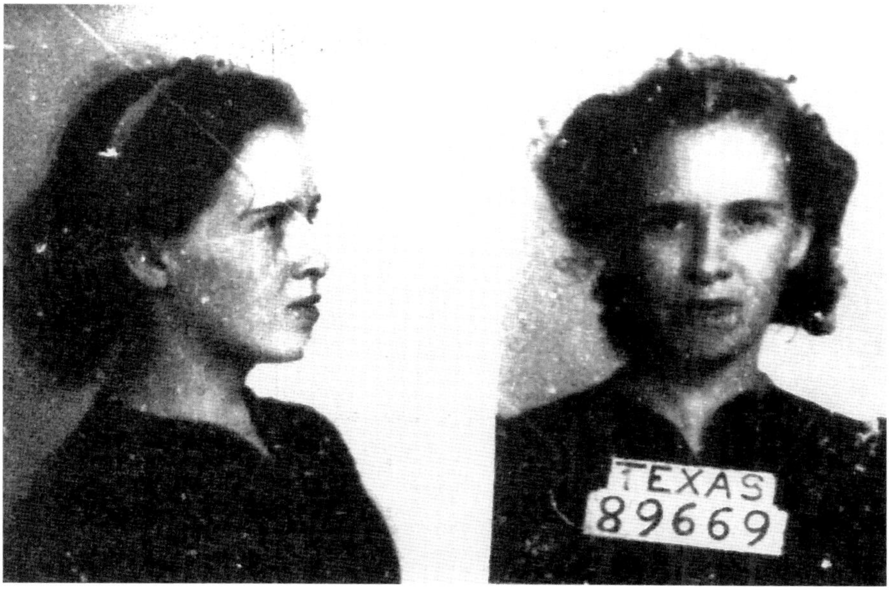

Mug shot of Burma Harris. *Texas Department of Criminal Justice.*

Harris was well liked among her fellow Goree residents and enjoyed star status in the Goree band until her departure in August 1941. Born in 1913 in Houston and committed to Goree in October 1938 with two convictions of heroin possession, along with receipt and concealment of stolen property, her prison records are forever marked with "Drug Addict" in large red script. Because of the unlikeliness of continued heroin use while in the prison—at least, in the 1930s—Harris attained some balance through the music while she was at Goree and soon became an exemplary inmate who held a leadership position.

Unfortunately, as had occurred with Jack Purvis, Harris continued to suffer from heavy addiction issues. Following her conditional pardon in 1941, the shining moments as a *Thirty Minutes* radio star faded back into obscurity. Harris's trail fades considerably after her release. She appears to have distanced herself from her Houston-based family, living a somewhat inauspicious lifestyle.

In her 1972 death certificate, the cause of death was listed as cirrhosis of the liver, along with hypertension. Fifty-eight-year-old Burma Harris, popular fiddler and Goree bandleader, died alone on January 7, 1972. Her death was reported by the Houston Department of Welfare, and all the fields for family and occupation are listed as "unknown."

Convict #94151

In February 1940, an article in the *Greeley Daily Tribune* in Colorado expressed concern for the welfare of one of its residents with the following statement: "Police today widened their search for Mr. and Mrs. Ray Scott of Aurora, Colo., whom officers said were the last known occupants of an abandoned bullet-riddled car found near Fort Sam Houston."[119] Because of the state of the car, officials worried that the pair had been murdered.

In the months before that bullet-riddled vehicle was found, young Bonnie Barron entered into a check-forging scam with her father, Jack Barron, a man of dubious background who'd already served thirty-three years of his life behind prison walls. He gallantly took responsibility for the crime, telling the courtroom how his daughter's role in the crime was due to his paternal influence, and was sentenced to another five to ten years behind bars. His daughter, Bonnie, was given probation.

As Jack Barron was carted away to serve out his sentence, he told the judge and anyone who would listen that he was worried about his daughter getting into "serious trouble."[120] Meanwhile, Bonnie Barron sat in the county jail awaiting her sentencing.

While Bonnie was in jail, a young soldier from Lowry Field came around to visit her a couple of times. After receiving probation, Bonnie Barron and her soldier, Raymond Scott, moved to 2109 East Sixteenth Avenue in Denver. Bonnie worked as a waitress while Raymond carried out his military duties, and after his enlistment was completed, the couple opened a café at 1937 Broadway in Denver. Soon enough, however, Bonnie started talking to a few of her friends about the couple's plans to head for Texas. In the first days of February 1940, Raymond Scott asked a mechanic buddy, R.L. Kenyon, if he could borrow his car to take Bonnie to the hospital, and Kenyon acquiesced. Off the couple went, and Kenyon didn't hear one word from them again, or see his vehicle, until Texas authorities found the car days later with the windshield shattered and bullet holes throughout.[121]

The mystery was solved within days. A week before the car had been found, the Dryden filling station in Randall County was robbed at gunpoint and the perpetrators escaped in a getaway car. Following leads provided, authorities soon located a man and woman driving a car matching descriptions of the alleged getaway car. Officers embarked on a high-speed chase with the suspects, exchanging volleys of gunfire with the vehicle (Bonnie at the helm and Raymond behind the gun). The chase ended badly for law enforcement officials because the newest "Bonnie and Clyde" couple—in this case, "Bonnie and Ray"—escaped in their fast-moving car.[122]

The following Friday, the same couple was apprehended after kidnapping a man named James Ruby in San Antonio and forcing him to drive them to San Marcos. Once near the town, the pair relieved Ruby of his wallet and jacket. When the getaway car with the bullet holes was located the next day, the Texas authorities knew they'd caught the bandits from the Dryden filling station. A marriage license, military identification and bloodstained clothing was found in the abandoned vehicle.[123]

Through reports of others who had encountered the couple along the way, it very soon became clear that the bandit couple were, in fact, the missing Mr. and Mrs. Scott from Colorado. It seems that Bonnie Barron of Denver had, in one fell swoop, made good on her promise to head for Texas and, in the process, actualized her father's fear that his Bonnie would end up in "serious trouble."[124]

A little over a month later, Bonnie and Ray were each sentenced to two to five years in prison for the kidnapping and theft of James Ruby. In August 1940, they were each slapped with an additional ten years for the Dryden armed robbery.

First entering the women's prison unit in March 1940, Bonnie Scott soon joined the Goree Girls, who were, at that point, rehearsing hard and heavy for their eventual appearance on *Thirty Minutes*. Despite not having any musical experience, Bonnie Scott joined the group on acoustic guitar and, later, bass fiddle. Her pretty, youthful appearance no doubt helped her become a good candidate for the group, and her sentence meant that she would stay in the prison for a time. Bonnie appears in many photographs of the Goree Girls between 1940 and her release in June 1943, with positive mentions from Reable Childs and other members of the *Echo* inmate staff, while she was there. Her husband, Raymond, was shuffled around between the Huntsville, Eastham and Retrieve units, at one point sustaining a serious injury in an accident at Retrieve, according to the *Echo*'s "Across the Back Fence" column, which offered its support to Bonnie, stating that the women at Goree "have our fingers crossed, Bonnie, and as Raymond is young and healthy, we feel sure that he will come through O.K."[125]

As with many inmates of the prison system—particularly those with common surnames—Bonnie's trail becomes indistinct after her 1943 release. What can be determined is that she never landed back in the Texas prisons for any reason after her full pardon in 1947, but it's unclear where or how long she lived after she got out or whether she remained married to Raymond Scott.

Convict #93371

In June 1939, young Ruby Dell Guyton and her husband, Eldon Guyton, were arrested for hijacking the bookkeeper of a feed store in Shamrock, Texas. They received a grand total of twenty-five dollars for their efforts. Listed as a "housewife" on her convict ledger, it seems Ruby was the leader of the two in the crime. For the robbery, during which a firearm was used, she received a sentence of five years in the Texas penitentiary; her husband got the same. While she was in the prison, Guyton worked in the garment factory, took part in the prison unit's sports activities and played acoustic guitar and sang with the Goree string band with harmonies and rhythmic instrumental backing. Paroled in 1942, during her incarceration, Ruby Guyton also exchanged letters with her husband, Eldon. Reable mentioned Guyton in her June 1940 column in the *Echo*:

> *Good natured Ruby Dell is sewing away like mad, no doubt she is wondering if that weekly letter from down Richmond way, will be in the evening mail. That usual letter from her "one and only" can change that gal's expression more than a full pardon would. And say, Ruby is somewhat of a ball player too, as well as an excellent seamstress.*[126]

Convict #94765

An inmate named "Fay Woodard" was frequently listed as one of the Goree band members according to the *Thirty Minutes* transcripts; however, no prison records exist for any inmate of that name. In his May 2003 *Texas Monthly* article, "O Sister, Where Art Thou," Skip Hollandsworth noted one of the Goree Girls as "Georgia Fay Collins, a blond, curly-haired divorcée with false teeth." A prison record exists for Georgia Fay Collins—a waitress serving two years for burglary—and lists identical attributes. In examining the convict ledger, a male inmate named Lee Woodard appeared as an inmate just a few lines down on the same page as Collins. His crime and sentencing date, as well as geographical information, matches that of Georgia Fay Collins. Collins was listed with a marital status of "divorced" in her convict ledger. She and Woodard went into the prison system for a crime they committed together, listed with separate surnames. It therefore seems that Georgia Fay Collins apparently chose to use, in an unofficial or social capacity, her middle name of "Fay," along with Lee Woodard's surname. It remains unclear whether Lee Woodard was the person Collins was divorced from at the time she entered the prison or if he represented a more recent common-law, or even marital, relationship. Little information is available about the crime that landed them both in the Texas prison or what happened to Collins after her release. But during her incarceration, Collins was a frequent featured vocalist on *Thirty Minutes*—especially after her bandmate Mozelle's release in December 1940—while singing western songs such as "Way Out There," popularized by the Sons of the Pioneers.

Convict #87910

Listed as a divorced woman who was five feet, three inches tall with dark blond hair and light brown eyes, Lillie Mae Dudley's story had remained something of a mystery compared to the rest of the Goree Girls. However, relatives recently came forward and agreed to talk about Lillie Mae Dudley's

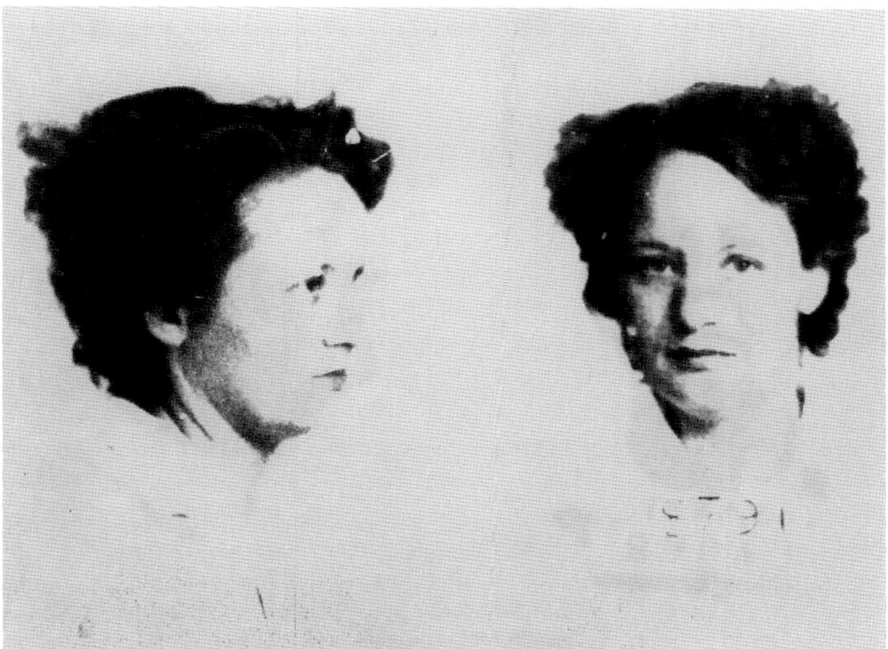

Mug shot of Lillie Mae Dudley. *Texas Department of Criminal Justice.*

life, both before and after prison. They preferred to remain anonymous, but the information they provided sheds some much-needed light on this mysterious inmate. As a result of this new information, one revelatory aspect stands out: unlike most of the other Goree Girls, Lillie Mae Dudley had a daughter *before* she went into the prison.

Her granddaughter stated that Dudley, one of many children in an impoverished, tenant-farming family, entered into marriage at a very young age and, with her husband (who was ten years her senior), gave birth to a girl child at age fifteen. The marriage did not last very long, and Dudley's daughter, Bettie Jo, was raised by her grandparents; her exact parentage was kept something of a family secret. Dudley and her husband divorced; described by her family as "wild," stubborn" and "independent" in her youth, Dudley found herself in a tight spot by her early twenties.[127]

On March 4, 1938, Marshall Trice of Denison, Texas, was assaulted and robbed by one Lillie Mae Dudley, future bass fiddle player of the Goree All-Girl String Band. A man named James Fred Crabtree accompanied Dudley during the robbery and was later named as her accomplice. Several weeks later, both were sentenced to seven years in the penitentiary after pleading guilty to the crime. Although Crabtree received a sentence of seven years for his role as accomplice to the robbery, it seems he may not have entered the prison after all because no records have been found for a prisoner of that name. However, Lillie Mae Dudley wasn't so lucky and entered the Goree Farm on March 28, 1938, just a few days after the inaugural episode of *Thirty Minutes Behind the Walls*.

No mentions of Dudley in the *Echo* were made until she became part of the Goree All-Girl String Band in early 1940. When the opportunity arose to participate in the all-girl string band, Dudley quickly volunteered to play the bass fiddle. Once she nabbed a spot in the coveted group, she worked hard to learn the bass fiddle, providing the rhythmic backbone for the entire group (in general, no drums were used with the string bands). Tasked with learning one of the group's most important instruments, she did excel at performance, according to a couple of reports in the *Echo*. Dudley appears in a number of photos of the Goree string band in its earliest incarnation, before being granted a conditional pardon by Governor O'Daniel in December 1940. While Dudley gleefully left the prison behind, she also left the Goree band without a bass fiddle player; the role eventually went to Bonnie Scott and then others. After her departure, Dudley kept to the terms of her release and was granted a full pardon in 1942. Dudley later told her sister that her prison experience was horrifying and that she'd resolved to get herself out of there as quickly as possible. According to her family, she was proud of her musical accomplishments in the Goree Girls and of her subsequent success in securing the clemency she so desired.[128]

In 1948, Dudley took another husband, Elmer Franklin, although he passed away in the 1950s. As a widow, Dudley moved to Houston for a time and worked as a bar manager there until moving back to Whitesboro later in life to take care of her aged mother. She stayed in Whitesboro until her death in May 1986.[129]

Even though many pieces are now in place, one part of Dudley's earlier mystery remains unresolved: even though Dudley's bandmate Ruby Mae Morace told her own family that she went to Arkansas to live with Dudley directly after Morace was pardoned, no direct evidence exists to prove that Dudley ever lived in Arkansas, and her family does not know of any such move. Even though there is a possibility that Dudley did move there—at least, for a time—and that Morace joined her there initially, it's not a strong one. Morace certainly ended up in Hot Springs with R.G. Matthews (she was listed as his wife), but some doubt can be cast on whether she was being entirely truthful with her family about her motives for moving to Arkansas. More likely, Morace added Lillie Mae Dudley into her story in order to keep her family from knowing she was moving to Hot Springs to be with Matthews.

Convict #83327

Part Two

In an era when female inmates of the Texas state prison were marginalized, stigmatized and even abused through punitive tactics like involuntary sterilization, solitary confinement, racial segregation and general mistreatment, Reable Childs's story is unique. Even though the Goree Farm women received more compassionate care at the hands of the unit's head matron, Mrs. Heath, Reable experienced considerably less ill treatment than the average female inmate. Perhaps because of her general gestalt—one that was pleasingly refined, good-natured and intelligent—she quickly rose through the prison's microcosmic hierarchy after her entry to Goree State Farm on October 2, 1936. Despite being portrayed as a cold-hearted seductress in the media during the furor of her highly publicized murder trial, by 1938, Reable had become a valued addition to the inmate

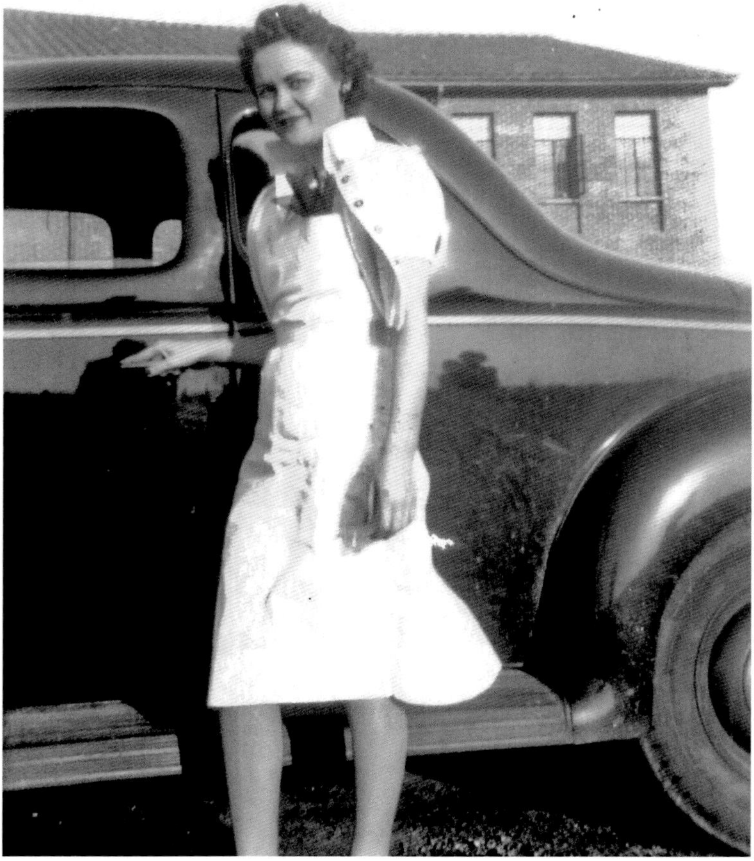

Reable Childs poses with a car in front of the main prison. *Gayle Royer.*

ranks. Not only was she a trusty, but she was also an *Echo* columnist, a *Thirty Minutes* radio star and a trusted leader to her fellow Goree inmates.

Reable began participation in *Thirty Minutes* not long after the broadcasts began. In addition to her good looks and charisma, Reable could really sing in a rich, strong contralto. Her daughter, Gayle Royer, spoke in an interview with the author on January 14, 2015, about her mother's singing:

> *I never saw my mother play a musical instrument. She never sang in any kind of choral group...I heard her sing at home and with her sisters. They*

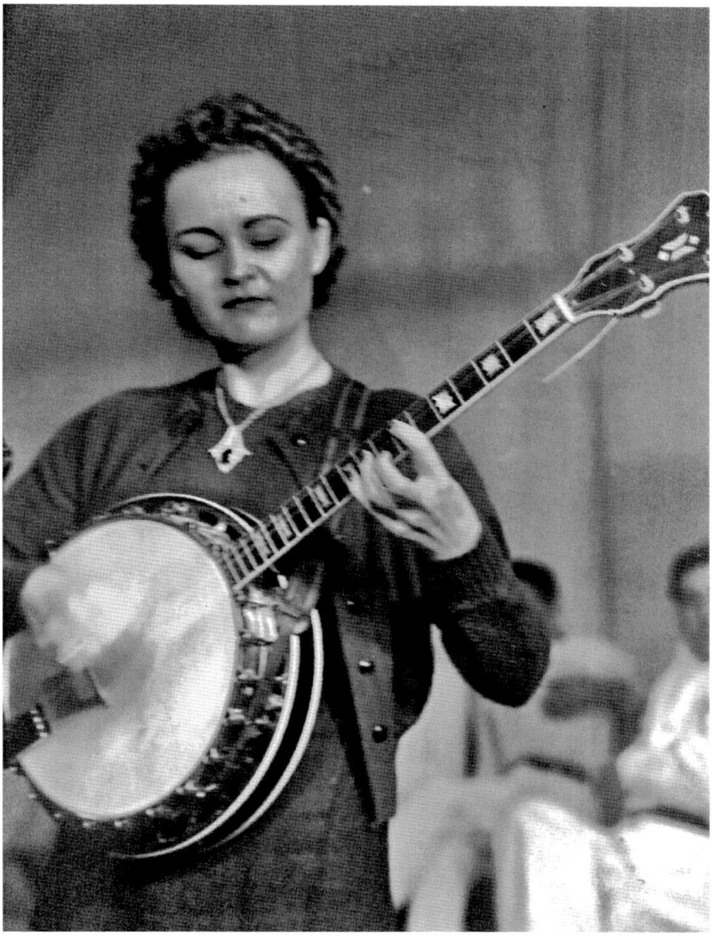

Reable Childs strums the banjo on *Thirty Minutes Behind the Walls*. *Gayle Royer.*

> *did something I'd never heard of before; they yodeled in harmony! We were on a trip and they were in the backseat of the car. I was sitting up front with my father and the women, with the two sisters, started singing, and I was enchanted. They were really good. But...a thin-voiced high soprano, that wasn't her. Mother could call the cows home! I have heard her* [do so]. *Strong voice, and not at all light and airy and soprano.*

At one point in recent years, Gayle Royer telephoned Sybil Vick (née Heath). As the daughter of Captain and Mrs. Heath, the officials in charge of the Goree prison unit, Sybil grew from a teenager into a young woman during the years Reable was incarcerated. In a recent interview, Gayle shared what she learned from Sybil about her mother's life in the Goree unit of the Texas state prison:

> *She* [Sybil] *said, "I have to tell you—I LOVED your mother…That was the sweetest girl. And I adored her and she was so pretty. I wanted to look like her SO much."*
>
> *And so, Mother…went to Goree and became the favored one of* [Captain Heath] *and his wife. Sybil told me, "My parents loved your mother. We lived on the grounds. We would have her over for dinner"…my own mother tried to match-make my uncle—her mother's brother—with my mother* [Reable]!
>
> *She* [Sybil] *said, "When I got married, your mother and I would sit and look through magazines together and decide what kind of wedding dress* [we liked]. *She was there for me, a young girl, just every way she could be—we had a real friendship. And when I got back from my honeymoon, I couldn't wait; the first person I wanted to see was Reable and tell her all my experiences."*
>
> *Because she worked in the office, she was granted special favors…because she was so well liked by the warden. For example, her dad would come to visit her and she was allowed to walk him out to the highway to wait for his bus…she was trusted to do that sort of thing.*[130]

It's probable that the marked affinity Captain and Mrs. Heath had for Reable led to the formation of the Goree All-Girl String Band. Of all the music featured on *Thirty Minutes*, this all-female country and western act was undeniably its crown jewel. Reable was instrumental in bringing her vision of the Goree All-Girl String Band to a reality, and Gayle Royer claimed that the band was even her mother's idea, with Reable telling Gayle, "I got the bright idea for something to do…I saw the privileges, the benefits that they [the male inmates] got."[131] Writer Skip Hollandsworth's 2003 *Texas Monthly* article, "O Sister, Where Art Thou," corroborates this claim, which was further substantiated by former Goree Girl Mozelle (McDaniel) Cash:

> *I think Reable must have figured that if she and her female inmates could create a female version of the Light Crust Doughboys, they could get noticed by Governor O'Daniel and perhaps receive an early parole. (They had, after all, seen other singers on the show get early parole.) At the least, Reable*

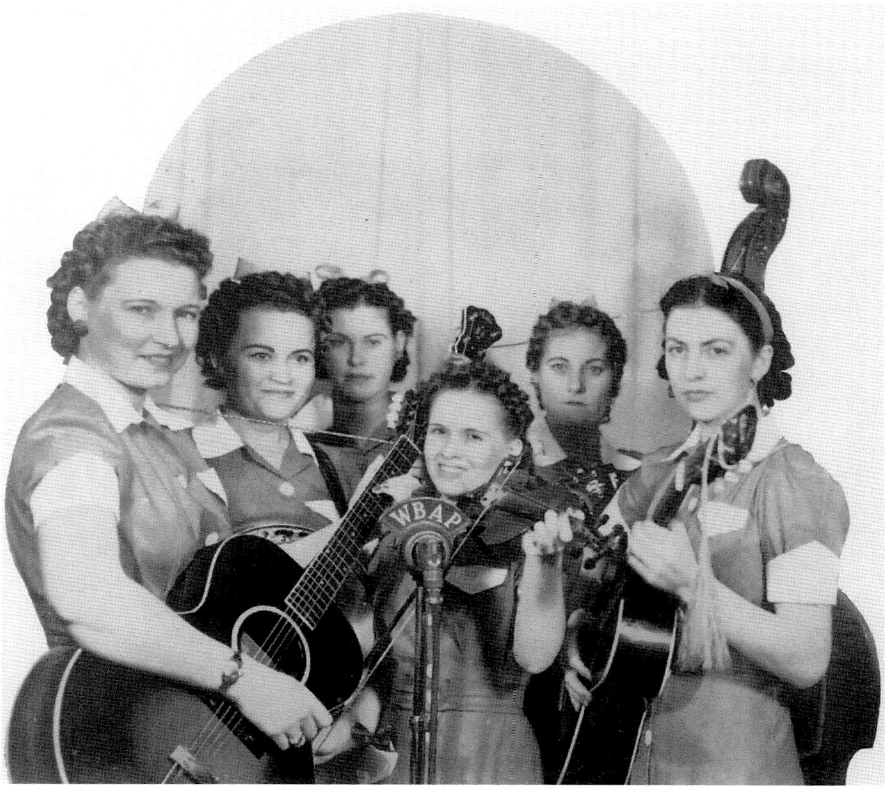

The Goree All-Girl String Band, circa 1940. *Texas Prison Museum.*

> *wanted to prove that the women of Goree, the state's most notorious outcasts, were capable of doing something that no one believed they could do. "She said we could be better than those men," Mozelle suddenly blurted…and then she started to laugh. "That's what she said."*[132]

On *Thirty Minutes*, however, the idea for the Goree All-Girl String Band was attributed to Captain and Mrs. Heath. Inmate Burma Harris—fiddle player for the Goree Girls while she served time on heroin and theft-related convictions—provided details on how the Goree Girls began. According to Harris's version, she and a number of other inmates worked in the prison unit's garment factory when Captain and Mrs. Heath entered the shop and asked whether the girls would like to start an all-girl string band to be featured on *Thirty Minutes*. The women voted and found the idea favorable.[133]

The differing stories on whose idea it was to start the soon-to-be hit string band may not be totally clear, but in assessing all sources, a likely explanation is that the all-girl band was an idea germinated by Reable Childs and conveyed to and supported by her friends Captain and Mrs. Heath, who in turn suggested it to the other women, thereby taking credit in an official capacity, avoiding any claims of favoritism. Furthermore, all inmates who were interviewed on *Thirty Minutes* were—whether spoken or unspoken—expected to laud the prison system and its officials at every possible opportunity. It certainly sounds loftier and more altruistic to state that the esteemed officials in charge of the Goree unit were responsible for the band's creation instead of one of the convicts. Whatever the truth may be, soon, a select few of the Goree unit inmates started rehearsals.

Stars Behind Bars

Playing in the Goree Girls was a demanding feat, but it was also a cherished privilege. In "Across the Back Fence," Reable related that the inmates held full responsibility for practicing their own instruments and developing their skills enough to appear on *Thirty Minutes*. Burma Harris said in her *Thirty Minutes* interview that the band rehearsed for six months in order to learn just a few songs—but learn them well—for the first public Goree Girls appearance, at a prison baseball game in July 1940. Individual rehearsals had to occur outside of a ten-hour workday, as mandated by Texas prison reform laws. Many full-cast rehearsals were held as well, with most of the day on Wednesdays devoted to crafting that evening's content.

In 1940, the Texas Prison Board passed a motion to allow some of the *Thirty Minutes* musical acts to perform at venues other than those within the prison system. Shortly thereafter, the best-known stars of the show—the Rhythmic Stringsters, Hattie Ellis and the Goree Girls—began making occasional forays into the free world outside the steel bars and high fences. The bands performed at festivals and fiddling contests, as long as the prison system's "General Manager provide[d] transportation for these inmates and special guards in the interest of the public and the inmates."[134] Bolstered by their radio success, the Goree Girls gained notoriety and their musical engagements outside of the prison—including actual multiple-date tours—proliferated, essentially becoming their occupation while in the prison system. Reable spoke of one such excursion in one of her "Across the

Back Fence" columns in the *Echo*, informing others what went on during a typical outing for the prison bands:

> *Before we go further we want to tell you a bit of something about the trip to the Black Eyed Pea festival in Center, Texas. Upon our early arrival, we were permitted to walk around the place and hear various school bands that were visiting from other towns. Later we were joined by the Rhythmic Stringsters and were given lunch at the courthouse. After a heavy meal the Stringsters and ourselves presented an hour-long program of lively vocal and instrumental numbers to a very attentive crowd of listeners. After the program, we were given a free ride on the Ferris Wheel.*[135]

The band's tour route in the fall of 1941 provides further eye-opening insight into their grueling schedule. On September 29, the Goree All-Girl String Band played the rodeo in Teague, Texas. The county fair and rodeo in Pittsburg followed on September 30, and then it was back to Huntsville to perform on *Thirty Minutes* on October 1. Shows in Bartlett, Crockett and Schulenburg followed from October 2 to 4, with the women returning once more to Huntsville to open the annual Texas Prison Rodeo on Sunday, October 5. There they remained for several days, no doubt picking up their usual assigned ten-hour workdays in the factory and other facilities.[136]

After the following Wednesday's *Thirty Minutes* performance on October 8, the Goree Girls traveled to Marlin, Palestine and Groveston, Texas, where they performed from October 9 to 11. This was again followed by a journey back to Huntsville to play at the prison rodeo and an additional performance at the Wynne unit of the Texas prison on October 12. Between the rodeo, prison ball games, *Thirty Minutes Behind the Walls* and their outside engagements, the Goree Girls played as frequently as—if not more than—most traveling country bands of the era. Professional acts on the *Grand Ole Opry* were required to return each week to the *Opry* stage from their tent show tours. So, too, were the Goree Girls required to return to the prison each Wednesday, in time to play the *Thirty Minutes* stage show and subsequent radio show.[137]

Around that same time, the board considered whether or not to curtail these outside shows, possibly because they were so numerous and left the inmates with little time to spend behind bars. But when grateful, praise-filled letters flowed in from the communities in which they played, the bands continued to be trotted out for the public's entertainment, albeit at the discretion of the prison management.

The Goree All-Girl String Band played so frequently that Reable Childs declared an "epidemic of sore fingers and thumbs in the ranks of the girl stringsters" while preparing for the rodeo in October 1941. "Owing to heavy practice and rehearsing, plus the many times we have played at various places in the past few weeks," she wrote in her *Echo* column, "we will have to carry a first-aid kit well-stocked with arnica, collodion, and 'nu-skin.'"[138]

Although the *Echo* and many Texas newspapers show a heavy performance schedule for the bands by late 1941, the trend was short lived. The *Thirty Minutes* stars' public engagements outside of the prison all but disappeared after the Pearl Harbor attack, when the United States officially entered into World War II. In January 1942, the Texas Prison Board approved a motion "that special trips by the Rhythmic Stringsters and the Goree Girl Orchestra be discouraged and discontinued during the present emergency and while the war lasts."[139]

Despite the war dampening their external excursions, being a cast member of *Thirty Minutes Behind the Walls*—with all the trappings required of its performers—commanded a staggering amount of time and commitment

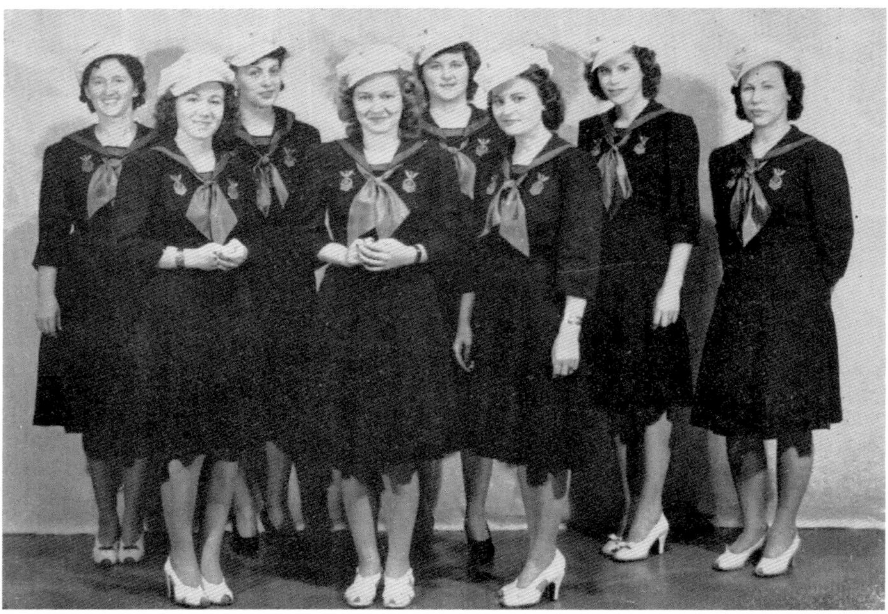

The Goree All-Girl String Band in early 1942; note the patriotic theme of dress as the United States enters World War II. *Left to right*: Juanita W., Shirley N., Bonnie Scott, Ruby Mae Morace, Bernice W., Reable Childs, Ruby Dell Guyton and Teddie G. *Texas Prison Museum.*

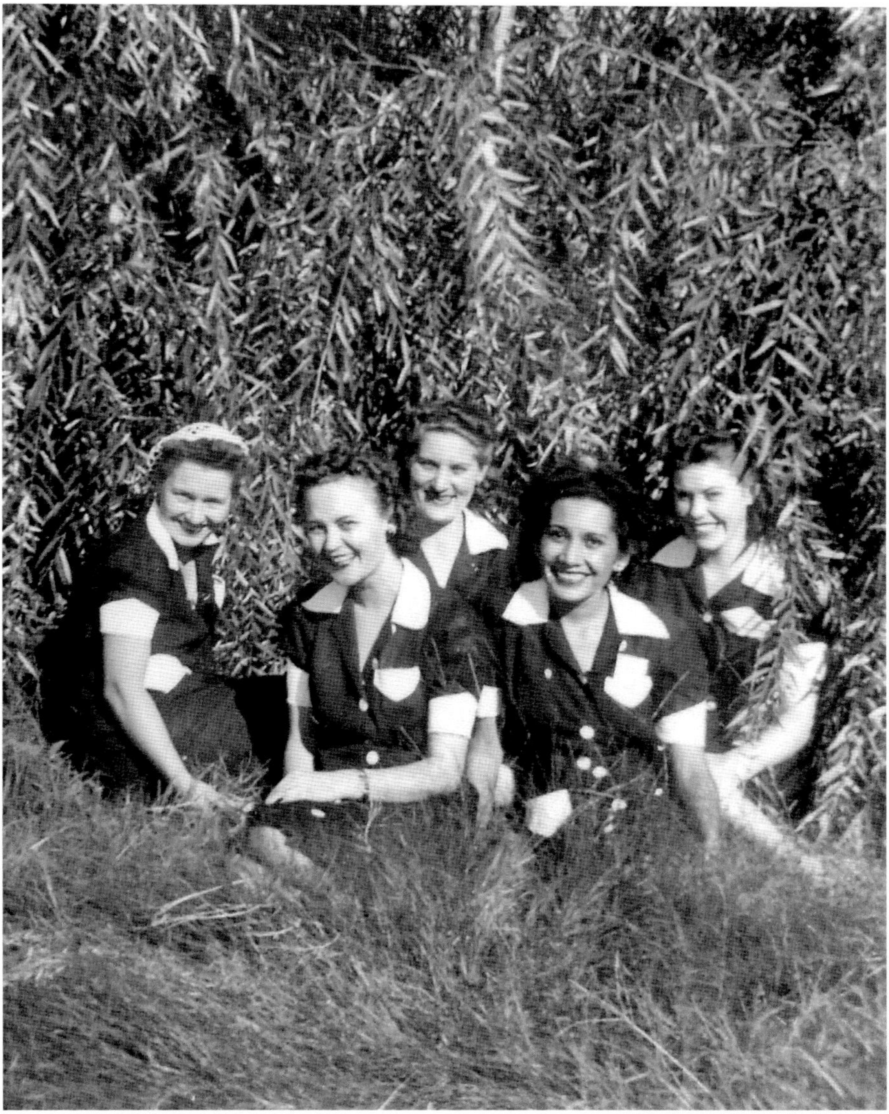

Goree All-Girl String Band members pose for the camera. *Gayle Royer.*

each week. As for the reasons behind their commitment, the original members of the Goree Girls don't seem to have been particularly motivated by love of the music or by performing. Rather, being part of the *Thirty Minutes* cast held personal importance to the inmates for infinitely more practical reasons. For many inmates, the travel they were required to do gave them an opportunity to eat real food—categorically described as exponentially superior to the fare served in the prison. For just as many others, the sight of an unfettered horizon beckoned the strongest—they wanted freedom. Still more inmates, like the prison officials, viewed their participation as evidence of their rehabilitative potential—both to the decision-makers of their fates and to themselves.

The radio show and the bands' public appearances led to public recognition and sometimes brought gifts of money from their fans that could be put toward clemency appeals. From an internal point of view, their musical performances both in and out of the prison also gave its inmate participants—whether male or female—a thrilling sense of accomplishment and all of its associated therapeutic effects. Perhaps most importantly, however, the notoriety these men and women received represented an opportunity to regain a positive reputation, a chance to again be seen by the public as fully human.

7

MINOR NOTES

Further Explorations of *Thirty Minutes Behind the Walls*

This program is as important as vocational training… [it] *fits the hand and mind to do useful work in life…it prepares us to be self-sustaining when we leave here…but what can the hands and mind do without a heart to give them life? If our spirits are broken by disapproval by the public, our vocational training is wasted…But now that WBAP has taken us to the public as human beings, we feel that our future is not hopeless.*[140]

—*Reable Childs,* Thirty Minutes Behind the Walls

Goree Girls

Image versus Reality

From Reable's words above, an understanding can be gleaned that, to the inmates of the Texas prison system, the definition of success was not to become radio stars. Above all, their primary desire was to regain personal autonomy in the form of clemency through early parole or even a pardon. Success on *Thirty Minutes* was the key to realizing this desire and represented an opportunity to convince the public—and the government—of their worthiness to be set free. The image they collectively and separately projected was, therefore, paramount to meeting their goals.

Inmate anecdotes reveal that the Goree Girls themselves spearheaded the approach to their visual representation with hand-sewn outfits and suitably "western" accessories. But how much consideration and calculation they applied to the social messages of their music is less clear. The variety of songs they performed consisted almost entirely of popular western and hillbilly songs of the 1930s, such as Rex Griffin's "The Last Letter," Stuart Hamblen's "Texas Plains" and WLS star Patsy Montana's "I Want to Be a Cowboy's Sweetheart." Most sources indicate that their musical choices were driven by logistics—technical familiarity with and current popularity of the song, personal preferences and, later, requests by fan mail—rather than by efforts to craft a repertoire that communicated their personal experience as inmates.

Country music motifs are, of course, rife with a variety of yearnings, including those of the prisoner who longs to be free. The simplistic, universal appeal of country music means that a listener could interpret many of its themes—such as freedom to roam or freedom to go home—from more than one perspective. However, lyrical analysis of a number of the Goree Girls' song selections from the *Thirty Minutes* transcripts indicates no obvious veiled subtext, such as pleas for freedom or better treatment beyond those standard to conventions of the country and western musical genre.

As for compositions of their own, no evidence exists that the Goree Girls joined their male counterparts in the use of songwriting as a method of expressing their personal experiences or desires, as Raymond Hall had done in his work with Jimmie Rodgers. Though *Thirty Minutes* occasionally devoted whole episodes to original compositions by inmates, announcing the authorship and genre style for each song played, all available radio transcriptions solely attribute the compositions to male inmates, usually the Rhythmic Stringsters.

From examination of existing documentation, only one original song by a female inmate of the Goree unit has been recorded. Hattie Ellis sang "Desert Blues" for John A. Lomax when he came through the prison in 1939, and the recording became part of the Library of Congress archives of his 1939 Southern States Recording Trip. According to Lomax's field notes, Ellis claimed the song was her own composition, and no other versions have been found to refute that claim. Nonetheless, numerous transcripts exist from Hattie's time on *Thirty Minutes* and show no evidence that her own song, "Desert Blues," was performed on the radio show. Perhaps they were not interested or encouraged—or, perhaps, it's simply not documented—but neither the Goree Girls nor any other female *Thirty Minutes* participants wrote their own material and performed it on the show.[141]

As women and as musicians, the Goree Girls' image appears to have involved careful consideration, if not orchestration. Other female-headed country and western acts—such as the Girls of the Golden West, Patsy Montana, the Coon Creek Girls and the Carter Family—were in high demand on barn dance radio throughout the late 1930s. As Skip Hollandsworth noted, on the local front, a proven formula already existed in the Light Crust Doughboys, a western-influenced string band that was lightning-hot on WBAP in its earlier years.

With the Doughboys attached to Wilbert Lee "Pappy" O'Daniel propelling his bid for governorship, it makes sense that they would come to mind when developing the music that appeared on *Thirty Minutes*. It's likely that the radio station managers, prison officials and the inmates—particularly Reable—intentionally developed the Goree All-Girl String Band using these acts as a prototype. However, their situation placed them in uncharted territory concerning the already-established roles of female country music performers. Unlike their professional peers, the Goree Girls—who were convicted felons—could not believably project the era's most common image used for female country performers: the moral or sentimental mother.[142]

In the world of barn dance radio, the role of the moral or sentimental mother appealed to mass audiences—even if the performer herself didn't resemble her projected image. This gentle, familial image combined a notion of autonomy with the quality of virtue, representing a model image to which other women should wish to aspire, especially when it came to country music. Because of the nature of their public reparation for crimes committed, the possibility exists that the women of the Goree All-Girl String Band could have achieved later success after they were released from prison by adopting a variation on the "moral mother" role—but, of course, only if they continued with their musical careers in a format like barn dance radio. But as long as they remained in prison, working the "moral mother" angle was out of the question. An incarcerated woman, by her very circumstance, had already been evaluated by the state judicial system and found to be immoral in one way or another. Also, the circumstance of their incarceration meant these women were already unequivocally assigned to a position of total dependence. This held true even if the same woman already had children when she entered the prison to serve her time. Essentially, she reverted to a child's social status, even as she left a family dynamic where she was the primary caretaker.

Unable to adopt the omnipresent "moral mother" role in their country music image, the Goree Girls assumed a different role in the same family:

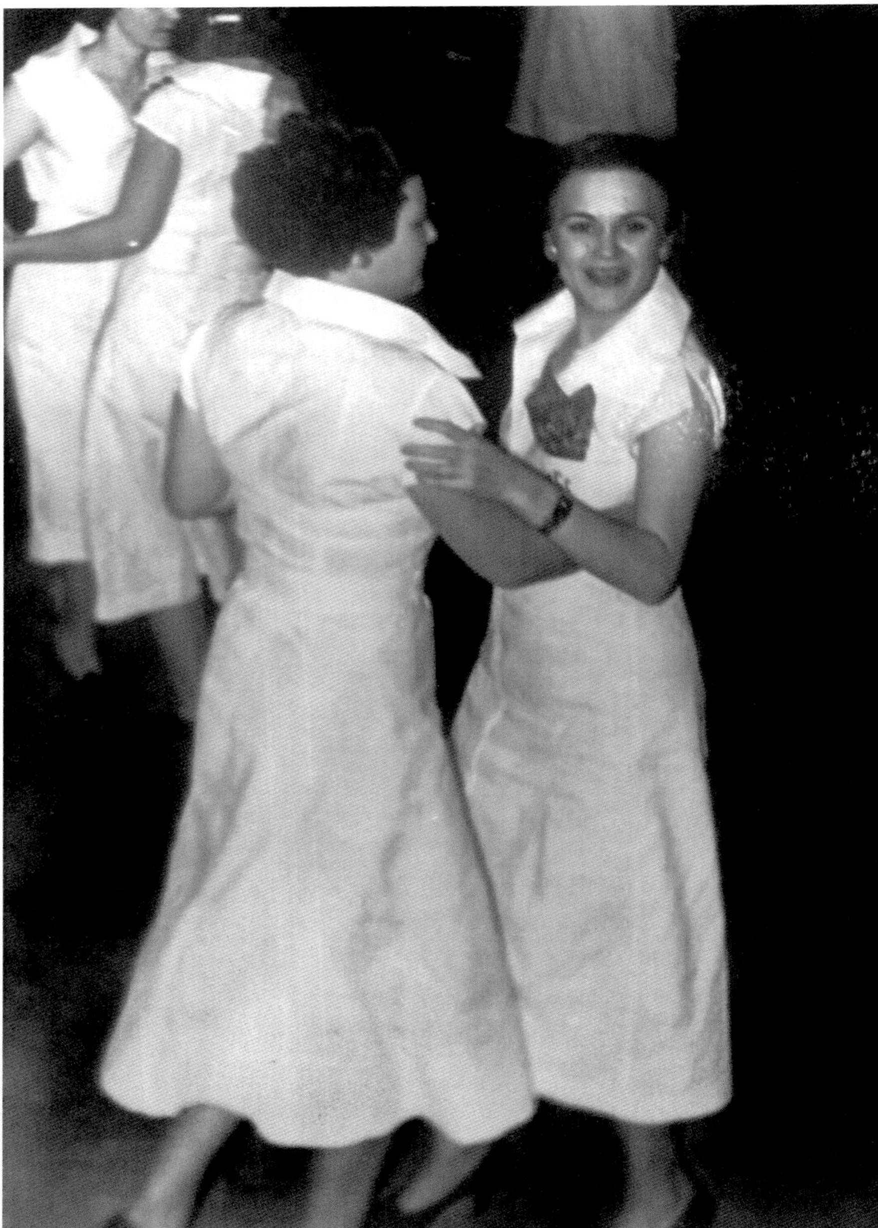

Reable Childs pairs up with a fellow Goree inmate at one of the unit's popular dances. *Gayle Royer.*

the obedient daughter. They projected the image of a convivial sorority of good daughters who lived together in harmony with their den mother—in the form of the prison matron, Mrs. Heath—and sung respectfully of their own sentimental mothers. Playing the "obedient daughter" enabled the Goree Girls to build a more superficial, glamorous image as an accomplished, attractive, sorority-like hillbilly band. It was an alluring combination and the best they could hope for to regain the autonomy they'd lost when they were convicted and sentenced to serve time in the penitentiary.

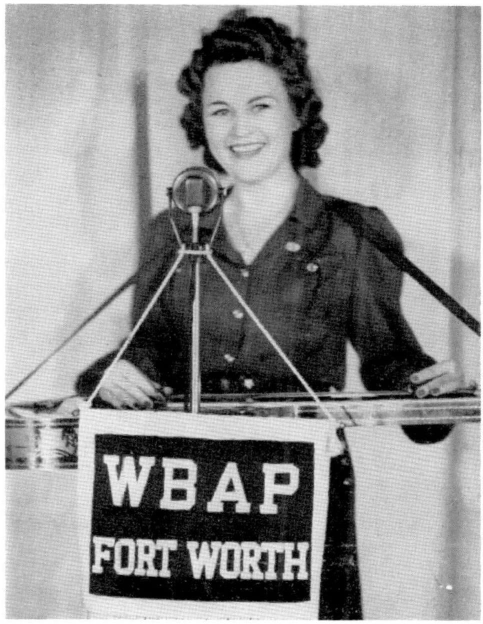

Reable Childs poses with her steel guitar, circa 1943. *Texas Prison Museum.*

Whether intentional or not, Reable Childs herself represented the ideal "obedient daughter," further borne out by the motherly support she herself received from Mrs. Heath. In a 1940 *Thirty Minutes* interview, for example, the much-beloved inmate divulged her twenty-five-year sentence but did not discuss in detail the court case that had landed her in the prison. Reable exemplified the model image of the rehabilitated prisoner: a pretty, articulate, musically talented young woman wanting only to work hard and earn an honest way in life so that her heart could be light again. Thus, the transformation of Childs's image was complete. No trace remained—indeed, if it had ever been there in the first place—of the "comely young widow," the sexualized Jezebel the media had fixated on just four years earlier. Regional listeners of the show no doubt recalled the Reable Childs murder case, but the trial had occurred years before the *Thirty Minutes* program began. Instead of recounting her crime or claiming that she was fully rehabilitated, as some other inmates had done, Childs spoke with heartfelt enthusiasm of *Thirty Minutes*, and the radio show gave them all hope for freedom and forgiveness.

> *WBAP has given us a nice dream…I mean a dream of the future. If the public is interested in us while we are in prison, it stands to reason that their interest will go with us when we leave here. We believe that we shall find happiness somewhere; that our mistakes won't be held against us…that we will be given another chance.*[143]

Given what is known about Reable Childs as a person, these were undoubtedly honest sentiments and an expression of sincere optimism rather than an effort to fool the public. In general, the inmates didn't try to "buck the system" because they were aware that every word printed in the paper, and every word spoken on the radio, could be counted against them in some manner and possibly extend their stays. Inmate columns and radio show interviews—particularly those of female inmates—appeared to stem from a genuine place, using humor or the veil of anonymity common to gossip columns as an outlet for anything that could be perceived as criticism of the system.

While their interview persona might have elaborated the figure of the obedient daughter, visually, the Goree Girls' figures were elaborately clad in

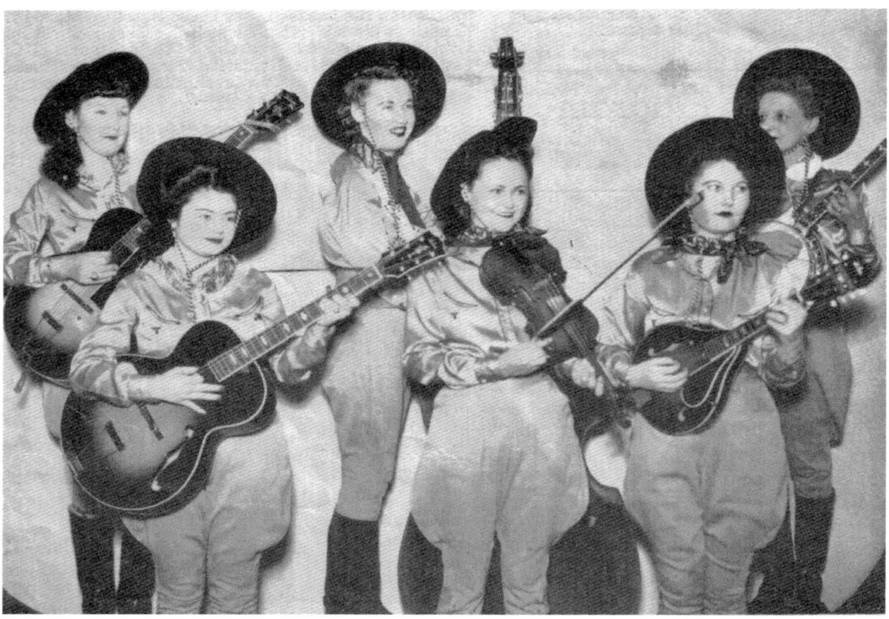

The Goree All-Girl String Band, circa 1943; Reable Childs poses with the fiddle. *Texas Prison Museum.*

gaily colored western outfits with cowgirl hats, under which coiffed hair—styled and set in the Goree Farm's "beauty school" classroom— nestled next to dimples on smiling, affable faces. Published photographs of the Goree Girls occasionally showed the band in prison whites and, as World War I entered the picture, patriotic sailor outfits. But for the most part, the Goree Girls were identifiably western in appearance. In one "Across the Back Fence" column, Reable ardently described some new outfits the Goree Girls planned to wear at the upcoming 1941 prison rodeo:

> *All the girls who are in the string band are tickled to death with their new riding habits. We have had many nice compliments from various officials and inmates of the Goree, and we are plenty proud of the new cowgirl ensembles…The cowgirl shirts are gold satin trimmed in black. Slaunch-cut double pockets with a black steer head set off the right pocket and a black horse's head adorns the left one. The ten-gallon puncherette hats are black with corded black and white band. Dude ranch khaki riding britches and glossy black English riding boots complete the riding habits. However, for a bit of individual adornment, each girl wears a silk scarf of varying design and color, and believe you me, some of them put a mad artist's palette to shame when it comes to a wide assortment of color.*[144]

One of the more widely distributed photos of the Goree All-Girl String Band shows them wearing the above-described ensemble. Such a winsome image leaves no doubt that the costumes delighted their audiences at the rodeo and the various festivals to which they traveled. The *Echo* extolled their talent, popularity and, in particular, the visually striking costumes in one October article:

> *Fully attired in their rodeo regalia, the girls from the Goree Farm, women's unit of the Texas Prison System…appeared at the opening performance of the Eleventh Annual Texas Prison Rodeo which opened at* [the] *Prison Stadium here Sunday, October 5th. Dressed in golf satin shirts trimmed in black, khaki riding jodphurs, black boots and hats to match, with other cowgirl accessories, this unique musical group, the only one of its kind in the world, received a tremendous ovation from the many thousands of rodeo fans.*[145]

By 1941, the members of the Goree All-Girl String Band had indeed become stars, adorably polished in their visual presentation and adept at performing hit songs on radio and various stages. One issue of the *Echo* reported that fan mail and sales of the *Thirty Minutes* souvenir booklets soared higher than ever before, attributing the show's popularity to the Goree Girls.[146]

The group was such a sensation that they were eventually featured in a number of "all-girl" special episodes of *Thirty Minutes*. Unfortunately, the "all-girl" radio shows commenced in April 1942, over a year after extant volumes of the *Thirty Minutes* radio transcripts end. The *Echo*, however, covered the shows in its columns and articles and provided some insight into the novel new *Thirty Minutes* format:

> *The All Girl Program that was broadcast from this unit on April 1, proved such a success and there have been so many requests for another program by the girls that one is promised for June 3. Reable is the manager of the band, and did the announcing and wrote the continuity for the program.*[147]

Even with the overwhelming success of the Goree All-Girl String Band, it's important to remember that their image was much more cheerful than the reality of their lives—after all, they were incarcerated in one of the country's most ruthless prison systems. Their bright smiles belied the tribulations that incarcerated women experienced in Texas during the 1930s and '40s. Whether their conviviality was real or not, the expression of it was encouraged at all times, if not coerced, by the officials. Not many of the audience members possessed a genuine understanding of what these women had gone through to get to the microphones through which they sang.

Harsh treatment and meager accommodations had never really ceased in the Texas prison system. Although the women did not often experience brutality and violence on the level of the all-male units, they certainly experienced their fair share of misery and emotional oppression. But perhaps most significantly, females in the Texas prison systems were physically—and systematically—subjugated in a way that the male population was not.

As discussed in earlier chapters, Texas never legally adopted the practice of eugenics, including those concerning involuntary sterilization. However, just because eugenics laws were not officially passed in Texas does not mean that the practice did not take place. The supervisory medical staff of the Texas prison system was largely left to do their own work as they saw fit, without much interference from the Texas Prison Board or other entities. It appears that sterilization of the women in the Texas prison was performed as a matter of course, although there were some exceptions. As for the rationale behind the conduct of this procedure, the old Basland system of inmate classification could be brought into consideration.

The female inmate population of the 1930s Texas prison system—150 or so out of nearly 7,000—was technically too small to process according to Basland's classification system, but nevertheless, it seems probable that the female inmates would have been categorized to some extent. This would be especially true if they exhibited one of the "undesirable" traits, such as drug addiction or feeblemindedness. Certainly prison records show that male and female drug users were frequently noted as such on the convict ledgers and the conduct registers. But even with such undesirable traits, if a female inmate exhibited good behavior, she could still be allowed to participate in recreational activities such as the prison bands, sports or the dances held at the Goree unit. Regardless, in dealing with some of the other undesirable traits such as insanity, physical ailments, homosexuality or feeblemindedness, one common method of resolving the issue—for the officials, at least—was to "treat" certain female inmates who fit into the system's subjective assessments of social pathology. This provides a little more insight and motive for why some of the women in the Texas state penitentiary may have been sterilized against their will.

Despite the assumption that involuntary sterilization would have only been performed on certain types of female inmates, of the Goree Girls, only Reable Childs appears to have remained unscathed—at least, from the earliest incarnations of the band. Journalist Skip Hollandsworth conducted interviews with the families of not only Reable but also with other former Goree Girls, such as Lillie Mae Dudley, Mozelle McDaniel and Ruby Mae Morace. Shockingly, the interviews revealed multiple assertions that these members of the Goree All-Girl String Band had undergone compulsory sterilization shortly after their incarceration.

The granddaughter of Lillie Mae Dudley avowed, in a recent interview, that, although she had given birth to her daughter a few years before she was incarcerated, Dudley was sterilized after her entry into the prison system.[148] Reable's daughter, Gayle Royer, was also recently asked about the possibility of involuntary sterilization as a typical part of female inmate management. She concurred with this conclusion, stating that her mother had said that involuntary sterilization was performed on all the other members of the band; her mother had told her that the only reason she had escaped the surgeon's scalpel was because of the esteem the prison manager and his wife—Captain and Mrs. Heath—held for her.[149]

During examination of these claims of involuntary sterilization, several supporting pieces of evidence have come to light about the actuality of performing involuntary sterilization on the women of the Goree unit. First, if surgical procedures of this nature were performed—on male or female prisoners—the operation itself would likely have taken place right there at the women's unit, one of the few units in the system with an operating room equipped to conduct major surgeries. If prison medical officials chose to discreetly dictate the reproductive future of the system's female inmates, the immediate proximity of surgical facilities allowed the considerably invasive procedures of female sterilization, in the form of hysterectomies, to occur without drawing much attention.

The inmate newspaper column "Across the Back Fence" also provided some loose support for the families' claims of sterilization in several of the Goree Girls. Mozelle McDaniel was committed to Goree on January 29, 1938. Eight months later, in August 1938, "Across the Back Fence" stated, somewhat mysteriously, that she was "recovering from a recent operation." Bonnie Scott was also noted as being hospitalized in August 1941, a few months after her entry into Goree. And in the May 1940 "Back Fence" column, Reable made a reference to Ruby Mae Morace being hospitalized for a time. In a 1941 interview on *Thirty Minutes*, Morace herself stated that she had missed several months of performing on the show the previous year. Furthermore, her niece Judith Bergeron told *Texas Monthly*:

> *You should have seen the tears form in my aunt Ruby's eyes when she'd talk about a certain doctor tying up her tubes so that she could never have children...She told me that a part of her life was taken away, that she was made to feel like she didn't deserve to be like other women because of that one mistake she had made on that highway.*[150]

Without direct access to inmate medical records from this era—all destroyed or lost, according to prison representatives—it is impossible to prove that forced sterilizations were carried out or to establish whatever justification officials might have offered for them. If the sterilizations did occur, the prison system's decision to sterilize Morace and McDaniel, two alleged cases, may be partly attributable to the severity of each woman's crimes. As detailed earlier, Ruby Mae Morace was incarcerated for assault and robbery, receiving a sentence of up to twenty-five years in prison. Morace's crime was considered a violent offense, which was perhaps sufficient for her to be judged "feebleminded" or even "insane," thereby providing a green light for the officials to sign off on her surgery.

Mozelle McDaniel, whose court case was also discussed at length in an earlier chapter, was also found guilty of a violent crime. Whether in her own interest or for her own protection, Mozelle McDaniel admitted to killing her stepfather when he threatened her and her siblings with a severe whipping. Perhaps, like Morace, McDaniel's spectacular violation of the passivity and submissiveness expected of a young woman met Basland's definition of either insanity or feeblemindedness.

Many questions are raised from this discovery. For instance, we can draw conclusions that the women were given hysterectomies while in the Texas prison, and some possible reasons have been presented above. But assuming that the claims are true and that forced sterilizations were regularly performed, more questions arise. Did the women know what was going to happen to them, or did they only find out afterward? Was consent ever obtained prior to the surgery, and if so, how? How long did this practice go on? How many women were sterilized, and why were some women spared while others were not? Was Reable's good relationship with the prison managers the only reason she herself didn't experience sterilization resulting from her own violent crime? The answer to these questions may never be known, but one arresting fact remains: while the information is not complete due to privacy laws, public records have been located on the original Goree band members after they left the prison. Aside from Reable Childs, no other members of the original Goree Girls—who were all of childbearing age—appeared to have given birth to any children after they served time in the Texas prison system.

Minorities Making Music

Women, of course, represented only one aspect of the marginalized populations within the Texas prison system. Even though they were a feature of the show, unfortunately, male and female *Thirty Minutes* participants of African American, Mexican or other ethnic heritage were not offered the same opportunities to excel and, therefore, to rehabilitate themselves as easily as the white inmates. Firmly ensconced in the Jim Crow era and on a plantation-style prison system, that pervasive attitude would not change for decades; in fact, many argue that it's never changed. Former African American prisoners even today speak of the spirituals and labor songs they played while toiling in the fields of the Texas prison units, even in the late

1990s. Certainly in Texas of the 1930s, the racial attitude of *Thirty Minutes* was made quite clear by the manner in which the inmates were spoken of.

The variety of music performed by the white, African American and Mexican inmates integrated the show in general, but racial lines seldom crossed when it came to the non-musical format. In addition to the music, *Thirty Minutes* also featured human-interest interviews and comedy acts. As Ethan Blue notes in *Doing Time in the Depression*, inmate announcers "consistently represented black prisoners with a mixture of opprobrium and condescension, while still emphasizing their musical skills to listeners." Thus *Thirty Minutes*, while evoking an air of tolerance, still relegated African Americans to what the station and prison officials felt was an appropriately submissive, or minor, role on the radio show. The unspoken message was that African American inmates were "entertainment," whereas white inmates could be taken seriously.

To give an example of racial roles on *Thirty Minutes*, one comedy act featured on the show consisted of two African American inmates (and sometime rodeo clowns), Charlie Jones and Louie Nettles, as "Fathead and Soupbone." Their duo act was strongly reminiscent of a blackface minstrel show, cleaving to the stereotype of African Americans to play a childlike buffoon or trickster, with a straight man or simple-minded sidekick. As inmates, it was also common for Fathead and Soupbone to make tongue-in-cheek jokes about clemency, as seen in the following excerpt from the transcripts:

> *FATHEAD: Looka' here, Soupbone. Did I tell you what happened to me out dere at de Rodeo grounds one Sunday?*
> *SOUPBONE: Go on, Fathead, tell me whot happened to you.*
> *FATHEAD: Well, you see I was a clowning out dere befo' all dem milluns o' white folks, an' wuz actin' kinda smart and graceful you know. When all of a sudden one of dem big Brahma bulls broke loose an' started toward me.*
> *SOUPBONE: He did, an' whot did you do Fathead.*
> *FATHEAD: I started to gittin' away from there in a hurry. I made a big razzo fo de fence, and I busted right into one o' dem big men whot was wearing one o' dem big hats. Well, I hit him so hard I bet he thot it was dat Brahma Bull instead of me.*
> *SOUPBONE: I'll bet yo' got into a jam, did'nt yo'?*
> *FATHEAD: I sho' did, but I come out of it alright.*
> *SOUPBONE: How's dat, Fathead?*

> *FATHEAD: Well yo' see, I gets up off de top o' hem and he gets up an' we both brush de dirt from our clothes, an' he sez…"Look here, don't you know I am?"*
> *SOUPBONE: Whot did yo' say then, Fathead?*
> *FATHEAD: I sez no I don't know who yo' is…an' he sez, "I'm the governor, that' who I am."*
> *SOUPBONE: Lawd have mercy on you! I bet yo started runnin'.*
> *FATHEAD: Oh no, I didn't. No No!*
> *SOUPBONE: Well whot in de world did yo' do then, Fathead?*
> *FATHEAD: I jes' sez in de mosest sweetest voice I knew how. "Pardon me Governor…"*[151]

Contrastingly, *Thirty Minutes* inmate interviews generally adopted an earnest tone. They began with a few casual personal questions, followed by disingenuous discourse about topics such as the length of the prisoner's sentence and rehabilitative prospects—all with an unspoken expectation that the interviewee exhibit a supplicant demeanor within his or her response.

This expectation of supplication was particularly notable with respect to race. While an overwhelming majority of the inmate interviews on *Thirty Minutes* were with white convicts, every six months or so, a minority interview was included—but usually this was done with a humorous tone, such as claiming ignorance about the name pronunciation for a reportedly heavily accented Mexican American prisoner or poking sly fun at an overweight African American female inmate at one of the Goree Farm dances.

With the white male and female convicts, the interviews focused on their remorse and reformative and rehabilitative potential. Occasionally, they took on a salacious tone when questioning "incorrigible" inmates, such as former death row prisoners or life-termers. Also interviewed were notorious prisoners such as Gene O'Dare, who, with his wife, Mary, had participated in many violent and illicit activities with the legendary gang of Texas desperadoes led by Clyde Barrow with Bonnie Parker. Even Reable Childs's former paramour, Terence Bramlett, appeared in an interview on *Thirty Minutes*.

On *Thirty Minutes Behind the Walls*, the inmates appeared to be one big, convivial, integrated family, and the prison system gave the impression of being more forward thinking as a result. Although *Thirty Minutes* displayed a clear racial hierarchy within the show's formats, the music itself was another matter. On *Thirty Minutes Behind the Walls*, African American inmates played "white" songs—although rarely cowboy songs—and similarly, sometimes the white musicians played the blues, jazz or even older gospel songs mainly known to the African American population. The music and its performers portrayed a true melding of cultures.

One of the first African American acts brought into the public eye was what Lee Simmons called the "Cotton Pickers' Glee Club." This large assembly of male inmates performed work songs and hymns for the public in the early years of the Texas Prison Rodeo. Later, they appeared on *Thirty Minutes Behind the Walls*. As the series progressed, the number of African American inmates increased. The Glee Club group sometimes performed as several choral ensembles of male inmates, such as the "Negro Quartette" and various gospel groups and duos with names that varied from episode to episode. Appearing much less frequently than their male counterparts, African American female inmates also performed as duos and quartets, nearly always singing gospel songs.

Hattie Ellis frequently performed as a featured vocal soloist, but she was one of a very few African American inmates who appeared on the radio show as such. In the early 1940s, after Ellis's departure, African American inmate Imogene King replaced Ellis as the resident blues singer on the radio show and at the Texas Prison Rodeo. King is immortalized in her role as solo singer in a photograph hanging on the wall of the Texas Prison Musuem. Occasionally, the African American inmates took center stage on special June episodes of *Thirty Minutes*, with time blocks set aside for Juneteenth celebration of African American heritage, featuring "Vera Jenkins, stellar blues singer and dancer; E.S. Shumake and his piano; A.B. Johnson, the harmonica wizard; Elyord Bailey and Adrian Kenney, the saxophone twins; the Cotton Pickers' Glee Club; the colored girls from Goree" and more.[152] Other than those special episodes, African American vocal solos were not frequent on WBAP's early years of *Thirty Minutes*; however, instrumental solos occurred more frequently, particularly with "folksy" instruments such as the harmonica. African American dancers also often appeared on *Thirty Minutes*, although the performances would occur at the live shows at the auditorium prior to the broadcast. Still, the photographs of African American dancers became part of the *Thirty Minutes* legacy when published in the radio show's souvenir programs.

Perhaps because the songs on the show were so intermixed, *Thirty Minutes* announcers attempted to keep the audience informed as to the performers' race. Overt and inferred both, racially oriented descriptions were given to African American inmates such as "dusky," "colored" or as being "from Darkyland." White inmates were not usually given a descriptive phrase unless it was to differentiate one instrumentalist—for instance, a harmonica player—from a similar performer of a different race.

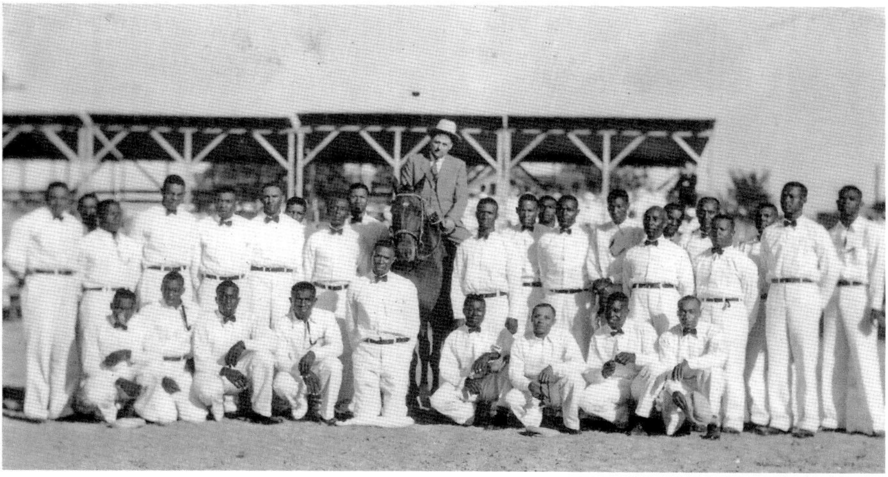

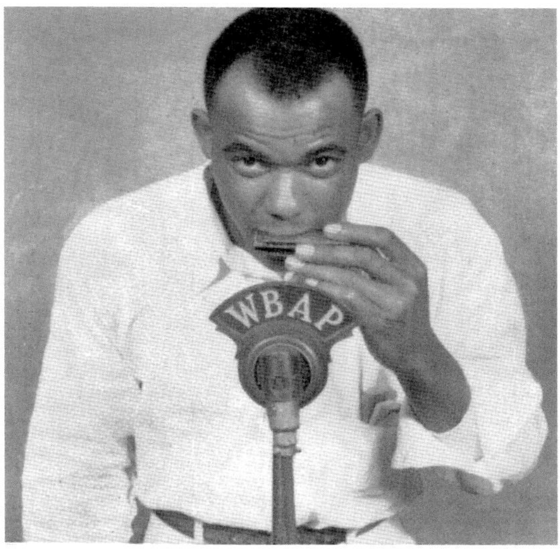

Above: Warden W.W. Waid (on horse) poses with the Cotton Pickers' Glee Club at an early prison rodeo. *Texas Department of Criminal Justice.*

Right: *Thirty Minutes* cast member A.B. Johnson plays the harmonica. *Texas Prison Museum.*

Thirty Minutes differed from many other radio shows of the era due to the diversity of its cast. However discriminatory the identifier, the radio audience may have been confused without them, at least if the intent was to provide listeners with a visualization of its performers in lieu of seeing them firsthand. For example, the transcription from a pre-Christmas broadcast in 1939 showed the announcer navigating one of the show's typical combinations of race and musical style so that listeners could make the distinction on the inmates' races. The announcer said, "Now, into the

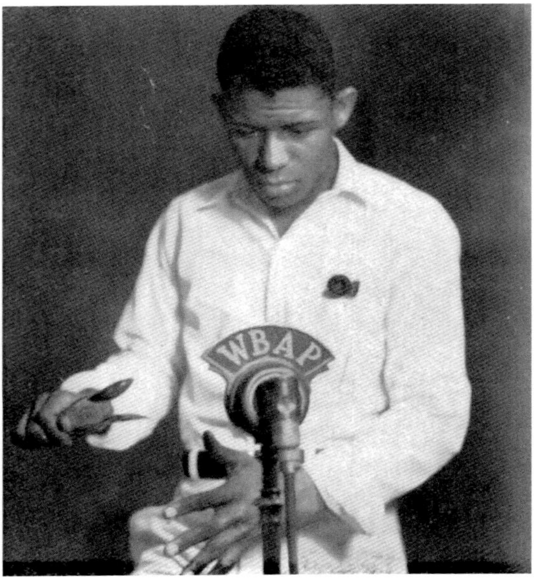

"The Deluxe Spoon Tapper," William Harold King, shows his talent on *Thirty Minutes*. *Texas Prison Museum.*

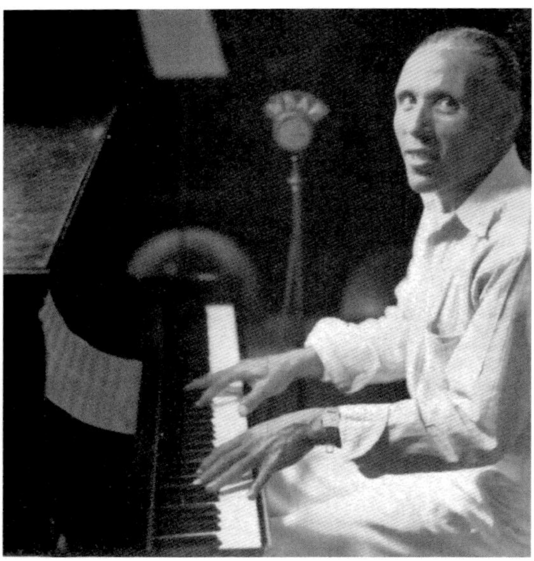

E.S. Schumake, "King of the Ivories," performs on *Thirty Minutes*. *Texas Prison Museum.*

spotlight steps Hattie Ellis, our Negro songstress. With a bit of aid from the Melody Trio [white], Hattie offers one of the most beautiful songs of the year…'Over the Rainbow.'"[153]

As she often did on *Thirty Minutes*, Hattie Ellis sang a popular song rather than a hymn or a blues number. The recordings done by John Lomax at Huntsville in May 1939 showed Hattie Ellis to possess a lighter, rather jazzy vocal style, so it's entirely possible that an audience member could have visualized her as a white singer had the announcer not made such a clarification.

Just the same, African American inmates were not the only ethnicity assigned patronizing descriptive terms on *Thirty Minutes*. The Latino inmate population—largely located at the Blue Ridge unit, also known as the "Mexican" unit—represented the second-largest racial minority in the prison system and also had a sizable role on *Thirty Minutes* throughout its lifetime. In terms of the admission of Latin ethnicity, *Thirty Minutes* did not make much distinction among

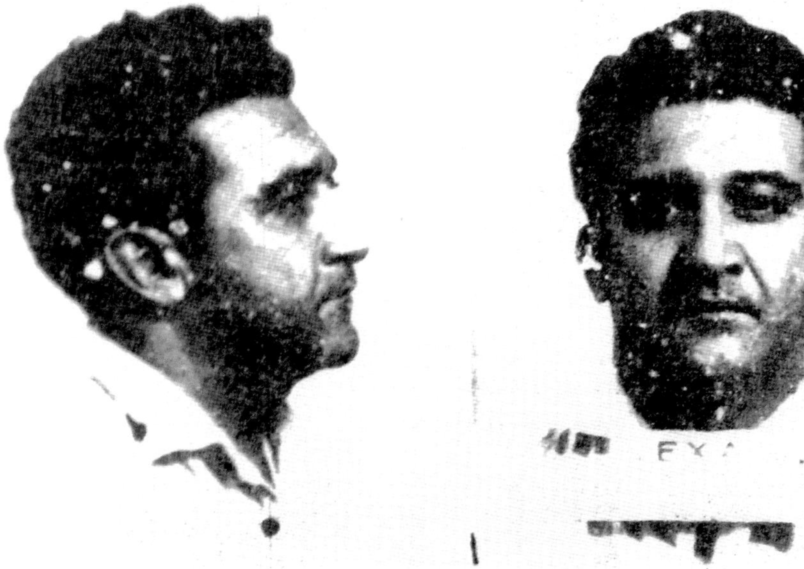

Mug shot of Humberto Boone. *Texas Department of Criminal Justice.*

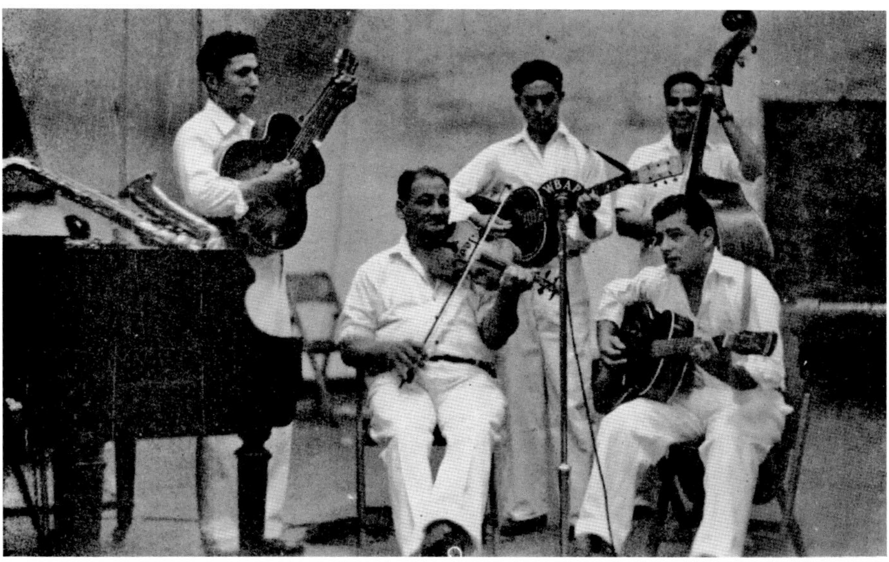

The Blue Ridge "Mexican" Stringsters perform on *Thirty Minutes*, circa 1943. *Texas Prison Museum.*

Mexican Americans, Mexican nationals, Cubans, Puerto Ricans or people of other Latin heritages. Each week, the various announcers simply changed assignations and appellations based on the song or sometimes the "mood" they were attempting to invoke during their musical introductions.

One of the earliest *Thirty Minutes* stars who was identified as having Latino heritage was Texas-born Humberto Boone. Born in Del Rio around 1912, Boone was listed as a musician when he entered the Texas prison system in May 1937. Serving five to ten years on a sodomy charge, Boone had already made inroads as a radio performer, allegedly singing on local Del Rio radio as well as border stations based in Mexico. He had many nicknames on *Thirty Minutes*, one of which was as a "diminutive Mexican singer," in reference to his five-foot-four frame. For a time, Boone was the voice for all songs of Latin designation on *Thirty Minutes*, whether a Spanish lullaby, a Mexican popular song or a Cuban rhumba (the most popular of all).[154]

For all intents and purposes, ethnic references to Latin cultures on *Thirty Minutes* were "Mexican" in designation. Frequently—and often indiscriminately—used descriptors were "Mexican," "South of the border," "Spanish," "mañana-land" and more. These were used when referring to any inmates of such heritage, as well as musical acts like the Blue Ridge Stringsters. The only exception was when introducing songs that were strongly identified as having a specific Latin heritage, such as Cuban rhumbas, which were very popular on the show.

As for the Latinas incarcerated in the Goree State Farm, very few seem to have appeared on *Thirty Minutes* as soloists, at least according to existing *Thirty Minutes* transcripts. Of the existing transcripts, the only notable Latina who appeared on the show was Eva Vigil, the "Little Spanish Nightingale," who performed with the Goree Girls for a time, playing bass fiddle and singing. When she sang a solo Latin-style song, the Mexican Stringsters usually backed her up rather than the Goree Girls. Possibly this was due to their own Latino status, but more likely because they possessed a stronger familiarity with the sometimes instrumentally complex music, and this also allowed Eva to sing without having to play an instrument at the same time.

Interestingly, even though Latina women seemingly were only allowed to sing songs related to their ethnic heritage, non-Latina inmates in the Goree string band also occasionally sang Latin-influenced popular songs, with the Stringsters (of either ethnicity) providing the instrumentation. Similarly, their male Latino counterparts were very seldom allowed to perform any non-Latin songs, although every so often, the non-Latino male inmates played songs such as the "Spanish Two-Step," among others.

The more general descriptor of "Latin" was occasionally used at that time, most often to identify performers like Boone—lighter-skinned inmates whose appearance and musical style could be considered more palatable to a white public—rather than, for instance, one inmate named Candelario Salazar. Scholar Ethan Blue wrote the following of Salazar's on-air interview with WBAP announcer Nelson Olmsted for *Thirty Minutes*:

> *On the rare occasions when black or Mexican prisoners were able to speak, announcers did their best to contain and alienate them. Such was the case in Candelario Salazar's interview. Olmstead* [sic] *begged the listeners' forgiveness on Salazar's behalf, as Olmstead condescended to struggle with the foreignness of Spanish.*
>
> "[B]*ecause he neither reads nor writes English, and speaks it only with the greatest of difficulty, we are going to ask you to be patient whenever he seems to stumble or falter in answering the questions we shall ask him. Now: Do you mind if we use your name?"*
>
> *Salazar: No—I do not…It is Candelario Salazar.*
>
> *Olmstead: I promised to spend all of last week learning to pronounce that name—Candelario Salazar…is that right?*
>
> *When Olmstead asked Salazar about the work he did prior to incarceration, Salazar quickly undermined Olmstead's claims to his implicit foreignness (as well as supposed inability to speak English): "Oh, I just do anyt'ing—farming—work in a foundry—and I fight in the World War, too!" By making this short reference to his presence as a soldier in the U.S. military, and as a veteran of the Great War, Salazar made claim to American nationality, valor, and patriotism.*[155]

As *Thirty Minutes* progressed through the war and beyond, the Latino male prison bands featured heavily in the rotation of songs. Photographs of the various musicians—groups as well as individual singers and instrumental soloists—also appeared in the souvenir radio programs.

Perhaps distinguishing the race of its performers on the air is unnecessary for the radio shows of today's society, but it was closer to a social necessity for a southern state in the Jim Crow era, if only to convey an open-minded approach by the Texas prison system (even as the "borrowing" of instrumental and vocal styles between races was well underway in popular music by the 1930s). Interracial musical genre appropriation undoubtedly helped form the melting pot that is today's popular American music, but in the 1930s and '40s, a station like WBAP nonetheless adhered to certain social and legal expectations concerning the race of its performers. Clearly, *Thirty Minutes*—at least, while it aired from the WBAP radio station—was a seminal radio show and a shining moment in the history of the Texas prison system, broadcasting unheard-of and unforeseen talent over the airwaves. But even so, it did not challenge the social and political limitations of its time.

Although the exact end date is unclear, documentation shows that the WBAP-sponsored *Thirty Minutes* episodes continued until sometime during 1947 or possibly 1948. The trail becomes unclear, but it appears that at some point in 1947 or 1948, *Thirty Minutes Behind the Walls* ceased airing from WBAP in Fort Worth. And in 1949, a new chapter of *Thirty Minutes Behind the Walls* began when the radio show quietly relocated to Houston, airing on radio station KPRC.

When *Thirty Minutes Behind the Walls* relocated to local radio station KPRC in 1949, Reable Childs was living in Houston. Perhaps she was feeding her young daughter when the radio show aired, or perhaps when the *Thirty Minutes Behind the Walls* intro floated across the air waves she snapped off the radio. It's unclear whether Reable ever heard the Houston version of the radio show, but it's an interesting idea to consider.

8

KEEPIN' THAT RHYTHM

Texas Prison Bands Shift Focus

Radio has gone behind prison walls and messaged to the outside world the almost forgotten fact that men and women behind the bars are human, that they have feeling…This changing public attitude well could make for reform instead of punishment. The prison problem is a public problem.[156]

Reable Childs and Life After Prison

After seven years of hard work through music, writing and leadership among her fellow inmates, Reable Childs was granted a conditional pardon in 1943. Soon, the war was over, and the postwar boom followed.

During her incarceration, Reable had gotten to know one of the male inmates, Paul Mitchell, quite well. Mitchell was the former death row inmate who never, ever played "Chicken Reel" on the harmonica after accompanying one of his own block-mates on his death march. The tall, blond Mitchell was a "man's man," masculine in appearance and interests, with few words, yet he possessed a substance underneath that was warm, straightforward and protective. Even in the newspaper articles that initially vilified him for his 1932 crime, the tireless efforts of his mother and those he knew helped get his sentence commuted from death to life. All throughout, Mitchell steadfastly maintained that he had never meant to shoot the grocery store worker, the gun had gone off accidentally in his hand and that he was wrecked from his own actions.

After his commutation, Mitchell acted as an occasional inmate announcer on *Thirty Minutes* and also drove the prison vehicles, accompanying the bands on their out-of-town sojourns. In this manner, Mitchell and Reable got to know each other. He made for her a beautiful end table with her first name carved into it, which was passed on to her daughter. He drew pictures of Reable, wrote letters to Reable and kept appearing on *Thirty Minutes* so he could have a few more moments in her presence.

During his incarceration, Mitchell's good behavior and amiable personality earned him multiple reprieves, one of which he voluntarily gave up to return to the prison. Incidentally, this was right around the time when the Goree Girls were embarking on a spate of performances throughout the state. Thus, he had even more opportunities to spend some time with Reable. Their relationship had become romantic and had solidified by the time Mitchell left the prison in early 1943.

On a 1943 six-month reprieve that was later extended another year, Mitchell was determined to build a life for them where they could start over. Reable left the prison in October 1943 and joined Mitchell, who had secured housing. They married shortly afterward, and in 1946, their only child, Gayle Mitchell, was born.

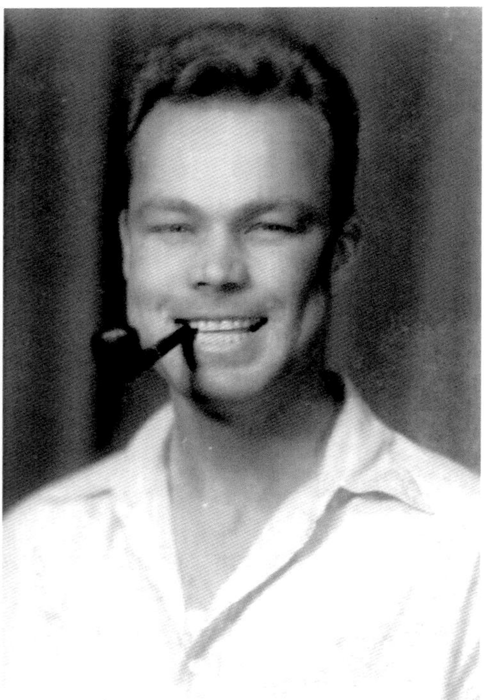

Paul Mitchell, free man with pipe, mugs for the camera. *Gayle Royer.*

Although required for a number of years to make reports to officials in order to maintain their freedom, they gladly did so. The war was over, the horrors of prison life were behind them and their lives had really, finally, started anew, and Reable and Paul Mitchell became part of a community in Houston. Both were determined that no one have any knowledge of what they'd both been through—especially their daughter. Maybe they'd tell her when she was older. Gayle Royer said:

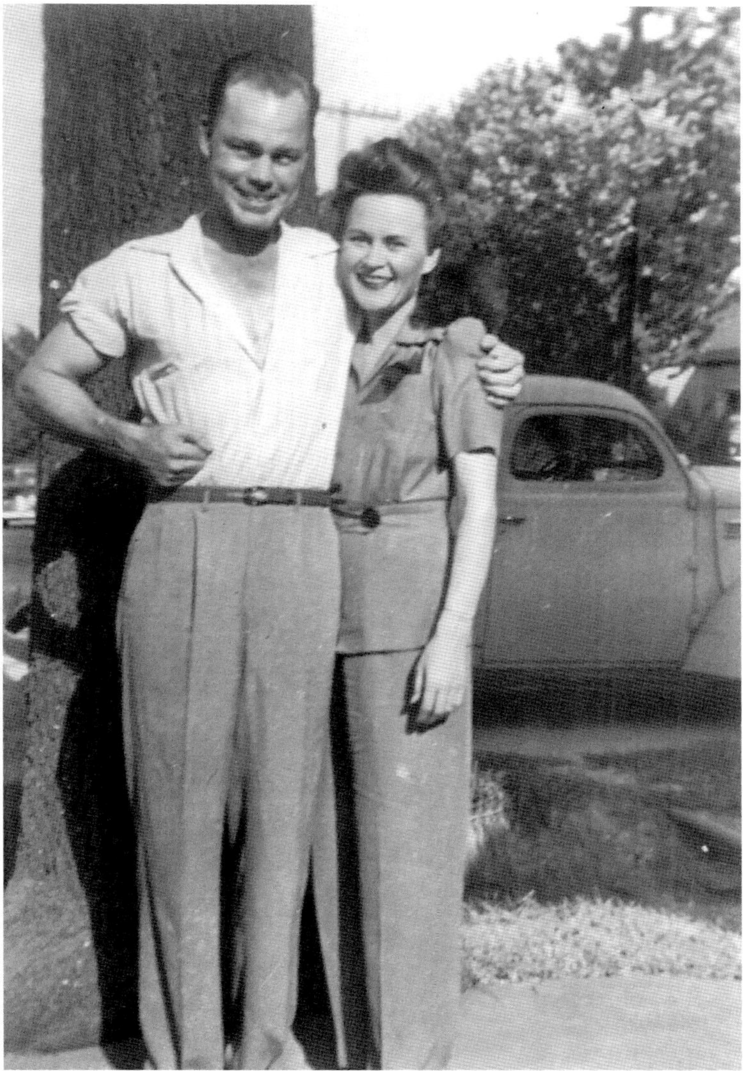

A newly married Mr. and Mrs. Paul Mitchell pose proudly in their front yard. *Gayle Royer.*

I never knew about my mother. They never told me a word. I grew up in a wonderful home with caring parents who never fought, never fussed. We were in church every time the doors opened; Southern Baptist [and] *community workers. Mother had blue ribbon awards for her yard; she kept a beautiful yard, I guess the country girl* [was] *in her still. And there could*

> *not have been a more secure, loving environment in which to raise a child. I'm an only child; there are no siblings. And looking back on it, it just simply was the American dream. Hardworking parents; not a lazy bone in their bodies, and caring very much about me.*[157]

Royer didn't find out the truth until she was nearly college age, and then only because a boyfriend's mother had recognized Reable when they met. Slowly, haltingly, her father told her the story of her mother. As she absorbed the information, he also told her his own story. The shock of finding out one's seemingly idyllic life had been built by not one but two convicted murderers was an enormous shock to Royer to say the least. In light of these revelations, questions followed and some family strife occurred over the secret keeping, but eventually, things settled back down and life went on. Although she never liked to discuss the matter—certainly not outside the family—Reable shared some, but not all, of her prison experience with her daughter over the years. She didn't tell her daughter that she used to write a column for the prison

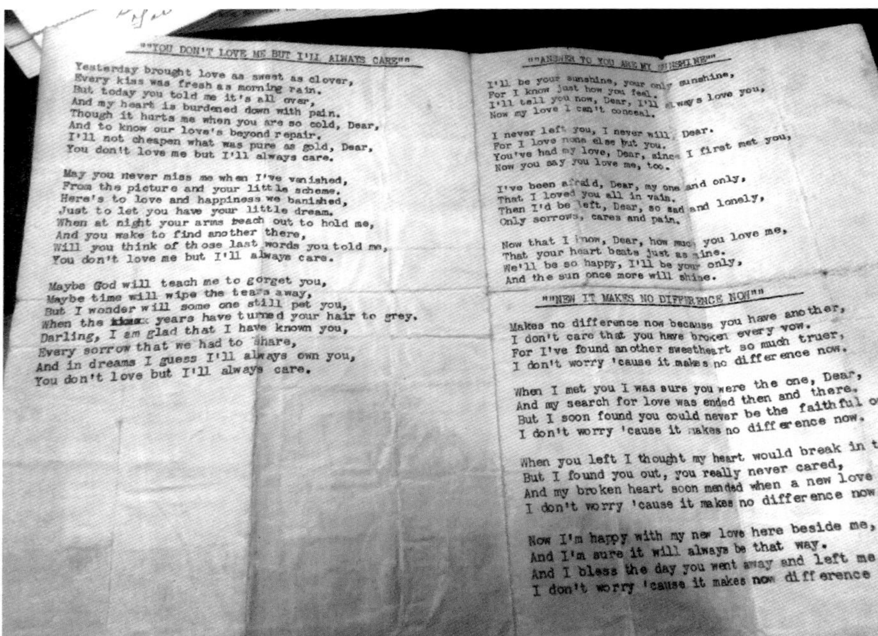

""YOU DON'T LOVE ME BUT I'LL ALWAYS CARE""

Yesterday brought love as sweet as clover,
Every kiss was fresh as morning rain.
But today you told me it's all over,
And my heart is burdened down with pain.
Though it hurts me when you are so cold, Dear,
And to know our love's beyond repair.
I'll not cheapen what was pure as gold, Dear,
You don't love me but I'll always care.

May you never miss me when I've vanished,
From the picture and your little scheme.
Here's to love and happiness we banished,
Just to let you have your little dream.
When at night your arms reach out to hold me,
And you wake to find another there,
Will you think of those last words you told me,
You don't love me but I'll always care.

Maybe God will teach me to gorget you,
Maybe time will wipe the tears away,
But I wonder will some one still pet you,
When the years have turned your hair to grey.
Darling, I am glad that I have known you,
Every sorrow that we had to share,
And in dreams I guess I'll always own you,
You don't love but I'll always care.

""ANSWER TO YOU ARE MY SUNSHINE""

I'll be your sunshine, your only sunshine,
For I know just how you feel.
I'll tell you now, Dear, I'll always love you,
Now my love I can't conceal.

I never left you, I never will, Dear.
For I love none else but you.
You've had my love, Dear, since I first met you,
Now you say you love me, too.

I've been afraid, Dear, my one and only,
That I loved you all in vain.
Then I'd be left, Dear, so sad and lonely,
Only sorrows, cares and pain.

Now that I know, Dear, how much you love me,
That your heart beats just as mine.
We'll be so happy, I'll be your only,
And the sun once more will shine.

""NEW IT MAKES NO DIFFERENCE NOW""

Makes no difference now because you have another,
I don't care that you have broken every vow.
For I've found another sweetheart so much truer,
I don't worry 'cause it makes no difference now.

When I met you I was sure you were the one, Dear,
And my search for love was ended then and there.
But I soon found you could never be the faithful on
I don't worry 'cause it makes no difference now.

When you left I thought my heart would break in tw
But I found you out, you really never cared,
And my broken heart soon mended when a new love
I don't worry 'cause it makes no difference now.

Now I'm happy with my new love here beside me,
And I'm sure it will always be that way.
And I bless the day you went away and left me,
I don't worry 'cause it makes now difference

Yellowed, typewritten lyrics of songs sung by the Goree Girls over the years. Reable Childs left behind many typed and handwritten lyrics from her time in the Goree Girls. *Gayle Royer.*

newspaper the *Echo*. When Reable got the occasional (unrelated) photo or article in the newspaper in later years, she fervently hoped no one would pry further into her early life and relied on her small family to help keep their past under wraps. Gayle eventually married William B. Royer Jr., the same Royer who was assistant director of the Iran-America Society and held in the 1979 Iran Hostage Crisis. He was freed triumphantly with many of the others in 1981, but Reable kept to the shadows while the camera crews covered the events.

What Reable did do, however, was relay the importance of the music to her daughter. She told her about the band, the radio show and the camaraderie she had with her fellow Goree inmates. She kept the photos they took on the prison grounds all those years and many photos of them in their full cowgirl regalia. Yellowed lyrics of many popular songs sung by the Goree Girls, both typed and handwritten, remain in Gayle Royer's possession. After all Reable Childs had gone through in her early life, the music she made held its importance.

KPRC's *Thirty Minutes Behind the Walls*

KPRC Houston and the Rotary Clubs of Texas are collaborating with the Texas Prison System in a unique campaign to rehabilitate parolees who leave prison with good records, Jack Harris, KPRC general manager, has revealed. Beginning June 4 the station will air a weekly series of programs titled Thirty Minutes Behind the Walls *and featuring prison talent.*

Prisoners' records and job qualifications are to be reviewed, and listeners will be asked to find them jobs. Programs will emanate each Saturday at 6 p.m. from the central prison unit at Huntsville. The series will be offered to Rotary Clubs throughout the state if it becomes effective and KPRC will make transcriptions for use by other Texas stations, according to Mr. Harris.[158]

Transcriptions of KPRC's version of *Thirty Minutes Behind the Walls* have not been located, nor have any recordings or evidence of job placement based on the radio show, but the show did proceed, airing for at least two years. The show often featured penitentiary units other than just Huntsville, and photographic and newspaper evidence suggests the radio show continued at least into the early 1950s, with the KPRC banner waving proudly from their microphones. According to the above article, the *Thirty Minutes* talk portions

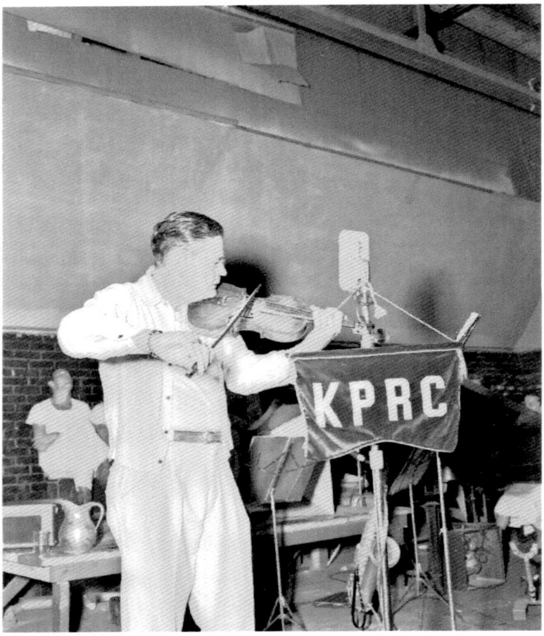

Left: An inmate fiddler keeps the rhythm on *Thirty Minutes Behind the Walls*. *Texas Prison Museum.*

Below: A female gospel quartet performs onstage for a KPRC *Thirty Minutes* production, circa 1950. *Texas Prison Museum.*

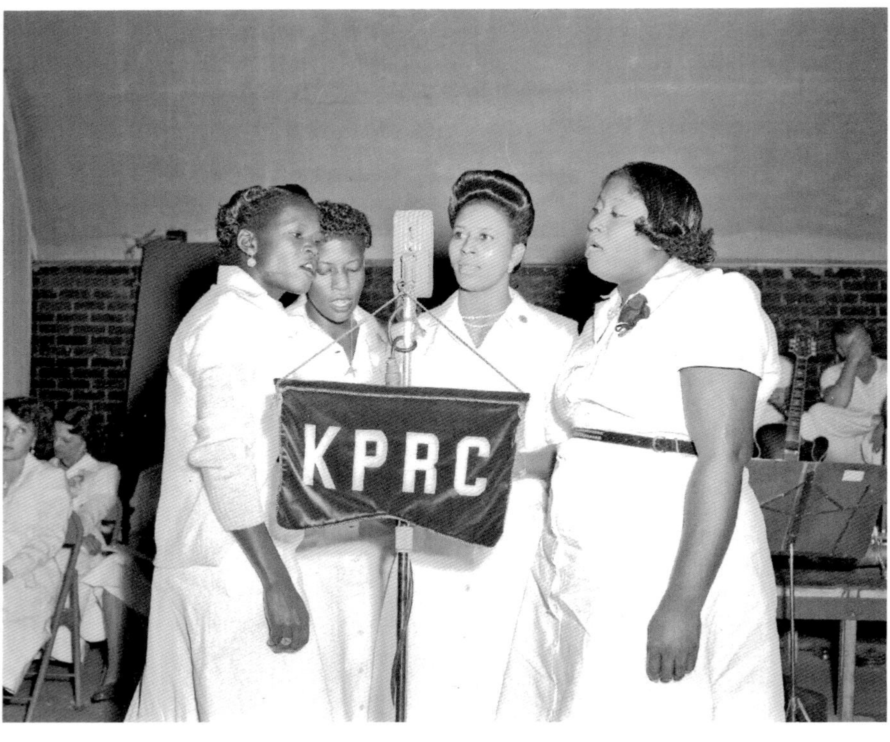

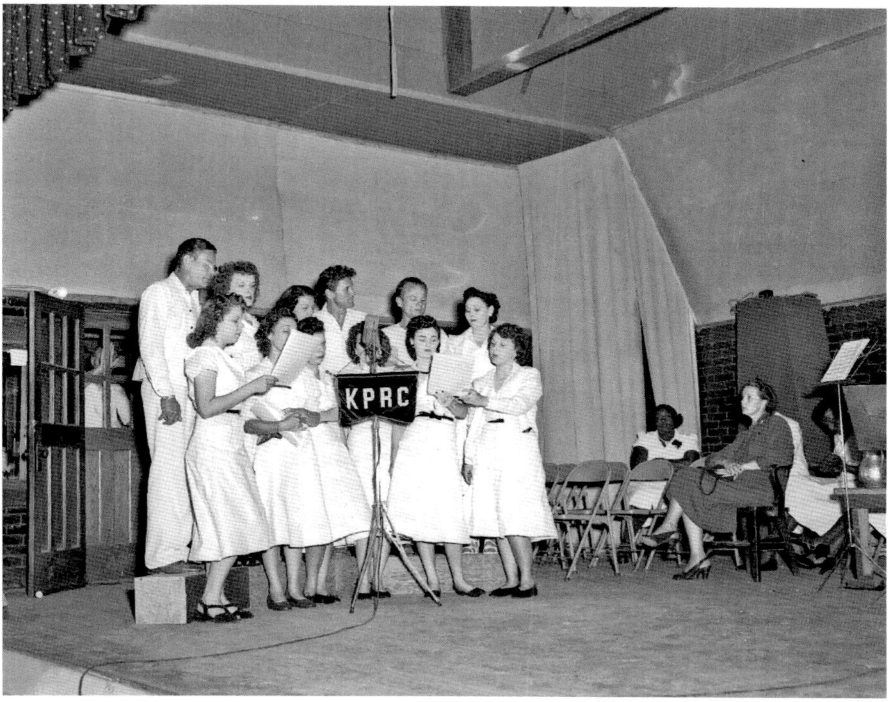

Above: A co-ed group of inmates performs on the KPRC stage, circa 1950. *Texas Prison Museum.*

Right: With the band urging him on, an inmate dances on KPRC's *Thirty Minutes*, circa 1950. *Texas Prison Museum.*

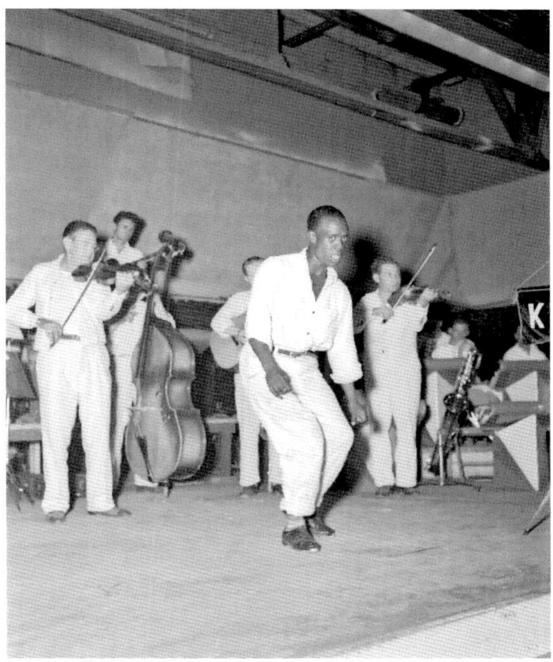

evolved from simple human-interest interviews to more personalized and genuine rehabilitation as the public got to know the inmates through their responses on the show.

Perhaps transcriptions, video or audio footage from this era do exist somewhere, even if none can be found from the WBAP version. In the photographs of KPRC's *Thirty Minutes*, the female entertainers from Goree continued to provide entertainment on the show, and the male entertainment expanded to feature more from the other units of the prison system, such as Ramsey, Wynne and Clemens. African American and Latino participation also expanded, with many male and female groups fully participating.

1950s and Beyond

As always, the Texas Prison Rodeo continued, featuring the inmate bands heavily each October; the only exception was 1943, when the rodeo was temporarily halted due to the Second World War. Many photographs of the

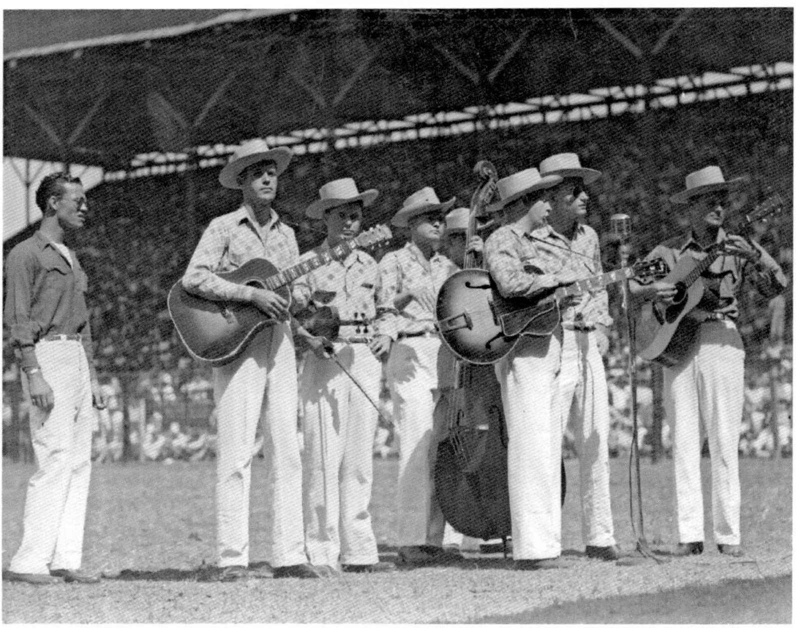

The Rhythmic Stringsters perform at the 1947 rodeo. *Larry Jene Fisher Collection, Lamar University.*

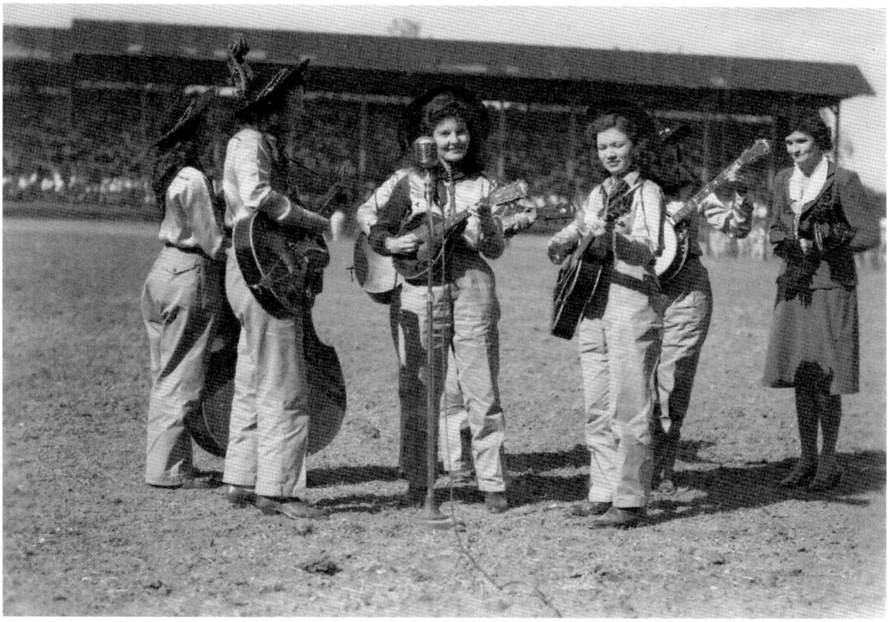

A late 1940s incarnation of the Goree Girls performs at the prison rodeo with Mrs. Heath standing by. *Texas Department of Criminal Justice.*

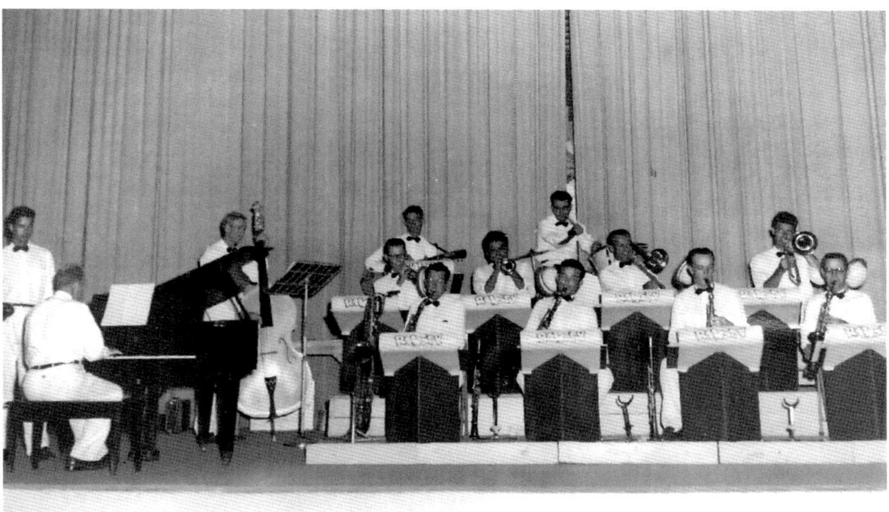

The Ramsey Unit Band, circa 1955. *Texas State Library and Archives Commission.*

prison rodeo in later years have been found, and documentation kept by the Texas State Library and Archives Commission, the Texas Prison Museum and others promises a rich history with ample opportunity for further study.

The temporary ban on musical groups performing outside the prison was lifted after World War II ended, and newspaper reports abound showing that the Goree Girls and the Rhythmic Stringsters performed outside prison walls at state-run functions like awards dinners and law enforcement

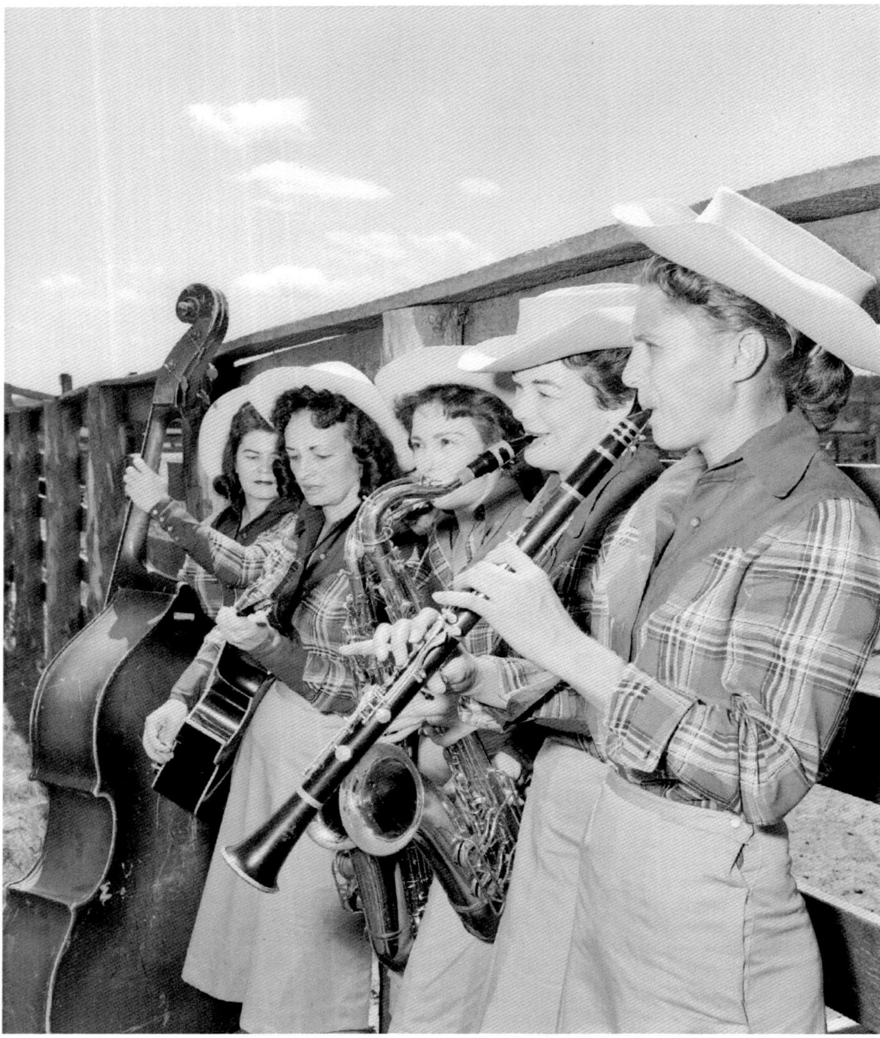

The Goree Girls at the Texas Prison Rodeo, circa 1963. *Texas Department of Criminal Justice.*

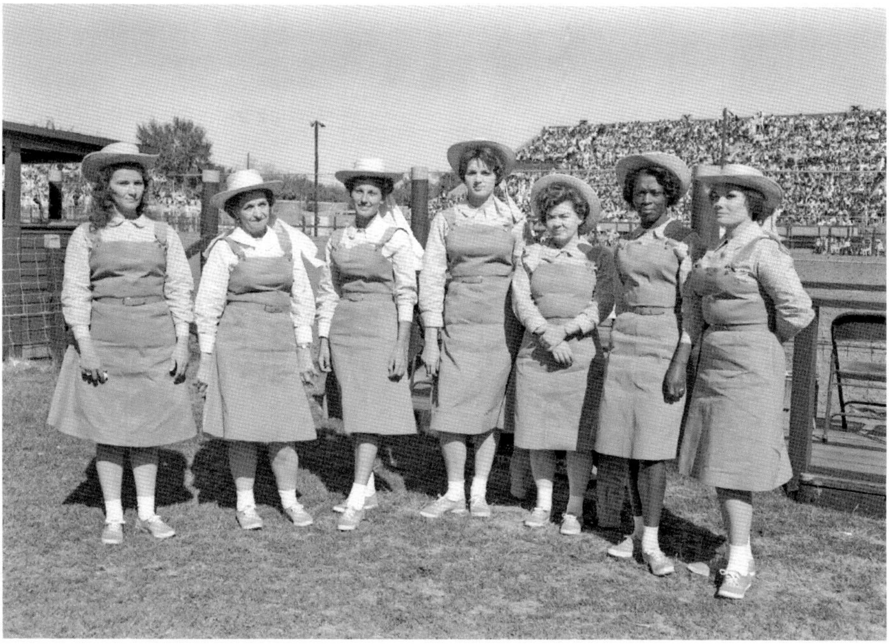

The 1964 Goree Girls at the Texas Prison Rodeo. *Texas Department of Criminal Justice.*

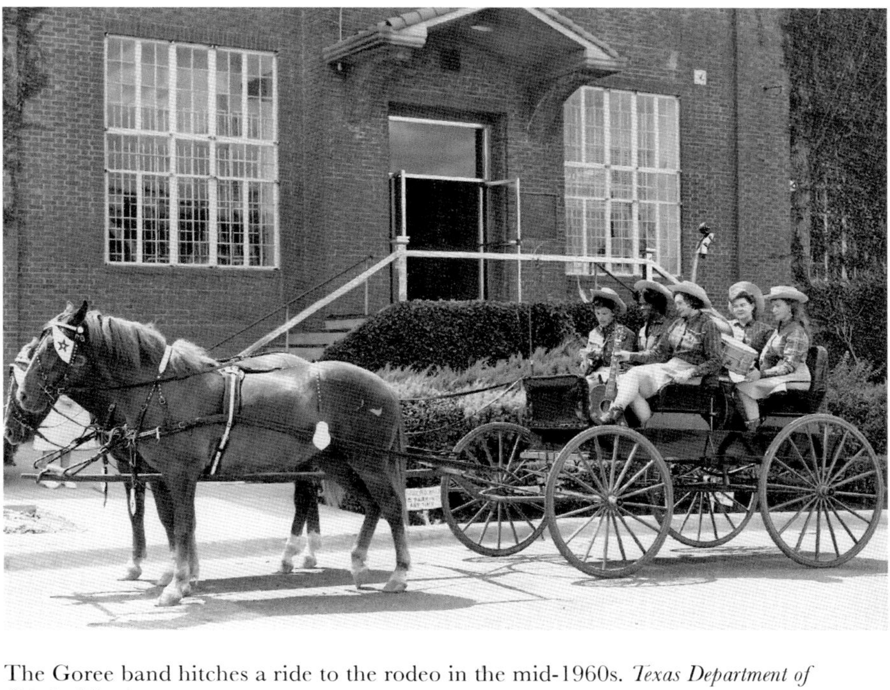

The Goree band hitches a ride to the rodeo in the mid-1960s. *Texas Department of Criminal Justice.*

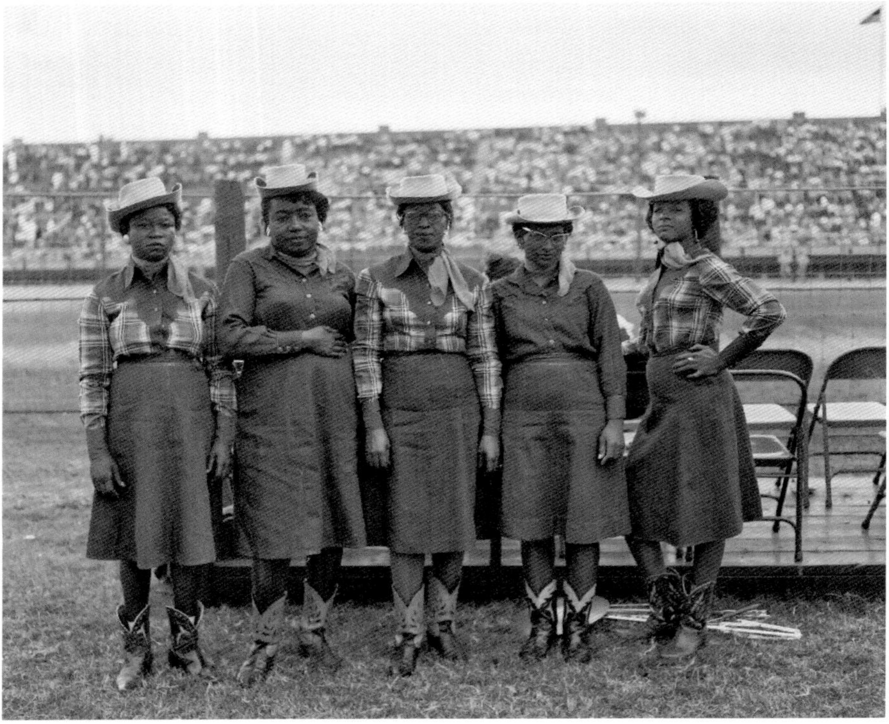

Members of an African American musical group from Goree strike poses in their full western dress. *Texas Department of Criminal Justice.*

social gatherings, as well as fiddle contests all over the state. In a multitude of incarnations, the Rhythmic Stringsters and the Goree Girls lasted for three to four decades after they each began. Media acknowledgment and photographs of the "Goree Girls" band and various "Stringsters" have been found as late as 1968.

It has become more difficult to learn the stories of the inmates in the Texas prison bands since their early days. For confidentiality purposes, among other reasons, convict records are not publicly available after 1945. Therefore, to get any sense of the story, one must rely on newspaper articles—possibly later issues of the *Echo*—or, better yet, firsthand accounts of those directly involved in the prison bands, either as an inmate or as a musical director. One notorious member of the Goree Girls later wrote of her own experiences in the band. In 1960, the Goree Girls had a star in their midst even before they stepped out onto the rodeo field: Candy Barr.

Convict #153781

Born in Texas to Elvin and Sadie Mae Slusher in July 1935, Juanita Dale Slusher had a hard childhood, fraught with sexual abuse from "trusted" neighbors, friends and extended family. Beginning when she was molested at four years old by an eighteen-year-old neighbor, Juanita learned only to say yes and exhibit all the charm and agreeability expected of a polite little girl, even as reprehensible acts were forced upon her. At the age of eight, with her father away serving in World War II, one person entrusted to care for her held frequent poker games in her family home while her mother was out working. The cherubic-faced, green-eyed little girl was dressed up in high heels, lipstick and dresses, with "breasts" made out of fruit placed strategically under the clothing. She was then placed on a table to be literally served up as the plaything of the winning player (whoever that might be) and was expected to endure whatever they wanted to do to her. It was an awful existence for a little girl who was way too young to understand and whose father was not there to protect her.[159]

In another couple of years, her mother, Sadie, died, and her father remarried. By the time she left her home in South Dallas as a runaway at age thirteen, her stepmother and cousin had also made their mark on her, rewarding her with candy and money in exchange for her performing certain sexual favors. Juanita wanted to be free, but she knew no other world than that of a sexual plaything for men and women alike.

Knowing this background, it's not surprising that new runaway Juanita almost immediately fell into the clutches of several men who targeted her for their Dallas-based prostitution ring, which she refers to as "the Capture." This sex trafficking ring's clientele consisted of a number of supposedly highly moral, often high-profile citizens of Dallas such as politicians, preachers, philanthropists and public officials. Eventually, however, she removed herself from the life in the Capture and began to let her own star shine as a dancer with a new name: Candy Barr. As Candy's dancing prowess took her from the Colony Club in Dallas to the bright lights of Vegas and back to Dallas by the late 1950s, she seemed invincible—if formidable. One journalist wrote that hers "was the face and the body and the telltale blonde hair that seemed to focus all the guilts and the fantasies of the fifties. She epitomized the conflict between sex as joy and sex as danger. The body was perfect, but it was the innocence of the face that lured you on."[160]

The "highly moral" men of her earlier days were still on her trail, however. With her mystique deepened due to her Las Vegas mobster associations,

Candy Barr strongly believed, as do many biographers, that they were responsible for landing her in the Texas prison. To Candy Barr's mind, the Dallas police force in particular resented that a good-for-nothing female like her had achieved some success, even as their highest ranks had used her for sexual favors long ago. No matter what the real story is, however, a charge of marijuana possession, stemming from two conveniently appearing marijuana cigarettes that were suddenly found in her apartment, culminated in a fifteen-year sentence for Candy Barr at the Goree State Farm for Women.

Recently married again after a couple of earlier failed attempts, Candy wanted to settle down with her husband and have children. When the court case came about, she was forced to postpone her plans to start a family until her release. But even in prison, Candy Barr found herself a victim of sexual trauma yet again.

> *The doctors discovered she was pregnant...* [they] *would later claim that she was suffering from the ravages of the sexual abuse she had endured as a prostitute. Her body was in such bad shape that the fetus was either being rejected prematurely, or the fact of pregnancy alone was seriously endangering her health. Whatever the reasons, Juanita miscarried, after which the doctors performed a hysterectomy...*
>
> *There was no informed consent. There was no discussion. Once again Juanita was back in the hands of the Capture, this time at the hands of a doctor, and again the experience was emotionally overwhelming. "When I found out what was done to me, I prayed to go insane. I was so wild, so out of my head, that I was given heavy doses of the tranquilizer Thorazine."*[161]

Kept in the hospital ward for weeks upon her entry into the prison, eventually, Candy fought to join the general population at Goree. She'd been isolated first because of her physical condition, but the ward was also a convenient place to keep her due to her fame, which had caused uncertainty among the officials about how to manage her incarceration. After some weeks, she was allowed to join the other Goree inmates in the general population, but this did not necessarily make Candy Barr a willing participant in the Goree Girls.

In her biography, Candy had plenty to say about the Goree prison while she was in there, and it seemed to be quite a change from the one the women described in the 1940s, although almost certainly the Goree women's words were censored somewhat due to the radio show and the necessities of writing approved copy for the *Echo*. Nonetheless, Candy's

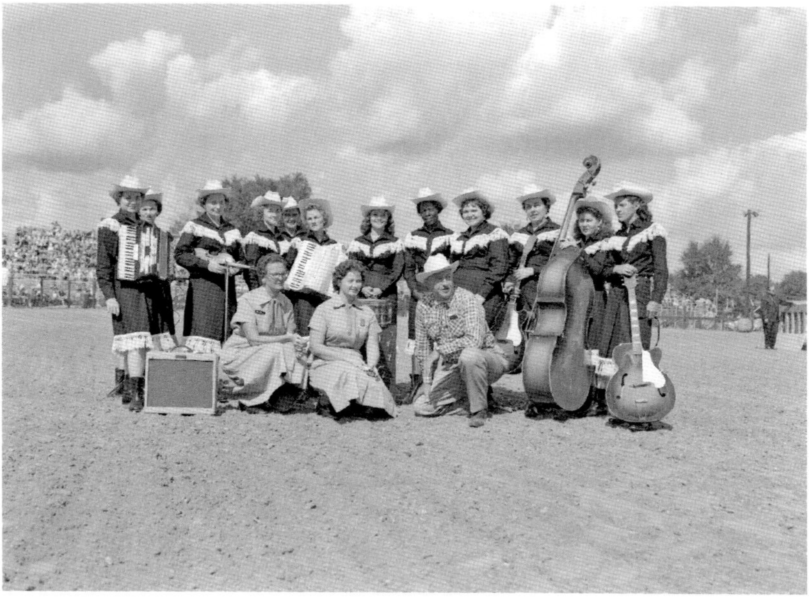

The Goree Girls at the 1960 rodeo posing with prison officials. Note Juanita Slusher, aka "Candy Barr," in the center posing with her snare drum. *Texas Department of Criminal Justice.*

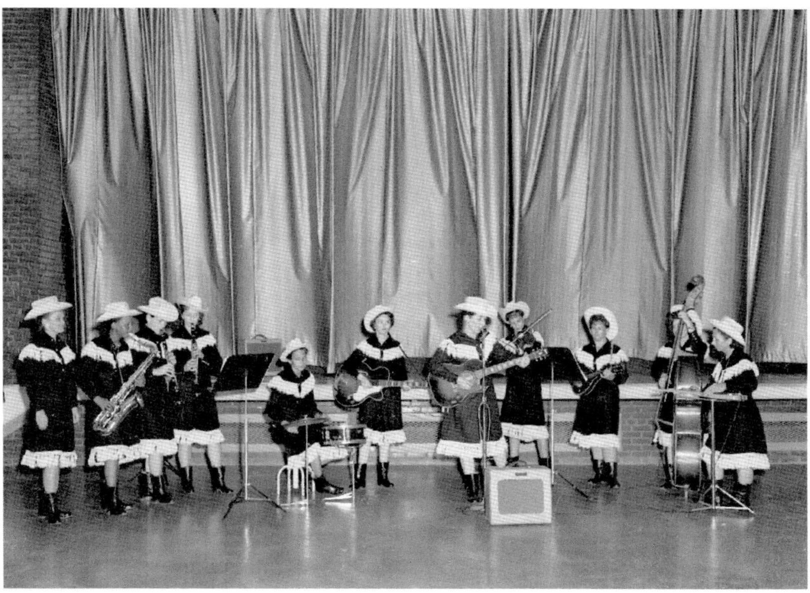

The Goree Girls play onstage; Candy Barr is on the far left. *Texas Department of Criminal Justice.*

account shows a much rougher, more realistic environment in the Goree unit than that of earlier years.

According to one of Candy Barr's biographers, she was unaware that she was being billed as the star attraction in the Goree Girls at the Texas Prison Rodeo—until she was told by an outside visitor who'd seen her name on the bill. Being in the Goree Girls had been a privilege for many women before her, but still, it was not a required activity for the inmates. Candy Barr felt that even behind bars her name was still being exploited, although perhaps less violently. But this gave her some leverage, so Candy Barr instead negotiated her way onto the rodeo bill. She parlayed her appearance into a job in the prison library instead of the garment factory where she'd been working; she felt she could read and learn more if she worked in the library. She was granted this request, and so she appeared in the Goree Girls at

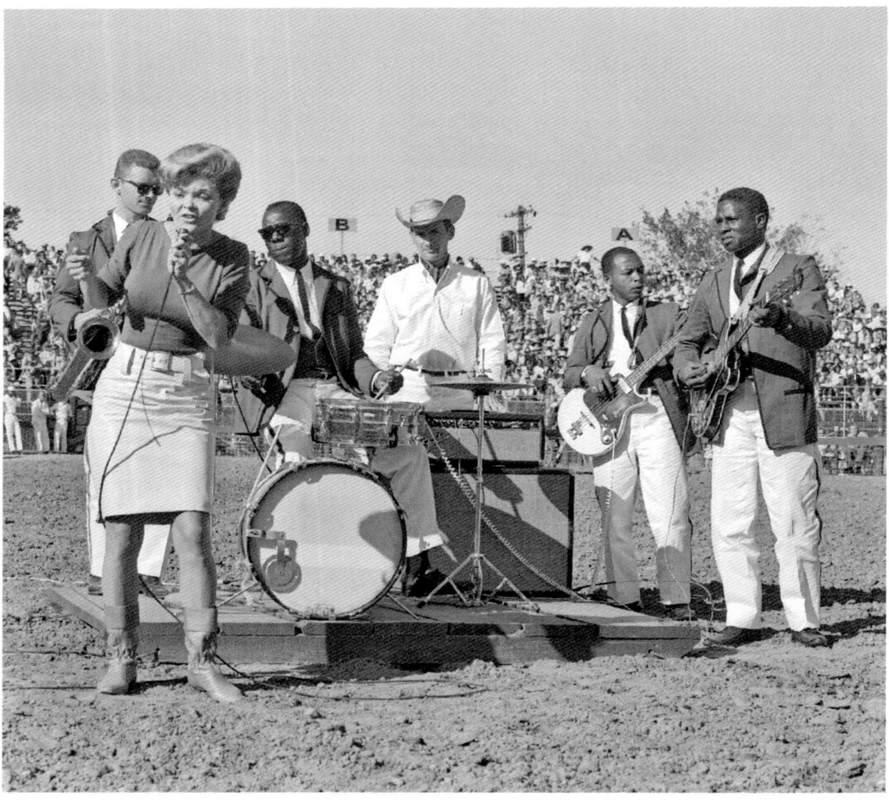

Candy Barr sings "Fever" at the 1966 Texas Prison Rodeo—this time as a free woman. *Texas Department of Criminal Justice.*

the prison rodeo for the duration of her prison stay. With the Goree Girls, Candy played the drums behind the other singers, and when her turn came, she sang spirituals, western songs or even Elvis Presley. Meanwhile, her job in the library allowed her to improve her education, take more classes and instruct some of the less literate inmates on reading and composition.

A model prisoner, Candy Barr was released only three years into her fifteen-year sentence. After her release, she continued to return to the rodeo throughout the 1960s. This time, she was booked on the rodeo bill as an outside performer rather than an inmate. Thus, her own transformation was complete, and Candy Barr lived for the rest of her life in Texas—generally out of the spotlight after the 1970s—and passed away in 2005.

Keepin' That Rhythm

In the 1960s and '70s, the Wynne unit of the Texas prison became known for its music programs, developed and executed by Harley Rex, who also served as the prison bands' music director for many years, followed by Gregory Gathwright, among others. Under their guidance, the inmate music programs flourished mightily during the 1970s and '80s. This is also when the sounds of Texas inmates can really be heard. Recordings from the 1970s and '80s were sold at the rodeo each year, and they can still be found from time to time, although only on LP. They offer unique glimpses into the music of bands from various units performing (often original) country, soul, blues, jazz, rock-and-roll and everything in between.

This era of the Texas prison bands is being researched further by some Texas documentarians, with the cooperation of Rex and others who were involved at the time. Rock star David Crosby of Crosby, Stills & Nash (and, later, Young) served time at the Wynne unit in the mid-1980s following a highly publicized court case for a drug-related sentence. Crosby's biography, *Long Time Gone*, tells of his transformational time in a Texas prison:

> *I was assigned to the Wynne Unit…They knew I was a musician and Wynne Unit was the place that had the best band and a tradition of playing good music. In the days of the Huntsville Prison Rodeo, they used to furnish the music for the big show, which was nationally known… They still had little concerts on major holidays and they staged an annual country and western show. Wynne Unit always provided the band. Gregory*

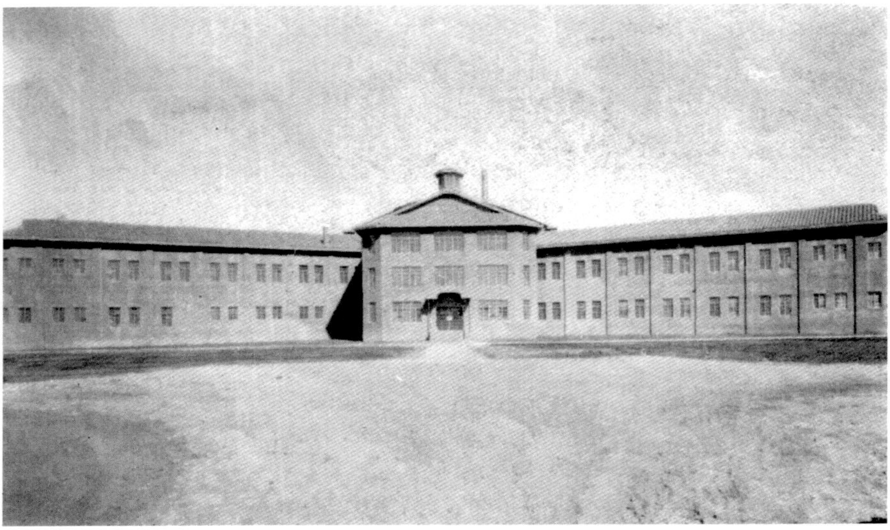

An early photograph of the Wynne unit of the Texas state prison. *Texas Department of Criminal Justice.*

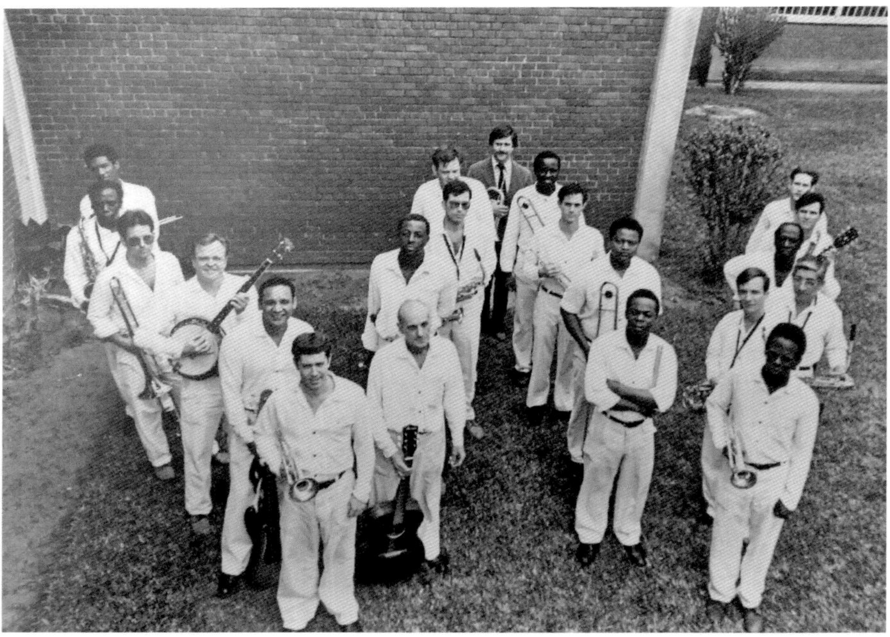

The Wynne Unit Band in the early 1960s. *Texas State Library and Archives Commission.*

> *Gathwright was the music teacher, an employee of the Texas Department of Education, not a prison guard or administrator. He was there on a contract basis to run a music program as part of the process of inmate rehabilitation. Wynne Unit was the only real musical scene in the Texas prison system.*[162]

In *Long Time Gone*, Crosby doesn't mince words about the difficulties he encountered with prison life. It was hard and definitely not fun, but he does give the music credit for providing him with some comfort and happiness while he was incarcerated:

> *When I was in the room playing with these guys, I was actually happy. I started being creative. I'd write these lyrics to myself in the middle of the night. I'd dream about a song and wake up to write down the lyrics. Then I'd write more lyrics. I'd try to be alone, separate from the band a little while, so I could work on more tunes…*
>
> *Playing for our block was great because all our friends would come in in gangs, they'd go crazy and cheer, and we loved it. It was good rock 'n' roll and they got to have a break in the prison routine and see our live show, which they treasured…I was singing well. I looked very funny onstage, but I could sing and play and we rocked it out. It was a hot little band.*[163]

Back to Silence

As the prison system legislation changed over the years, inmates continued to sing their way to that old freedom train via the Texas Prison Rodeo, which endured until the mid-1980s. The Texas Prison Rodeo ended in 1986, and the rodeo arena was later condemned and torn down.

Changing penal methodologies meant many changes for the inmates. Stricter management meant less brutality and violence than the early years of the Texas prisons. There are programs that assist with inmate rehabilitation—such as arts and crafts, drug and alcohol abuse treatment and education—but music as a rehabilitative tool is largely forgotten, with the exception of the choirs during faith-based services. There are many logistics involved with the creation and maintenance of such a large undertaking. Certainly the opportunities for playing in the "outside world" have diminished considerably, and rules and regulations prohibit still more.

Given the rich history of music in the Texas prison system, it may be beneficial for the officials of today to take a cue from their own past and see the power and possibilities of music: music learned and played for rehabilitation, inspiration and comfort. Even back in 1940, the *Amarillo Daily News* made a compelling point: "Radio has gone behind prison walls and messaged to the outside world the almost forgotten fact that men and women behind the bars are human, that they have feeling...This changing public attitude well could make for reform instead of punishment. The prison problem is a public problem."[164]

Appendix 1

SUGGESTED LISTENING

At the heart of this book is a statement on the power of music to transform one's life experience. Therefore, in order to enhance the readers' experience of *Texas Jailhouse Music*, I have created a "suggested listening" list of songs, albums and artists, inspired by the prison bands covered in our chapters.

I am listing recorded music of actual inmates when I can—even if they weren't in Texas—to draw an aural picture of the times in which these inmates lived.

It's unfortunate that no extant recordings have been found for most of the musical acts appearing in this book, such as the Goree All-Girl String Band or the Rhythmic Stringsters. If no recording is available, I have listed either a similar-sounding group or another artist performing a song they sang on *Thirty Minutes Behind the Walls* (since the prison bands mostly performed covers of current popular songs).

Aside from a few online clips on the Library of Congress website, I have made the below list using commercially available recordings. Some will be difficult, if not impossible, to find—but take heart! Many of these songs can be heard on the Internet through video or music websites. I encourage everyone to take the opportunity to learn more about the music of these inmates and the times they lived in.

APPENDIX 1

Chapter 3

Ellis, Hattie. "Desert Blues." *Field Recordings Vol. 6: Texas (1933–1958)*. Document Records, 1997. CD or MP3.

Head, Iron. "This Heart O' Mine." *1939 John and Ruby Lomax Southern States Recording Trip*. http://cdn.loc.gov/master/afc/afc1939001/afc1939001_02604b2.wav.

Ledbetter, Huddie "Lead Belly." *Lead Belly: The Smithsonian Folkways Collection*. Smithsonian/Folkways, 2015. CD or MP3.

———. *March of TIME Newsreel: The Folk Legend Lead Belly (1935)*. http://content.time.com/time/video/player/0,32068,30862122001_1918195,00.html.

Platt, Moses "Clear Rock." "Wild Geese." *1939 John and Ruby Lomax Southern States Recording Trip*. http://www.loc.gov/item/lomaxbib000204/.

Chapter 4

Hinton, Sam. "Chicken Reel." *Master of the Solo Diatonic Harmonica*. Eagle's Whistle Music, 2005. MP3.

Purvis, Jack. "Dismal Dan." *1930s Jazz: Small Combos*. Sony, 1990. CD.

———. *1928–1935*. Jazz Oracle, 2003. CD.

Chapter 5

Rodgers, Jimmie. "Gambling Polka Dot Blues" (by Raymond Hall). *The Essential Jimmie Rodgers*, 2013. MP3.

———. "Moonlight and Skies" (by Raymond Hall). *Frankie and Johnny: The Blue Yodeler Volume 2*, 2011. MP3.

———. "Ninety-Nine Years Blues" (by Raymond Hall). *The Complete Recordings of Jimmie Rodgers*. Doxy Collection Remastered, 2014. MP3.

Chapter 6

Davis, Jimmie. *The Jimmie Davis Collection, 1929–1947*. Acrobat, 2013. CD.

Girls of the Golden West. *Home Sweet Home in Texas*. British Archives of Country Music (BAMC), 2002. CD.

Appendix 1

Griffin, Rex. "The Last Letter." *Hillbilly Fever, Volume 2*. Rhino Records, 2002. CD.

Montana, Patsy. *Cowboy's Sweetheart*. King Records, 1997. CD, MP3, Vinyl, Audio Cassette.

Chapter 7

Coon Creek Girls. *Lily May, Rosie & Susie*. County Records, 2011. CD.

Ellis, Hattie. "I Ain't Got Nobody." *1939 John and Ruby Lomax Southern States Recording Trip*. http://cdn.loc.gov/master/afc/afc1939001/afc1939001_02650b1.wav.

Chapter 8

Fender, Freddy. *Freddy Fender: Recorded Inside Louisiana State Prison*. Power Pak, 1975. Vinyl.

Various Artists. *Behind the Walls: Original Country and Western Music, Volume 1 (Composed and Recorded by Inmates of the Department of Corrections)*. Texas Department of Corrections, 1972. Vinyl.

———. *The Texas Prison Rodeo Presents: Behind the Walls (Featuring the Wynne Unit Band)*. Texas Department of Corrections, 1980. Vinyl.

Appendix 2

A NOTE ON SOURCES

While most of the sources are acknowledged in the notes section of this book, several of them are located in repositories that bear further explanation.

Newspapers: First, although the Texas Prison Museum and other archives house copies of the *Texas Prison Echo*, all issues appearing in citations for this book are located at the Dolph Briscoe Center for American History at the University of Texas. No other physical repositories of the *Echo* were utilized in researching this book. Unless otherwise noted, all other newspaper articles cited in this book are from the online repository www.newspapers.com, a subscriber-based service with thousands of fully scanned and archived historical newspapers from all over the United States.

All radio industry magazines cited in this book (such as *Broadcasting* or *Rural Radio*) are accessed from the online repository www.americanradiohistory.com, which contains a wealth of information in its hundreds of scanned and archived radio fan and industry magazines, free of charge and available to the public.

Prison Records: The Texas State Library and Archives Commission has thoughtfully and conveniently placed digital images of two major sets of Texas prison records on the genealogical website www.ancestry.com: the Texas prison *Convict Ledgers* and the Texas prison *Conduct Registers*. Both the *Convict Ledgers* and the *Conduct Registers* cover all years up until 1945. These documents (among many others) are available to ancestry.com subscribers.

APPENDIX 2

A description of each follows:

The *Convict Ledgers*' records are completed upon any inmate's initial entry into the prison system and are arranged in consecutive order according to the convict number. The *Convict Ledgers* track the inmate's name, sex, age, race, physical description (including any identifying characteristics such as scars, tattoos, etc.), demographic information (i.e., state in which they were born, previous occupations, current residence) and crime and sentencing information.

The *Conduct Registers* are records kept throughout the inmate's stay and are arranged in consecutive order according to the convict number. The *Conduct Registers* cover all significant inmate status and notable conduct during their incarceration. The registers include the inmate's name, age, sentence, status (i.e, whether they were a "trusty"), various units they were housed in (and when) and dates and brief descriptions of the following: infractions, punishments, hours completed toward their sentence, reprieves, conditional pardons and paroles, full pardons and revocation of any privileges.

Although each instance is not cited in the chapter notes, the *Convict Ledgers* and *Conduct Registers* were consulted and cross-checked for all applicable inmates appearing in this book. These two sets of documents are the primary source of much of the information provided. Similarly, public records are available for any individual on ancestry.com (birth, marriage, death records, United States census, public directories and so on). As such, these records may have been consulted to help build the inmates' biographical sketches. With that said, public records are tricky to navigate, and the information on any individual must be carefully cross-checked with other public records, lest someone be confused, for instance, with another person who happened to have the same name or birthdate. This is one of the more difficult aspects of ancestry.com, because many users are not genealogical experts.

For any public records that are used in this book, a careful cross-reference has been performed and every effort taken to ensure the public records used for this book are accurate and refer only to the inmate or their family members.

Unless otherwise noted, almost all of the photographs in this book stem from a few major sources. The Texas Prison Museum's collections contain many photographs from the Texas Department of Criminal Justice. The Texas Prison Museum also holds the Buster Moore Collection, the Tom Miller Collection, the Prison Rodeo Program Collection and the *Thirty Minutes Behind the Walls* Souvenir Programs, Radio Program Collection. The Texas Department of Criminal Justice has been a source for mug shots and historical photographs. The Texas State Library and Archives Commission is another; specifically, I have utilized its TDCJ archives of the Texas Prison Rodeo and general photographs, as well as its Texas Prison Rodeo souvenir programs. The Library of Congress has also provided a few photographs that are in the public domain. Lastly, Gayle Royer has generously provided a number of photographs from her mother's personal collection, thus rounding out our story.

NOTES

Introduction

1. Robert Perkinson, *Texas Tough: The Rise of America's Prison Empire* (New York: Henry Holt & Company, 2010), 5.
2. New York Correction History Society, "Auburn & Osborne," http://www.correctionhistory.org/auburn&osborne/brochure2.htm.
3. *Texas Department of Criminal Justice* (Paducah, KY: Turner Publishing Company, 2004), 11–12.
4. *Thirty Minutes Behind the Walls: One Hundred and Fifty-Six Penitentiary Broadcasts, Presented each Wednesday night at ten-thirty from the Huntsville unit of the Texas Prison System, through the facilities of WBAP, in Fort Worth* (Huntsville: Texas State Prison, 1941), transcriptions, program 106, March 27, 1940. Held at the Dolph Briscoe Center for American History, University of Texas at Austin, Austin, TX.
5. Ibid.

Chapter 1

6. *Thirty Minutes*, transcriptions, program 1, March 23, 1938.
7. Perkinson, *Texas Tough*, 182.
8. Lee Simmons, *Assignment Huntsville: Memoirs of a Texas Prison Official* (Austin: University of Texas Press, 1957), 52. Held at the Dolph Briscoe Center for American History at the University of Texas, Austin, TX.
9. Perkinson, *Texas Tough*, 205.
10. Simmons, *Assignment Huntsville*, 52.

11. Perkinson, *Texas Tough*, 205.
12. Ibid.
13. Ibid., 207.
14. Ethan Blue, *Doing Time in the Depression: Everyday Life in California and Texas Prisons* (New York: New York University Press, 2012), 46.
15. Carl Basland, *Classification in the Texas Prison System* (Austin: University of Texas, 1938), 9–10.
16. Ibid., 10.
17. *Thirty Minutes*, transcriptions, program 23, August 24, 1938.

Chapter 2

18. Melba Newton George, "Girl Reporter Gets Out of Prison and Recommends Woman Matron of Goree Farm," *Houston (TX) Post*, October 11, 1937, 1.
19. Jack Martin, "So Common Sense Is Always the Detective's Best Weapon," *Salt Lake (UT) Tribune*, November 8, 1936, 33.
20. Ibid.
21. Ibid.
22. *Dallas (TX) Morning News*, "Widow of Rich Texan Tells of Plot to Kill Him," May 1, 1936, 1.
23. Gayle Royer, interview with the author, January 14, 2015.
24. Ibid.
25. Ibid.
26. Ibid.
27. *Port Arthur (TX) News*, "It's Her Birthday! Confessed Slayer Buys Present," May 1, 1936, 1.
28. Ibid.; Robert Utley, *Lone Star Lawmen: The Second Century of the Texas Rangers* (New York: Berkeley Publishing Company, 2007), 169–70.
29. *Harlingen (TX) Valley Morning Star*, "Love Triangle Tragedy Told," September 17, 1936, 5.
30. *Port Arthur (TX) News*, "Testimony in Murder Trial Ends: Bramlett Says Woman Guilty," September 23, 1936, 1–2.
31. Skip Hollandsworth, "O Sister, Where Art Thou?" *Texas Monthly* 31, no. 5 (May 2003): 136–41, 178–81, 197.
32. George, "Girl Reporter Gets Out of Prison," 1.
33. Ibid., 5.
34. Ibid.
35. Ibid.
36. Ibid.
37. Ibid.

38. Ibid.; Royer interview.
39. *Brownsville (TX) Herald*, "Testing Prison Conduct," October 21, 1937, 4.
40. Kelly McAdams, "A Social Study of the Women's Penitentiary of Texas," master's thesis, 1932. Archives of the Texas Prison Museum, Huntsville, TX.
41. Ibid.
42. "Bull-daggering" is a prison term for a woman who engages in lesbian sex with other female inmates, often by force or coercion.
43. McAdams, "Social Study."
44. *Houston (TX) Post*, "Charge of Theft: Negro Woman Arrested by the Police Department," August 9, 1906, 16.

Chapter 3

45. John Lomax interview with Dr. Miles Hanley, October 1933. Transcribed by author from *Jail House Bound: John Lomax's First Southern Prison Recordings, 1933*, Global Jukebox, 2012, CD.
46. Charles Wolfe and Kip Lornell, *The Life & Legend of Leadbelly* (New York: Harper Collins, 1992), 85–86.
47. Lead Belly, "Governor Pat Neff," *Lead Belly: The Smithsonian Folkways Collection*, 2015, CD. Lyrics transcribed by the author.
48. *Time*, *March of Time: Folk Legend Leadbelly*, http://content.time.com/time/video/player/0,32068,30862122001_1918195,00.html. Script transcribed by the author.
49. Letter from James "Iron Head" Baker to Lomax, John Avery Lomax Collection, Dolph-Briscoe Center for American History, University of Texas at Austin, Austin, TX.
50. John A. Lomax, *Adventures of a Ballad Hunter* (New York: Macmillan, 1946), 165.
51. Library of Congress, Prints & Photographs Division, Lomax Collection, Washington, D.C., http://www.loc.gov/pictures/item/2007660009.
52. Lomax, *Adventures of a Ballad Hunter*, 166.
53. Ibid., 165.
54. Alan Lomax, *The Land Where the Blues Began*, rev. ed. (New York: The New Press, 2002), 286.
55. Lomax, *Adventures of a Ballad Hunter*, 173.
56. Ibid., 174.
57. Ibid., 177.
58. *Massillon (OH) Evening Independent*, "Loses Reprieve Won by Singing," August 12, 1937, 2.
59. Lomax, *Adventures of a Ballad Hunter*, 178.
60. Ibid., 179.

61. John A. Lomax, *Field Notes: 1939 John and Ruby Lomax Southern States Recording Trip* (AFC 1939/001), American Folklife Center, Library of Congress.
62. Jerrod Hirsch, "Modernity, Nostalgia, and Southern Folklore Studies: The Case of John Lomax," *Journal of American Folklore* 105, no. 416 (Spring 1992), 183–207.
63. Hattie Ellis, "I Ain't Got Nobody," *1939 John and Ruby Lomax Southern States Recording Trip* (AFC 1939/001), American Folklife Center, Library of Congress, http://cdn.loc.gov/master/afc/afc1939001/afc1939001_02650b1.wav. Lyrics transcribed by the author.
64. Lomax, *Field Notes.*
65. Skip Hollandsworth, "Blue Notes," *Texas Monthly* (May 2003), http://www.texasmonthly.com/articles/blue-notes.

Chapter 4

66. *Thirty Minutes*, transcriptions, program 52, March 15, 1939.
67. Richard Sudhalter, *Lost Chords: White Musicians and Their Contribution to Jazz, 1915–1945* (New York: Oxford University Press, 1999), 471.
68. *Indianapolis (IN) Sun Star*, "Wealthy Kokomo Man Sued," November 20, 1910, 26.
69. *Kokomo (IN) Daily Tribune*, "Jack Purvis Puts Across Sly Getaway," June 26, 1919, 1.
70. Sudhalter, *Lost Chords*, 473.
71. Ibid.
72. Dick Hall, "An Unusual Story of the Life of Musicians Behind Prison Walls," *Down Beat Magazine*, November 1938, 12, Hogan Jazz Archive, Tulane University, New Orleans, LA.
73. *Texas Prison Echo* (Huntsville, TX), "*Thirty Minutes Behind the Walls* Starts 3rd Year," (March 1940), Texas Newspaper Collection, Dolph Briscoe Center for American History, University of Texas, Austin, TX.
74. *Thirty Minutes*, transcriptions, program 1, March 23, 1938.
75. *Broadcasting Magazine*, "WKY Scores Big Hit with Broadcast from Oklahoma's Big House," August 1, 1937, 46.
76. *Broadcasting Magazine*, "Prisoners Take the Air: Carolina Inmates Reform as They Perform on WRAL Prison Feature," August 1, 1940, 130.
77. Don Hinga, "Texas Prison Radio Program is a Great Morale Booster," *Texas Prison Echo*, January 1942. Reprinted from the *Baltimore Sun*.
78. *Thirty Minutes*, transcriptions, program 8, May 11, 1938.
79. *Amarillo (TX) Globe Times*, "Paul Mitchell Pointed to as Holdup Killer," January 31, 1933, 1.

Chapter 5

80. Don Hinga, "Texas Prison Radio."
81. Bill Malone, *Don't Get Above Your Raisin'* (Urbana: University of Illinois Press, 2002), 14, 66.
82. Hall, "Unusual Story."
83. *WFAA/KGKO/WBAP Combined Family Album*, 1941. The Miller Collection, Archives of the Texas Prison Museum, Huntsville, TX.
84. *Broadcasting Magazine*, "No Air for Inmate," May 1, 1938, 63.
85. *Corpus Christi (TX) Caller Times*, "Escaped Convict Captured During Drunken Spree," April 20, 1938, 1.
86. Hall, "Unusual Story."
87. *Thirty Minutes*, transcriptions, program 153, February 26, 1941.
88. Herman "Mexico" Brown, "Stringsters," *Texas Prison Echo* (Huntsville, TX), September 1942.
89. *Amarillo (TX) Globe-Times*, "Old Fiddlers Contest Gets 2,000 Persons," March 21, 1921, 7.
90. Ibid., "They Play Again," April 26, 1928, 5.
91. *Vernon (TX) Daily Record*, "World Famous Fiddler, Former Resident of Vernon, to Appear in Program at High School Here," September 28, 1928, 5.
92. Ibid., "Vetrans [*sic*] of Gray Leave Saturday for Chattanooga," October 25, 1921, 1.
93. Ibid., "Vernon Ready to Celebrate Span Opening," July 2, 1937, 1.
94. Ibid., "Lewis Franklin Charged in Chillicothe Slaying," August 9, 1937, 1.
95. *Texas Prison Echo* (Huntsville, TX), "Inmate Writer Gains Place in Who's Who," March 1941.
96. Ibid.
97. Nolan Porterfield, *Jimmie Rodgers: The Life and Times of America's Blue Yodeler* (Urbana: University of Illinois Press, 1979), 57.
98. Ibid.
99. NEA Service, "He Couldn't Wait for Freedom," *Ada (OK) Weekly News*, August 15, 1928, 2.
100. Porterfield, *Jimmie Rodgers*, 252.
101. Ibid., 253.
102. U.P., "Atrocities at Pen Reported," *Amarillo (TX) Globe Times*, April 3, 1935, 1.
103. *Thirty Minutes*, transcriptions, program 11, June 1, 1938.

Chapter 6

104. Reable Childs, "Across the Back Fence," *Texas Prison Echo* (Huntsville, TX), March 1940.
105. *Thirty Minutes*, transcriptions, program 143, December 17, 1940.
106. Ibid., program 50, March 1, 1939.
107. Ibid., program 155, March 12, 1941.
108. *El Paso (TX) Herald Post*, "Admits Beating to Get Money," June 22, 1938, 1; Hollandsworth, "O Sister."
109. *Thirty Minutes*, transcriptions, program 155, March 12, 1941.
110. Laura (no last name), "Across the Back Fence," *Texas Prison Echo* (Huntsville, TX), June 1942, 14:6.
111. Hollandsworth, "O Sister."
112. U.P., "Stepfather Slaying Brings 7-Year Term," *El Paso (TX) Herald Post*, January 29, 1938, 1.
113. U.P., "Mozelle McDaniel Kills Step-Father," *Chillicothe (MO) Constitution-Tribune*, August 16, 1937, 3; *Abilene (TX) Reporter News*, "Girl Free on Bond," August 17, 1937, 11; AP, "Farm Girl, 17, Held After Her Stepdad Dies of 11 Bullets," *Dallas (TX) Morning News*, August 16, 1938, 3.
114. Hollandsworth, "O Sister."
115. Ibid.
116. Ibid.
117. Reable Childs, "Across the Back Fence," *Texas Prison Echo* (Huntsville, TX), August 1940, 12:8.
118. Ibid.
119. AP, "Girl on Probation from Greeley Court May Have Been Murdered on Honeymoon in South Texas," *Greeley (CO) Daily Tribune*, February 10, 1940, 1.
120. Ibid.
121. Ibid.
122. AP, "Riddled Auto Case Cleared," *Paris (TX) News Sun*, February 11, 1940, 5.
123. AP, "Arrests End Mystery," *Harlingen (TX) Valley Morning Star*, February 11, 1940, 9.
124. AP, "Girl on Probation," 5.
125. Laura (no last name), "Across the Back Fence," *Texas Prison Echo* (Huntsville, TX), September 1942, 13:9.
126. Reable Childs, "Across the Back Fence," *Texas Prison Echo* (Huntsville, TX), June 1940, 12:6.
127. Dudley's granddaughter (who wished to remain anonymous), interview with the author, January 3, 2016.
128. Ibid.

129. Ibid.
130. Royer interview.
131. Ibid.
132. Hollandsworth, "O Sister."
133. *Thirty Minutes*, transcriptions, program 143, December 17, 1940.
134. *Meeting Minutes of the Texas Prison Board*, May 6, 1940, Texas Department of Criminal Justice Collection, Texas State Library and Archives Commission.
135. Reable Childs, "Across the Back Fence," *Texas Prison Echo* (Huntsville, TX), August 1940, 12:8.
136. Ibid., October 1941, 13:10.
137. Ibid.
138. Ibid.
139. *Meeting Minutes of the Texas Prison Board*, January 5, 1942, Texas Department of Criminal Justice Collection, Texas State Library and Archives Commission.

Chapter 7

140. *Thirty Minutes*, transcriptions, program 106, March 27, 1940.
141. Hattie Ellis, "Desert Blues," May 14, 1939, *1939 John and Ruby Lomax Southern States Recording Trip*, http://memory.loc.gov/cgi- bin/query/S?ammem/lomaxbib:@FIELD(OTHER+@od1(+ellis,+hattie+)).
142. Kristine M. McCusker, "'Bury Me Beneath the Willow': Linda Parker and Definitions of Tradition on the National Barn Dance, 1932–1935," *A Boy Named Sue: Gender and Country Music*, ed. Kristine M. McCusker and Diane Pecknold (Jackson: University of Mississippi Press, 2004), 23; Pamela Fox, *Natural Acts: Gender, Race, and Rusticity in Country Music* (Ann Arbor: University of Michigan Press, 2009), 61.
143. *Thirty Minutes*, transcriptions, program 106, March 27, 1940.
144. Reable Childs, "Across the Back Fence," *Texas Prison Echo* (Huntsville, TX), October 1941, 13:10.
145. *Texas Prison Echo* (Huntsville, TX), "Goree Girls to Entertain Newspaper Folk," October 1941, 13:10.
146. Ibid., "Goree Girls' Band on Air Two Years," August 1942, 14:8.
147. Laura (no last name), "Across the Back Fence," *Texas Prison Echo* (Huntsville, TX), June 1942, 14:6.
148. Dudley's granddaughter interview.
149. Hollandsworth, "O Sister."
150. Ibid.
151. *Thirty Minutes*, transcriptions, program 85, November 1, 1939.

152. Ethan Blue, "Hard Time in the New Deal: Racial Formation and the Cultures of Punishment in Texas and California in the 1930s," PhD dissertation, University of Texas, Austin, TX, 2004, 429; *Thirty Minutes*, transcriptions, program 117, June 12, 1940.
153. *Thirty Minutes*, transcriptions, program 92, December 20, 1939.
154. Blue, *Hard Time*, 347.
155. Ibid., 336.

Chapter 8

156. *Texas Prison Echo* (Huntsville, TX), "Songs from Prison" (as reprinted from *Amarillo Daily News*, editorial, March 21, 1941), March 1941, 13:3.
157. Royer interview.
158. *Broadcasting Magazine*, "KPRC Program to Assist Texas Parolees," May 30, 1949, 45.
159. Ted Schwartz and Mardi Rustam, *Candy Barr: The Small-Town Texas Runaway Who Became a Darling of the Mob and the Queen of Las Vegas Burlesque* (Lanham, MD: Taylor Trade Publishing, 2008), 15–20.
160. Gary Cartwright, "Candy: Taking the Wrapper Off a Texas Legend," *Texas Monthly* (December 1976), Texas Monthly online archives.
161. Schwartz and Rustam, *Candy Barr*, 228–29.
162. David Crosby and Carl Gottleib, *Long Time Gone: The Autobiography of David Crosby* (New York: Bantam Doubleday Dell Publishing Group, 1988), 446–47.
163. Ibid., 459.
164. *Texas Prison Echo* (Huntsville, TX), "Songs from Prison."

INDEX

INDEX

W

ABOUT THE AUTHOR

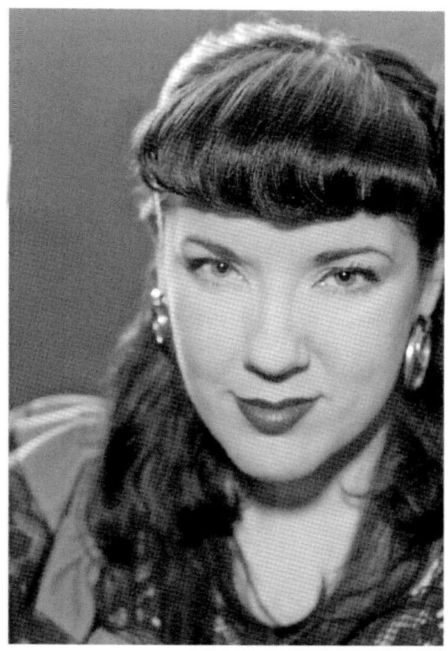

Kenneth Gall Photography.

Caroline Gnagy is a music writer and musician based in Austin, Texas. As a musician, Caroline has played many rockabilly and Americana festivals throughout the United States and Europe with her rockabilly group, the Casey Sisters, and her country act, Caroline Casey and the Stringslingers. Caroline has released several successful albums with both musical acts and also appears in the 2003 Grammy-nominated documentary film *Welcome to the Club: Women of Rockabilly*.

Caroline has served as contributing writer and music editor for a number of independent local and national publications. Since 2011, she has probed into the history of prison bands in Texas and other states and presented her research at numerous academic conferences. She is the author of "As If They Were Going Places: Class and Gender Portrayals Through Country Music in the Texas State Prison, 1938–1944," an essay appearing in *Country Boys & Redneck Women* (University Press of Mississippi, 2016). Caroline is currently working on her second book, about the lives and careers of female rockabilly performers from pioneers to the present day.

Visit us at
www.historypress.net

This title is also available as an e-book